Praise for C

'A wonderful story, beautifully written, filled with heart and humour.'
Liane Moriarty (reviewing *Ciao Bella!* on 3pm Pick Up, KIIS 1065)

'Kate Langbroek's voice . . . the one that emerges from this terrific memoir is an easy blend of light, funny, sad and occasionally bleak. You can taste the pasta, the local reds, the thrill of meeting new friends and sense the adventure of daring to live differently.'
***The Sydney Morning Herald* (Steven Carroll)**

'[A] delicious, wise and honest read. Langbroek's intelligence and wit imbue every page . . . I've read every family travel memoir around. This is by far the best.'
Better Reading

'This book makes you want to experience a new culture. It makes you want to travel again. It makes you want to go to Italy. *Ciao Bella!* is an inspiring story for anyone who likes a good yarn.'
Glam Adelaide

CIAO BELLA!

CIAO BELLA!
SIX TAKE ITALY
KATE LANGBROEK

SIMON & SCHUSTER

London · New York · Sydney · Toronto · New Delhi

CIAO BELLA!: SIX TAKE ITALY
First published in Australia in 2021 by
Simon & Schuster (Australia) Pty Limited
Suite 19A, Level 1, Building C, 450 Miller Street, Cammeray, NSW 2062
This edition published in 2023

10 9 8 7 6 5 4 3 2 1

Sydney New York London Toronto New Delhi
Visit our website at www.simonandschuster.com.au

© Kate Langbroek 2021

All rights reserved. No part of this publication may be reproduced, stored in a retrieval system, or transmitted in any form or by any means, electronic, mechanical, photocopying, recording or otherwise, without prior permission of the publisher.

A catalogue record for this book is available from the National Library of Australia

ISBN: 9781761420849

Cover, endpapers and internal design: Christabella Designs
Cover shot and endpaper images: Tina Smigielski (Kate); Incomible/Shutterstock (tiles)
Back cover photograph: www.paulstuart.co.uk (Kate & family).
All photographs in picture sections are from the author's personal collection.
Images for chapter openings all courtesy of Shutterstock by: Katsiaryna Pleshakova: Introduction, Chs 4, 14, 20, 22, 37, 38 & 42, Postscript; GooseFrol: Chs 1, 2, 6, 8, 16, 19, 24, 25, 26 & 47; Cosmic_Design: Chs 13, 36; GoodStudio: Chs 27 & 34; icon99: Ch 3; mspoint: Ch 5; Vibrush: Ch 7; Alekksall: Ch 9; js-studio: Ch 10; Alexey Pushkin: Ch 11; Martial Red: Ch 12; Yogesh Ponkshe: Ch 15; lapas77: Ch 17; Yulija Murtazina: Ch 18; OrangeVector: Ch 21; SunshineVector: Ch 23; Iconim: Ch 28; SViktoria: Ch 29; Sudowoodo: Ch.30; be_u_and_i: Ch 31; Sergio Carlis: Ch 32; stocksolutions: Ch 33; robuart: Ch 35; Ramona Kaulitzk: Ch 39; IGORdeyka: Ch 40; Win Art: Ch 41; All for you friend: Ch 43; Eva Cornejo Coba: Ch 44; Tetiana Peliustka: Ch 45; rin-rin: Ch 46.
Typeset by Midland Typesetters, Australia
Printed and bound in Australia by Griffin Press

The paper this book is printed on is certified against the Forest Stewardship Council® Standards. Griffin Press holds chain of custody certification SCS-COC-001185. FSC® promotes environmentally responsible, socially beneficial and economically viable management of the world's forests.

For the adventurers

CONTENTS

INTRODUCTION — xiii

PART 1

1. ITALIA: FALLING IN LOVE — 3
2. WHY, WHY, WHY? — 11
3. WHERE, WHERE, WHERE? — 18
4. *ARRIVIAMO*: FAMIGLIA LEWIS ARRIVE! — 25
5. BALONEY, BALONEY, WE ALL LOVE BALONEY — 33
6. CELEBRATION OF THE ART — 43
7. THE AMBASSADOR AND THE SHOWGIRL — 51
8. BOO HOO, POOR LUCKY ME — 57
9. THE FIRST OF MANY — 63
10. HAMSTERDAM: NEAR CANAL; FAR CANAL — 70
11. BASKET CITY — 76
12. BE CAREFUL WHAT YOU WISH FOR — 82
13. I BELIEVE IN MIRACLES — 90
14. I CAN SMELL FREEDOM — 96
15. IN BED WITH MADONNA — 100
16. I AM, YOU ARE, WE ARE ITALIAN — 104
17. THE HOST WITH A GHOST — 111
18. TWO TAKE THE AMALFI — 114
19. WHEN THE MOONEY HITS YOUR EYE LIKE A BIG PIZZA PIE . . . — 119
20. THE FIRST TIME I CRY — 127
21. DON'T GO CHANGING (WE CAN'T, YOU'VE LOST OUR SUITCASE . . .) — 137

| 22 | WHEN NOTHING IS EVERYTHING | 143 |
| 23 | WHAT DO YOU DO ALL DAY? | 152 |

PART 2

24	HOW DID I GET HERE?	163
25	VENICE: A TALE OF TWO CITIES	166
26	CARNEVALE: THE BALL	182
27	WHITE WEEK	193
28	WE LIKE-A LUCCA	197
29	SUPERMARKET SWEEPS	203
30	THE FIRST DAY OF SPRING	209
31	WHEN LIFE SERVES US LEMONS, WE MAKE LEMON TART	217
32	HAPPY ANNIVERSARY	225
33	GOOD BAD FRIDAY	233
34	STOCKHOLM SYNDROME	244
35	SUNDAY'S BIRTHDAY	250
36	MAY THE FOURTH BE WITH US . . .	256
37	THE FIRST SUPPER	260
38	STEPPING OUT	269
39	STRAWBERRY THICKSHAKES	272
40	THE BEE IN BEE-ACH	284
41	PLEASURE. PAIN. PUGLIA	287
42	SICILY: MOLTO, MOLTO GIOVANNIS	293
43	SIX MAKE A PARTY	306
44	TIME TO LEAVE	313
45	THANKS FOR THE GIVING	318
46	THE LAST SUPPER	325
47	THE BIG ARRIVEDERCI	334

POSTSCRIPT: THE RECIPE FOR HAPPINESS	347
ACKNOWLEDGEMENTS	357
ABOUT THE AUTHOR	361

INTRODUCTION

There is a lot of talk in this world about making dreams come true.

Dare to dream, we are told. Chase your dreams. If you can dream it, you can do it.

Well, in 2016 I had a dream. My dream – shared so fully and immediately with my husband Peter Lewis that neither of us can remember the moment we actually formulated it – was to live in Italy for a year. For us it meant a circuit breaker; an adventure; a chance to spend more time with our four children – Lewis, Sunday, Artie and Jannie – in a country we had been swept away by since our first visit in 2015.

But all dreams dissolve in waking hours and when uttered aloud in the stark light of day suddenly seem like madness. We didn't speak Italian. We knew no one in Italy; in fact, we had only been in the country for a few weeks on rose-tinted, aperol-spritz-toasting, basil-scented holidays. My parents hated the idea. I also had the best job in the world: hosting a top-rating afternoon drive radio show with my friend and colleague of eighteen years, Dave Hughes – in Australia. Not in Italy. As for the children, by the time we planned to leave on our grand adventure, two of them – Lewis and Sunday – would be teenagers, reluctant to uproot their lives, and leave all they knew.

So what we swiftly discovered was this: the world doesn't necessarily share your dream.

This is the story of an Australian family making their way across the world to a foreign land, trying to find an apartment, a car, a supermarket, a basketball team, a school, a cafe that would serve them a cappuccino after 11 am (no milka after morning!) and – hopefully – their place in a foreign place.

And it is also the story of our sixteen-year-old son, Lewis Lewis. The boy who lived. The child who at six was diagnosed with childhood leukaemia and survived – and who, because of this, was the unwitting motivation behind our bold move. The deep irony is that, though we wanted to seize life because he nearly lost his, he would rather not be in Italy.

It is about the day-to-day of Italian life, trying to learn a new language and make new friends, and what you discover about yourself when you are a stranger in a strange land.

It is about stepping up and falling down. On cobblestones.

It is about the Australian spirit – about wearing thongs as footwear and leaving the swimming pool with wet hair and laughing when many would weep. It is about fear and courage; about having a dream and living it.

Mostly, it is about love.

PART ONE

1

ITALIA: FALLING IN LOVE

It is no great revelation that certain countries or cities can become shorthand for a feeling; that their very name becomes one with an ethos or experience. Hawaii. Thailand. New York. The name of the place automatically conjures a mental picture. So much so that when you say you are going there others immediately intuit what sort of holiday or experience you will have.

Hawaii, for instance, is cocktails in tiki bars and old dudes doing the shaka, surfing on longboards, garlands of leis, Elvis Presley movies, volcanic rock and swimming with giant turtles. In Thailand you will float in aquamarine waters, eat green curry, drink fresh mango juice, tuk-tuk to markets and marvel at strange foods and maybe wash an elephant in a village stream. New York is the subway and musicals and eccentricity on the streets. It is The Met and 'Empire State of Mind' and *Sex and the City* (hopefully not the lamentable second movie) in a glittering, tumbling, urban front-loader.

Of course, this is not necessarily the case. You could be in any of these places working as a nurse or a builder covered in limestone and dust. You may be a free-running, teetotalling instafluencer who consumes their surrounds for likes. You may spend the day in a funk, weeping in your fourth-floor, red-brick, freeway-facing apartment. Just as we don't know the inner workings of each other's lives, so it is with a foreign country. We have no idea of the way in which it will open up to us, and us to it. And yet we think we do.

Few places on earth, it seems, conjure up more of an emotional response than Italy. It is a land that transcends cliché by simply piling on more of them: afternoon slumbers and wine, church bells and saints, terracotta-coloured villas and washing hanging over balconies, grapevines and pasta, and glittering seas and venerated old people. It is cobbled thoroughfares and picture-book villages, Pinocchio and families in the piazza, sliced meats and summer fruits, and music on the streets and romance. It is golden light caressing – not just the ancient stone buildings upon which it alights but also those blessed to bask in its rays. Falling in love with a country is like falling in love with a person. You are initially tentative. You start off with a few dates. With a country drive; with dinner. If that goes well, you return for more. Magical outings in which it feels everything is brushed with possibility. Suddenly, your heart is singing. You have never looked better. You feel alive – like your true, unfettered self. You are open and happy and free. You laugh. You see things differently.

Mostly, falling in love is not so much about the reality of the other person as it is about how they make you feel *about yourself*.

I wasn't looking to fall in love with Italy. I wasn't expecting it. It just happened.

There were seminal moments that made me fall in love. Many were as fleeting as feelings. Sometimes, tellingly, they emerged from chaos.

In Milan, we were driving along a narrow street, jammed with parked cars on either side. I was looking down from my perch in our idling van into the pit of an adjacent building site. Instead of construction vehicles busying themselves, I saw an archeological dig. A few muted worker bees were sectioning portions of dry earth, or brushing off pieces of broken pottery meticulously laid out alongside their roped-off dig. The scene was, we were to discover, a not uncommon occurrence in this old, old country, where the earth, when it is moved, will often reveal the past. To us, it was fascinating – so mesmerising that it actually took a while to realise our progress had been halted. We were alerted to our inertia when the drivers around us, impatient with being patient, started leaning on their horns and yelling.

One of the children hopped out of the back seat to scout the thoroughfare and see what was causing the holdup. Their report, breathlessly delivered on their return, was so remarkable we all had to lean out the windows to confirm it for ourselves. Ahead of us, a delivery van had stopped, right in the middle of the street. The driver had left his vehicle and was standing on the narrow footpath, at the counter of a cafe. There he was, casually downing a shot of espresso. The exasperated tooting and catcalls from the other drivers reached a cacophony before he deigned to acknowledge them. His coffee finished, he twirled his arm in an unflustered 'yes, yes' motion. Returned to his van. Got behind the wheel again, and we all moved off.

Near Siena, we were searching for our hillside accommodation in a tiny village intersected rather cruelly some years back by a freeway. The town, once an armoury, was called Armaiolo and was now a relative ghost town: bakery shuttered and the only restaurant seeming permanently closed. We were looking for an *agriturismo*, farmstay accommodation, we had booked several weeks prior. We had been misled – as so often happens in Italy – by Google Maps, and ended up on a narrow dirt road flanked by tiny plots of farmed land. In the absence of any street numbers and very few houses, we pulled up in front of some old wrought-iron gates, behind which was a two-storey, slightly crumbly, dusty-rose villa. It seemed like the place, but when we rang the bell no one answered. Weary of being car-bound, the kids scrambled out and found a track leading up the hill alongside the house. We followed them, and suddenly popped out through the bushes to a scene straight from a European film.

There, surrounded by a sparse orchard of olive and stone-fruit trees, was a glittering blue swimming pool. Perched on the stone edging, her legs trailing in the water, was a mahogany-skinned goddess in a scrap of a bikini. Lying alongside her, his head cradled on her lap, was an equally bronzed Adonis. He was staring up at her as she stroked his hair. They were smiling and murmuring to each other as an Italian pop song blared tinnily from one of their phones.

Even the children were caught short by this idyll. We all stood, transfixed for a moment, hot and panting from our thrash through the scrub. Then, feeling like creepy, pink interlopers, we called out to them. Apologetic. Tentative. The lovers looked up at the sound of our voices – not even slightly put out. They sprang to their feet, beaming, welcoming us with profuse apologies, kisses and handshakes. It was indeed our villa. The girl gave us a tour of the house, unselfconsciously still in her damp brown bikini. Then, after showing us the bedrooms (shuttered and lovely), and the kitchen (tiled and spacious), and offering to take us into Siena that night to watch the spectre of the *Palio* (a mad horserace and fistfight that takes place in the city square), she walked us back into the far reaches of the backyard and explained the only place the wi-fi might work (and why she hadn't responded to our earlier messages).

'*Italy!*' She laughed, simultaneously shaking her head and her phone. Her boyfriend got on a motorbike and roared off, coming back minutes later with milk and bread and coffee.

Four days later, some beloved friends from Australia – Nick and Kanye – joined us. We convened first at a castle on a local hill where we mistakenly ordered tripe and – deliberately – crispy porchetta and jugs of local Chianti. They came back to our villa and spent three days by the pool where we drank spritzes (aperol), and they chain-smoked and laughed with my mother-in-law Maree. We heard about their travels and tried to mount the giant inflatable popsicle that was the children's hotly contested pool toy. We drove to the village and nibbled from platters of prosciutto and melon and tomatoes and cheese. There was minor major adventure: Jannie and I went foraging roadside for wood for a barbecue and the old flat-capped farmer from below caught us stealing from his pile. We were guilty and apologetic; he sternly pinched Jannie on the cheek, then gave us half-a-dozen split logs, finger-waggingly warning us not to take more.

There is a perfect moment captured in memory. I am floating in the water, face-up, eyes closed. The summer sun is projecting spangled rainbows on my eyelids, when suddenly I am brushed on the shoulder by something. Startled, I open my eyes to see Peter, swinging the pool-cleaning net towards me. He is laughing, and as he manoeuvres the blue mesh towards me on its long pole, I see something nestling inside. It is an apricot he has picked from one of the trees festooning the yard. The fruit is still warm from the sun; its blushing skin studded with freckles. I fish it out of the net and, swimming to the side of the pool, share the apricot with my husband. It is the sweetest, most glorious orb. It is summer in the mouth. It is a gift of love.

Again in Milan. We have checked into a small hotel, where the seven of us have been allocated a trio of modern rooms plonked on top of a four-storey building. It is peak summer, a 44-degree heatwave, our rooms are being belted by the blazing sun, and the air-conditioning doesn't work. The rooms are brutally hot – in one, there is the faint emphysemic panting of air with a telltale whiff of mould, but the others are simply unbearably stifling. We go back and forth to the front desk to enquire about the progress of the 'engineer' who is supposed to be fixing things. The charming man on the front desk explains that, yes, they are having problems with the aircon, but they will have it fixed by the afternoon. This is a lie. As the day wears on, the rooms get hotter and hotter. It is too hot to go out; we are trapped in the sour soup of our rooms, literally dripping with perspiration. In between, an ancient valet appears. He is well over seventy, immaculately dressed in a maroon waistcoat and matching pants, despite working in a furnace. He speaks no English, and I speak no Italian, but he is well aware there is a problem. In a nod to Manuel from *Fawlty Towers*, his solution is to shift our suitcases from room to room. Every half hour he appears, moves the suitcases, and pauses to mop his brow with an immaculately white handkerchief. He shakes his head uncomprehendingly when I ask about the aircon before he disappears.

Eventually I realise our patience and polite smiling is not helping. I return downstairs again, this time with purpose. I ask the man at the front counter to move us to another hotel. He explains they have already tried to find us other accommodation, but the World Expo is on and every room in the city is booked. Peter and I have already confirmed this for ourselves, upstairs. What about portable air conditioners? I ask. He shrugs. The mobile coolers are already being used by other guests. He is sorry, but there is nothing more they can do.

I think it is the shrug that finally sets me off. I am too hot and frazzled for him to 'Italy' his way through this. I take things up a notch. The rooms are impossible to sleep in. It is his hotel. He has taken our booking and our money, and it is his responsibility to find somewhere for us to sleep that is not dangerously, ridiculously hot. We have four children who are already exhausted. Now, I inform him, they also have a mother who is angry.

I don't know what it is that finally breaks the impasse; whether it is my annoyed tone, or the mention of the children. It may even be my status as '*madre*' but, whatever it is, the hotel manager comes over and, after an impassioned back and forth with two other staff members, proffers his hand. He is sorry. I am right; this is unacceptable. Perhaps we can all share a room on the ground floor they have found for us tonight, and they will have things fixed by tomorrow. The ground floor room is large; it has a loft where they will set up extra beds and, he assures me, the air-conditioning works. I am so relieved. Finally, a solution. I thank him, and he calls over the old valet, who heads off up the stairs to move our suitcases once again.

As we all troop back downstairs to our temporary ground-floor solution, the manager beckons me and Peter over. By further way of apology, he explains, they would like to offer us dinner at a local restaurant. It is a very nice restaurant, he explains, and we would dine as guests of the hotel.

We accept his offer, and after taking turns to shower in the bathroom of our new room, we venture out to the restaurant he has recommended. From the outside it is unprepossessing; dimly lit, with a ripped lace curtain hanging raggedly in the window, where something is scrawled in texta across the glass. Peter, still wary from the day's fiasco, is sceptical about what lies in wait for us; especially as it seems the manager's peace offering is preferable to him actually offering a refund on our rooms.

The restaurant turns out to be a gem. It is owned by a couple who have had it for over forty years – a husband, who runs the front-of-house, and his wife, who does the cooking. They are expecting us; amongst the locals dining, there is a long table set for seven, with waiting pitchers of wine and water. The ensuing hospitality brings us all back to life. The children eat first; serves of homemade tagliatelle with tomato sauce and cubes of fried bread, with tiny squares of omelette and sliced meats and cheese. We feast on risotto Milanese, then veal with mushrooms, crumbed chicken and fried fish and roast potatoes, salads of mixed leaves with tiny multicoloured tomatoes, a dish of wilted wild greens and baskets of homemade bread. Lured from the kitchen by her curiosity and our appreciative applause, the cook emerges, where she accepts our accolades with a head-ducking, shy smile. In Italian, she addresses Maree. We use our phone to translate; she is happy about how many of us there are, and the beauty of our children. She is herself a *nonna*, and is thrilled that we are travelling with Peter's mother.

After cheesecake and gelato and liqueurs and coffee with tiny sugared biscuits, we are beyond sated. We go to leave, and among the exchange of thanks and farewell salutations, *la nonna* re-emerges from the kitchen, wiping sudsy hands on her apron. She motions for us to wait for a moment. Then she reappears and, after gently pressing the back of her hand against Sunday's cheek, presents my daughter with a punnet of strawberries.

It is such a lovely gift. Such an evening of riches. It is life-affirming and nourishing and humbling, and a reminder that, sometimes, things that seem too good to be true are actually possible. That feeling describes so much of our experience of Italy – just as things seem hopeless and lost, magic happens.

We return to our hotel, drowsily happy, to have our faith further restored. In our absence, the temporary room has been expertly set up. Peter and I share the king-sized bed downstairs with our youngest Jannie gleefully sandwiched in the middle. Artie sleeps on a mattress that has been wheeled to the foot of our bed. Maree, Lewis and Sunday have three trundle beds on the mezzanine loft above us. The aircon, though grumbling and complaining, is enough that we pull the crisp sheets up around our shoulders and fall into a deep, untroubled slumber.

Tomorrow, though we do not know it yet, we will swim in Lake Como. We will emerge from sparkling fresh water – four hundred metres deep – pooled at the foot of mountains, and while the children jump off a long wooden jetty, Peter and I will hobble across white stones to a food truck on the shore. Because this is Italy, the food truck will have an attached timber deck with bookcases, yellow-striped wallpaper, and a chandelier. We will drink prosecco while the hippy girl behind the counter makes us delicious pizzas and fried potatoes. Then she will show us behind the van where there are folded deckchairs we can use, and when we ask how much we owe her, she will say proudly, 'These are free. Like the beaches in Australia, no?'

And everything will be perfect.

Better than a dream, because it is real.

When it is time to leave Milan, I wake early, as I often do on a travelling day. I slip out of the hotel room, and walk through the quiet streets.

I pass a *tabaccheria* where two men, suited, are standing outside, downing short coffees, Italian style; as though they are cars filling up their tanks at a service station. I smile as I walk past. They smile back.

'*Ciao, bella*,' they say.

Hello, beautiful.

It is ridiculous how much this thrills me.

2
WHY, WHY, WHY?

In Italy, they say: *Perché*? (Why?)
And the answer often is: *Perché*. (Because.)

There are six of us in this family, and as my husband Peter Lewis says, only two of us do any work. That would be me and him.

Mainly, it's because the other four members of the family are children. There is the eldest, my fifteen-year-old son Lewis. Actually his surname is the same as his alleged father's, so his full name is Lewis Lewis. There is his sister, our artistic and slyly deadpan daughter Sunday Lil, thirteen, named for her beloved nanna's mother, Lil. Then there are The Two Little Boys, who we refer to by that moniker, so much so that everyone thinks they are twins – and they are so close, they practically are. They share a room, play basketball together, giggle into the night and wrestle like cubs. They are Artie, my green-eyed, studious eleven-year-old, and Jannie, our clog-dancing, mischief-making nine-year-old elf, named for my tall Dutch dad, Jan.

Those who are good at maths (or biology) would have worked out that somehow, somewhere, I went from not having any children, to having four under six. This, I assure you, is what is legitimately known as a quantum leap. Those who haven't set foot on the parenting yellow brick road may not understand its significance, but no matter. Just google any stand-up comedian talking about parenting (the women about their ravaged nether-quarters, their stretch marks and their pathological love of wine; the men bemoaning their lack of sex life and no longer being able to go to the movies or enjoy weekend sleep-ins). Multiply it by four and then by the factor of SHOCK and DESPAIR, temper it with moments of pure happiness and elation, and you are pretty well in the vicinity of modern parenthood. I am not, you understand, complaining about this. I understand that it was my choice, and to bleat about the attendant responsibilities is as pointless as to stand on the edge of an abyss and moan about gravity. But, oddly, they are not dissimilar experiences. In both instances you are left resolutely earthbound, where once you may have thought you could fly.

Imagine, if you will, that everything you hitherto loved and enjoyed has been stripped from you, and replaced by a life of dawn-to-dusk (and dusk-to-dawn) servitude in which your tiny, irrational masters not only relentlessly demand things that can only be delivered by you, but they are also prone to bed-wetting, tantrums, squabbling, endless questions and food fights. It may be less galling if your overlords could actually speak, or read, or wipe their own bottoms or were taller than two feet high. But though you are convinced you know more, you know nothing when it comes to them. Only that you are there to serve. And here is the irony. You do so willingly. Wearily, but willingly.

Because this much I have learned: nothing enslaves you more effectively than love.

I remember reading that the idea that childhood should be an idyllic state governed only by play and leisure is a fairly new construct. Of course, it's also a mainly Western world luxury because kids all over the world still have to work. They help out on farms, milk cows, pick cocoa beans and make bricks out of mud, and in some countries they have some dire responsibilities, sorting through rubbish piles or working in factories under diabolical conditions. And only a couple of hundred years ago, these very children, my fortunate children, now sitting around the table eating corn fritters and slyly flicking each other with rubber bands, would have been put out to work. Where? I wonder. Up chimneys? Down mines? Below decks on cargo ships? Wheat fields or weaving mills? But the fact is that we are Westerners. We are Australians, from what was once ironically deemed The Lucky Country but in many ways actually still is. And it is not the 1700s. It is 2018, so our children do nothing. I mean, they go to primary school, where they mainly seem to dance around maypoles and learn about recycling and how the world is going to end, and they do their homework (which always seems to entail a parent cutting shapes out of cardboard at 1 am and trying to find a glue stick to make a diorama of how the world is going to end) and then they go to high school, where they attend mental health workshops because they're all suffering anxiety, possibly from constantly being told the world is going to end. But I digress.

When it comes to the heavy lifting of household chores, modern children – or, at least, mine – seem blessed with the cloak of invisibility, and rendered positively leaden with an inertia so powerful that it would have stumped Isaac Newton. So Peter and I have found ourselves increasingly mumbling that mantra of defeated parents everywhere, as we stoop to pick up where the children left off, as we wash dishes and hang out laundry and sweep floors and empty rubbish bins and find lost single shoes: *It's easier to do it myself.*

I hate this thinking, and I know it is deeply flawed along the 'teach a man to fish' principle, yet I am way too weary/lazy/defeated/modern/overwhelmed/disempowered/exhausted/impatient to challenge it in myself.

In my fantasy family, you see, some metaphorical figure (a cross, perhaps, of the Captain from *The Sound of Music* and a stern but crisp Mary Poppins) would have trained the children in their early years – maybe even brutally – to be disciplined and helpful and cheerful. Of course, I say 'early' because I want the hard work to have already been done. By someone else. What I want is for me, years down the track, to reap the rewards. This desire, by the way, is not my fault. It's not just millennials who have been led to expect they can get what they want, when they want it. And in this case, I want McDonald's parenting. Fast-food, convenience parenting, where I can drive through, in maximum comfort, and pick up children to order. 'I'll have one medium Polite, please, a serve of Pretty and

Piano Playing; a Large Helpful with extra Loving Cuddles, a couple of Random Talented and Tidy Rooms, and a side of Diligent and Well-Mannered. Oh, and give us a large Enthusiastic and Happy, while you're at it. No sauces.'

In 2009, we had four children under the age of six. Peter was running a bar. I was doing a breakfast radio show with my on-air partner Dave Hughes. Our children were happy. My youngest baby, Jannie, was five months old, and so little I had only just stopped taking him into work with me. We were busy, busy, busy. We thought we knew exhaustion. Then we met cancer.

My firstborn, our beloved Lewis Lewis, was diagnosed with leukaemia and the diagnosis sent ripples of pain and shock and fear through everyone we knew. I thought I could not bear it, but I did. I could not panic and I could not run. Because I was his mother. And because he was frightened, I could not be. His treatment plan was to take four long years. To say it was a tough time is an understatement.

It was horrendous. Terrifying. Dread-inducing. Knee-buckling. Stomach-dropping. It was everything you could imagine, but worse. In fact, don't imagine it. Our family and friends were fraught and frightened (some of them even frightened away) and, while I never spoke about it publicly, we were consumed by our battle. Many of our friends rallied to support us and our suddenly fragile, ravaged family. There were meals dropped off to us, and constant messages, and a small but stoic front-line battalion of visitors to the hospital on long, long days and weeks when Lewis's immunity – smashed by chemo drugs and then radiation – was so low we couldn't be anywhere else.

We were trying to live a 'normal life', as we had been instructed at the start of Lewis's cancer diagnosis, but this was increasingly difficult. People showed their love in myriad ways. My love for Hughesy deepened as I bore witness to his strength and valiance. He was a rock – though he and his beautiful wife Holly (who had also had their firstborn, Raffy, that year) were both shaken to their foundations by the diagnosis of our boyo, whom they had both known from the womb. Comedian friends – notably Pete Helliar and Mick Molloy – filled in for me at a moment's notice on our breakfast show, sometimes taking the call at 3 or 4 am when I found myself unable to leave home or hospital.

Our beautiful butcher Gary made Lewis his favourite ham without nitrites (he found out how to do this with pineapple). My former boss sent Lego. Our friends Rob and Janie dropped off food for the children and airline-sized bottles of wine in case we ever felt like we needed a drink but couldn't commit to a whole bottle. My girlfriend Chrissie Swan, with awkward 'I don't know what to say' (and we *always* know what to say) kindness, brought me a chicken pot pie from her radio station to mine and presented it to me outside the lifts. There were books and blankets and baskets of homegrown veggies and pots of pesto dropped at the front door. My girlfriend Mac gave me a bracelet that said: *One devoted person can initiate change* (I wore it for five years, until the writing became scratched and faint).

And there were prayers; so many prayers. From Mum and Dad's Christian, mainly Dutch church. From our beloved Persian babysitter, Mitra. From hippie friends and Catholic friends and Jewish friends. The battle of our blue-eyed, blond-haired, beloved Lewis Lewis, it seemed, had brought everyone to their knees, and while we were down there, we may as well pray.

I tried to take each fear-filled, leaden step evenly. Each stroke of his little bald head with my hand was calm and reassuring. Every word I spoke, I uttered quietly and lightly, to make sure I would not betray to my child the quivering fear inside me. I made little jokes, and his father and I smoothed his pyjamas, and we lifted his tiny body onto his hospital bed, and everything was white and bright and clean and surgical, except for his fluffy blanket we had brought from home, and I smiled and murmured and comforted my boy, and the kindly surgeon said to me, very gently, 'I will take good care of him, I promise'. And I could only whisper 'Thank you', and I had to turn away because inside I was fluttering and weak like a captured, wild, dying thing.

That was more than five years ago. I could barely dare to dream that Lewis would one day be a strapping, lanky teenager. But he is. He has finished treatment and – praise be – is well.

For so long, we couldn't go anywhere, we couldn't travel anywhere; we just went to the hospital, and then we went home. So, once Lewis was cleared and we had regathered ourselves, the ultimate sign of his wellness was that we could have a travelling adventure. All of us, together. Everyone who has been brushed with cancer's icy witch-finger will attest to how it changes you. And for me, cancer changed my attitude about the opportunities you have in life – the biggest opportunity is life itself.

I guess this is part of what led us to this meeting around the table – the table where we have shared countless family dinners with Peter's parents and mine, where the aforementioned homework is done, where friends come for pancake parties on the weekends, and children's birthdays galore, where we look out onto our small but green backyard to the concrete yard of the next-door flats we have pilfered to turn into a basketball court. It is in the very fabric of this house that, for thirteen years, our trials and tribulations have been met. It is here that we have had, like so many other families, riotous dinner parties and impromptu gatherings. In this old wooden house we have wept and celebrated and staved off leukaemia and a kitchen fire, and a flood and an attempted home invasion. It sounds a bit biblical, and I guess in a way it is, because it feels like end times for us. And yet it is a home of optimism and energy. We are happy. We are fortunate. But we want to be happier. We want to test our fortunes.

So here we all are, six of us at the table that extends to seat twelve, and is often full. We are gathered to discuss our future as a family. The metaphorical boat Peter and I are about to launch is born partly from wanting to put an end to our own grinding non-decision – the to-ing and fro-ing we have engaged in, deep into the night – and partly from excitement. It is sprung from a desire to break the circuit we find ourselves in, even though much of the circuit is a fine one. Increasingly, Petie and I want to divest ourselves of the grind of the urban, modern life we have forged for ourselves, and have had foisted upon us. 'Simplicity' and 'being in the moment' have become modern touchstones, and yet they feel like extra chores to cross off on a seeming endless to-do list; between school runs and making lunches and forms for excursions and what's for dinner and fights about technology and uniforms and basketball five times a week and work–life and deadlines and groceries and doctors' appointments and swim squad at 5.30 am and why can't I have a phone.

And although we have barely addressed it with each other, Peter and I have, independently and jointly, had a growing dissatisfaction at clocking up miles, racing to meetings, attempting to negotiate the physical evolution of our children and their emotional and spiritual needs, while juggling, juggling, juggling our own. Sometimes it feels like we just come up for sips of air or to stroke each other's faces gently and helplessly between our work and parenting and a welcome schedule of social obligations that are supposed to be fun, but may as well be the ascent of Everest, so empty is our tank of oxygen.

It is, I realise, not even really a plan that Peter and I have devised, so much as a yearning.

We have barely thought through any logistics; more often than not, just trying to leave for a long weekend seems like disentangling ourselves from a skein of silken, sticky web. And yet we know this – as soon as we deliver the news to our charges, we will be speaking it into existence. This dream, this shimmering mirage of a new life, will take on a momentum that will compel us – propel us all – from our lovely home at the bottom of the globe to the other side of the world. And it will shift everything in our family. We will be asserting ourselves, not only as parents who make decisions for their children, but also as two adults who want something more. There are four expectant faces at the table. Two resolute ones.

'It's about next year,' Peter says, reaching for the last of the corn fritters before Jannie can add it to the pile on his plate.

'Next year, we are all going to live in Italy.'

3

WHERE, WHERE, WHERE?

It is a deep irony in life that too many choices can be as hobbling as not enough.

This has been evident throughout my life, particularly when it comes to deciding on a career. I have always marvelled at those who have a calling, who know from childhood or early adulthood that they want to be musicians, lawyers, plumbers or work with animals. I have never been like that – frankly, I am overwhelmed by the choices on a cafe menu. Do I want scrambled eggs, boiled eggs or poached eggs, Bircher muesli or pancakes? White bread or wholemeal? Avocado or bacon or mushrooms? Hang on a minute – corn fritters? This changes EVERYTHING! (Disclosure: I actually never want eggs. I baulk at runny yolks – liquid chicken – and it is nearly impossible to get them cooked hard in restaurants. Also, I would never order Bircher muesli.)

Anyway, in my working life, one pursuit has led to another – studying journalism, then moving from my home state of Queensland south to Victoria to go to acting school. This led, along a meandering route, to television writing and then community radio. It was really only by accident that I ended up with anything that constitutes a 'career', though I think many people's life trajectories appear like this in retrospect. Especially in show business, so much of success seems to be a mix of talent, white-knuckled tenacity and, of course, that elusive gift from the gods – 'luck'.

Peter, though more cautious and ordered than me, is similar in his pinballing approach to work. He started three courses at university:

science and then medical instrumentation (which he was studying when we met) before finally completing a degree in electrical engineering. When I was pregnant with our third child, Artie, Peter jumped from the large engineering firm he had been working at (and where his boss was, consciously or not, punishing him for having taken paternity leave and returning part-time) to become joint owner of a rock bar in a graffitied laneway in inner-city Melbourne.

It's fair to say we have never been people who operate with a five-year-plan.

No surprise, then, that we were faced with a quandary when trying to decide where in Italy we wanted to live. I guess most people, when relocating to a foreign country, would do a lot of research. They would seek out other expats, or read articles and online forums, or study statistics about population and income and terrain and climate.

Peter and I are doing it our way. We are filling out a BuzzFeed quiz.

In the cold light of technological day, our phones have probably been eavesdropping on us, as they obviously do with those weirdly specific ads that pop up in your feed. (Note to ethernet overlords: please stop sending me 'Hairstyles That Suit Women Over Fifty' – they make me shudder with how little you dream for me.) Anyway, we are so desperate for guidance that when a new BuzzFeed offering pings on my phone it actually seems like a sign.

'What Italian city are you?' it asks.

And because, eight months out from our grand adventure, we still have no idea what Italian city we are, we decide to fill out the questionnaire. All we know is that we favour the north of the country, above the knee of the boot. Peter has travelled there with his mum and the children on a previous holiday when I had to return to Australia to work, and he has ridden his bike among the alps. This part of the country is at the full height of its powers in winter but is also beautiful in summer, with grassy slopes and steep-roofed chalets and big alpine cows wearing bells. While we won't be living in wildflower-strewn meadows and milking goats *Heidi* style in the actual mountains, Peter has dreams of skiing on snow-covered European slopes. And we have also settled on the reality that we need an English-speaking international school for the children. After initially toying with sending all four to local schools (partly for financial reasons; partly because we believe in the equality of state education and would love the kids to have a deep immersion in Italian language and life), we have now ruled it out. It seems too cruel to plunge them into Italian schools, given they will already be uprooted.

We also know we don't want to live in a huge metropolis, like Rome or Milan. Melbourne, where we live, is a large city; in Italy, we want something different. Initially – spawned, I guess, by books and films – I had a classic Tuscan-villa fantasy: pool, vegetable garden, shaded terraces dripping with wisteria. But when Peter pointed out that at least three months of the year is proper, freezing winter, I amended my vision. Instead, we will live in the centre of somewhere; in an apartment, with a cafe downstairs, and a bakery around the corner. Somewhere we don't have to drive so much. Somewhere we can walk to the shops. Larger than a village; smaller than a metropolis.

This is the powerful thing about fantasy, you see; it can take whatever form you like.

Anyway, the quiz.

We complete it in bed one night, giggling at how half-baked the whole notion is, and yet it is as good a lead as the 'none' we already have. As my mother likes to say, 'In the land of the blind, the man with one eye is king', and when it comes to forging our phantom life in Italy, we are definitely working blind.

The questionnaire instructs us to make selections from an array of pictures: our favourite pasta, our favourite car, our favourite apartment/villa/house, our favourite scenery (beach or mountains?). It is surprisingly difficult, but I guess that is because we have a lot riding on it. We submit our answers and wait eagerly for the result.

Verona – it is decreed – is the Italian city for us.

We have heard of it. Verona is best known as the setting of Shakespeare's *Romeo and Juliet*. A city built on a river, it seems romantic and poetic and perfect (if you ignore the despair and the joint suicide at the end). So we add it to the places we are going to check out. The list now reads:

Florence.

Verona.

Bologna.

In July, when I have my two-week survey break – our designated radio holidays in which there are no ratings collated – and the children have school holidays, we will go to Italy, specifically to scope out those three cities, and their schools. My beloved mother-in-law Maree, who accompanied us on our first-ever holiday to Italy in 2015, will come with us again. We trust her judgement and enjoy each other's company so thoroughly we have shared many holidays together.

As well as being a gift of a mother and MIL, Maree Lewis is a rock. She was our third pillar in those dark days when Lewis was being treated for leukaemia. Together, we have sat vigil by his bed when things seemed at their darkest. We have cleaned up vomit and changed sheets in the middle of the night. We have made midnight trips to emergency, learned to administer chemo and clean feeding tubes. We have made each other endless cups of tea and drunk them, though our mouths were full of dust. We have stroked my son's naked head and waited with lead in our stomachs outside myriad oncology appointments. We have been silent together when things were too frightening to speak of. We have been cautiously exultant.

Maree is a shining example of a generation of bushy Australians who are strong, resourceful and practical. She is a great and natural traveller, and like most campers (she introduced me to the beauty of outside living) is adaptable and competent. She can chat to anyone and find common ground. She has slept on the dirt floor of a village hut with my Thai sister-in-law Bee, and has stayed in luxury, and is thrilled by both. She is humble and without pretence, but can spot a fool from fifty paces and richly enjoy them. She loves music and plays the guitar, reads books, does yoga and babies tell her their secrets. She has strong and lovely work-worn hands that can whip up scones or a hearty meal for ten from a seemingly empty fridge. The children adore their Nanaree. So do my parents. She has a great sense of humour and is unfailingly patient – except when Peter's dad, Bryan, refuses to use his hearing aid.

(I love my mother-in-law and am dismayed for friends who are not as fortunate in their relationships with their own loved one's mothers. How is it possible to adore the offspring, I wonder, and not find a way to respect and love the woman who shaped them?)

Anyway. Here are the results of our reconnaissance mission.

Florence: It is famously beautiful, amazing, stunning, breathtaking, awe-inspiring, jaw-dropping, art-filled magnificence. It is also crammed, jammed, rammed with tourists. The locals, though surprisingly pleasant, deal with the onslaught year-round, with millions and millions of visitors to their city that most of them can no longer afford to live in. They surely have tourist-fatigue, and we would only be adding to the problem. 'They are sick of us, and we haven't even arrived yet,' I say to Peter. Plus, the international school – a Fellini-film Tuscan villa on a hillside overlooking the city (and teeming with tourist buses) – would mean driving every day. Florence, it seems, is a 'no'.

Verona: The city itself is gorgeous; the river spectacular. We wander around the huge historical arena, which is hosting an open-air performance of the opera *Aida*. Outside are the giant props: fibre-glass elephants and boulders on wheeled pallets. We drive to the suburb which houses the international school. The building, surrounded by apartment blocks, looks like a low-level bunker: concrete, walled, impenetrable. The school is empty, but open – apparently there are exams on in some of the rooms – but the three or four women we introduce ourselves to in the office are incredibly unfriendly. We explain our quest: that we have come from the other side of the world and wish to have a quick look around. They are so brusque and rude, we retreat to our van, shocked. Peter says: 'If they think we are coming here to spend thousands of dollars and be treated like this, they are crazy.' No wonder Romeo and Juliet ran away, I think.

Which leaves us with Bologna.

When we arrive there's a glitch in our accommodation, and we end up staying fifty kilometres away, in a villa on top of a hill nowhere near the nearest town. The setting is idyllic; perfect for a holiday, but hopeless for checking out Bologna. Still, I have emailed the school and, although they are on holidays, I receive an instant response from the principal.

He would love to meet with us, he says.

So the next day, Peter and I drive into Bologna. We take the autostrada, then drive through the outlying suburbs of the town before we head through the old walls of the historical centre. The city is red and ancient. It is lovely. There is no tourist frenzy; just locals dressed for work, shopping or eating. We walk around, marvelling at the beauty and ease of the place, its elegance. Hardly anyone we meet speaks more than a smattering of English. We wander around the broad main piazza adorned with its fountain of Neptune, mermaids at his feet. Incredibly – audaciously – water is spurting from their nipples. We find ourselves in a narrow laneway, and stop for a drink at an outside table in the shade. The man who owns the bar comes out to take our order, and greets us heartily, marvelling that we are from Australia. Then he motions at me, at my sunglasses and my swimming-pool hair, held back with a couple of diamanté pins I have jabbed into my fringe at the last moment.

'*Fantastico!*' he says, beaming.

We return two days later with the children, and meet the school principal, a charming and polite Englishman. He is like a character from a novel, refined and thoughtful. He takes his time showing us around the school and then, in an empty classroom, we sit down together and he asks the children if they have any questions.

He would love to have us at his school, he says. But there is a waiting list for entry. And because of the difference in the curriculum (the European school year finishes in June and commences in September) and because this is Italy, it will be complicated. The upshot is that, if we are keen, we had better start with the reams of paperwork now.

We drive back to our house in the hills. The kids, released from best behaviour, jump in the pool. Maree and I begin to make dinner. Peter makes us an aperol spritz and we have a toast. He says he will begin the school application procedures immediately.

And so it is decided.

We are going to live in Bologna.

4

ARRIVIAMO: FAMIGLIA LEWIS ARRIVE!

After twenty-four hours of flying, two stopovers and myriad eye-glazing time zones later, we touch down at Bologna International Airport crumpled and tired. It is a crisp January afternoon, and though we feel we have been travelling forever, it is somehow the same day we left Australia: Saturday.

The children are clutching the remains of the paper bags our girlfriend Carla presented to them as our minibuses pulled out of our street in St Kilda to take us to the airport. In each are the dregs of an assortment of Australian specialties. There are Cherry Ripe chocolate bars. Bags of chicken and cheese Twisties. Burger Rings. Violet Crumble honeycomb. She roared into our street and handed out the treats with final hugs, while Mitra, our beloved and devoted babysitter of ten years, stood by with a jug of water, sprinkling it on the road behind us as we moved off – a Persian tradition that will ensure our safe return, she tells us, with water in her own eyes.

And now the six of us have been magic-carpeted to the other side of the world. Australian soil and its familiar hot, dry summer is far behind us, and in that always amazing travel trick of having flown like a bird over oceans and land, everything is now opposite. It is winter here; cold, but not brutally so. Still, I am wearing the only coat I own that will fend off the chill of a European winter – a quite spectacular but slightly demented white fur, an ankle-length covering I bought second-hand at a school flea market years ago. The children are variously layered in hoodies and puffer jackets and, after we have made our way through the snaking queue of immigration (our papers are in order!), we walk through the arrivals terminal, past groups of people eagerly scanning the crowd for loved ones.

There is no friendly family member waiting for us, of course. How could there be? We push our laden trollies past a gleaming yellow Lamborghini on display and a man at a table covered with a chequered cloth, making mortadella sandwiches on crunchy white rolls and there, suddenly, is a black-suited Italian holding a sign that says in scrawled sharpie: *Famiglia Lewis*. It is for us. We follow him outside, where amidst the standard Italian-flavoured chaos of jammed cars and farewell-and-welcome cuddles, and taxis and buses and huddles of smokers, there are two black minivans pulled up at the kerb.

After months of discussion and culling, we have brought from Australia only what we think we will absolutely need: a case each for the junior members of our posse, and two each for Peter and myself (one with winter clothes; one with summer). As well, there is sundry sporting equipment, two boxed bicycles for Jannie and Artie, five kilos of vac-packed bacon I have frozen (from our beloved market butcher, Gary), paintbrushes for Sunday and medicines (for hopefully no one). We have ten suitcases, plus backpacks and bodies, so we are squeezed into the vans like tinned Ligurian anchovies.

The trip into central Bologna only takes twenty minutes or so. Like every airport around the world, this one is on the outskirts of the city and the drive is not pretty. We pass concrete blocks of apartments, freeway ramps and the huge convention centre, and because it is winter, it is grey and the trees are stark. The overall impression is a little bleak. Looking through the tinted windows of our transport, I sense the bleary, unspoken apprehension of the children: *Where have you brought us?* And I must admit, even through the fog of my fatigue, it is an apprehension I share. Soon, however, we rumble our way to the outskirts of the walled city, and the buildings take on the famous red hue of the old city of Bologna, and everything is familiarly, unfamiliarly lovely.

As we pass through the entrance of the old walls – the thick, red-brick, crumbling structure common in so many ancient Italian cities and towns – that once formed an impenetrable barricade around the medieval centre, and bump along narrow streets covered in cobblestones and flanked with centuries-old buildings, Peter and I exchange looks. It is an eloquent, wordless exchange between two people who have been together a long time and are often surrounded by tiny eavesdroppers. A silent look and yet full of layered meaning. It says: *We are here. We have done it.* And it also says: *Aaarrrggghhh!* He reaches over and squeezes my hand as we make our unheralded entrance to our new home.

They call Bologna the city of red, and while that supposedly refers to its political leanings as a university town, it also applies literally. Every building is shades of terracotta and *rossa*. It is beautiful; beautiful enough to be another Florence or Milan, which are the nearest major cities, and yet it is somehow understated. This, I guess, is why Bologna is largely off the international tourist circuit. Even so, it is impossible not to be struck by its utterly charming *Italianness*. There are cobbled laneways and churches and apartment balconies sporting winter potted flowers. There are tiny shopfronts lit golden with twinkling window displays; restaurants with curtains framing immaculately set tables; mounds of brightly coloured fruit and vegetables outside corner stores; florists and shoe shops and tiny supermarkets. The streetlights are amber tiger's eyes warming the winter light. My own eyes are greedily trying to take everything in – so many shimmering jewels lie behind the arched porticoes for which Bologna is famous. It is spectacular, and I am momentarily reassured about the decision Peter and I so definitively made in haste seven months ago.

The upsweep of my triumphant heart is short-lived. When we finally drive through the old walls of the city centre, we encounter our first obstacle: the traffic in the city is blocked on the weekend. Central Bologna is a pedestrian precinct every Friday to Sunday night, when it becomes the domain of the vigorous local shoppers and diners. Today being Saturday, we cannot drive through the centre.

It takes a while to work out what the solution to this dilemma will be, but after much gesturing and explaining in impenetrable Italian, our driver pulls up at the nearest spot he is allowed to drive to – a narrow corner near the brown sweep of the main Piazza Maggiore. The convoy van carrying the rest of our luggage butts up behind.

Our driver, clearly itching to vacate the area before he incurs a fine, gets out and confers with his colleague then, with much gesticulating, the pair of them indicate that we will have to carry our cases across to a red-awninged building, three or four hundred metres away across the square. So here we are, hastily decanted from our vehicles with an enormous mound of luggage, and there, across the way, somewhere, is an apartment that we have never laid eyes on but have to find. It reminds me of the farmer who has to cross the river with a goose, a fox and a bag of grain, but can only transport one at a time. Obviously, the goose cannot be left with the fox, nor the goose with the grain. What to do?

We settle for leaving Jannie and Artie standing sentry with our pile of cases, while Sunday, Lewis, Peter and I schlep across the piazza dragging suitcases. Then we embark on the traditional *Lord of the Rings* like quest to find the building that matches the address we have been given. We finally find Via Clavature, a long laneway bustling with shoppers and diners, and then – *ta-da!* – the narrow doorway which matches our instructions. It is hidden behind a cluster of tables next to a tiny bar where people are eating and drinking. We have to ask people to move their chairs from the table blocking the doorway before we can squeeze past them with our unwieldy suitcases, negotiating the twisting and worn marble stairs that will lead to our new home.

Upstairs, there is a man from the holiday rental company waiting for us. He has buzzed us in, but nonetheless seems surprised when we arrive at the door, panting and heaving cases. Just as the van driver seemed astounded that the streets are closed off every Friday to Sunday, though they apparently have been for the last seven years or so, this new guy seems totally flabbergasted that people have arrived to stay in the holiday apartment his company is letting. (This strikes us as very Italian, and conjures up memories of many encounters we have had in our previous Italian trips. Basically, the scenario goes like this. Us: 'Hello. We have a booking for a hotel room.' Them: accusing stare, firm shake of the head, emphatic, '*No!*' We have learned not to panic at this. Five minutes later, after Peter has calmly riffled through his bag, painstakingly producing booking confirmation forms, there is inevitably a long and suspicious perusal of the paperwork, then furious tapping on a computer, and eventually: 'Your room! It'sa ready!')

When we finally communicate to our rental concierge – he using his welcome smattering of English, and we the international language of mime – that we have been dropped off across the way, he springs into apologetic action. He produces a portable trolley, and scurries across the piazza, with us following. Then he kindly trundles back and forth with our excess of luggage before giving the six of us a tour of our new home.

The 'tour' doesn't take long. We procured this apartment at the last desperate minute, after the elderly owner of the one we had initially found after months of searching developed cold feet about (a) renting to foreigners for (b) only a year. (Italian leases are generally for four years at a time and then are renewed for four years, pretty well guaranteeing housing security. Just not for us. As well, Italian law forbids evicting any family with minor children, which means a lot of landlords are hesitant to rent to a family with four of them.) When the first landlord cancelled on us three weeks before we were due to leave Australia, we were forced into a wormhole of bureaucratic terror: without a lease we couldn't get visas; without visas, we couldn't stay in Italy. Eventually, after a desperate day-and-night deep dive into every apartment in Bologna, and dozens of negative responses (or even no responses at all), Peter stumbled upon this holiday apartment, and had the temerity to ask if we could rent it for a year. Amazingly, they agreed, and this where we are now standing.

Real estate websites, we have found, are often Tinder-date deceptive – except while Tinder dates, in the flesh, tend to be larger than their flattering pictures, dwellings are the opposite. Certainly this is the case here. Our apartment is undeniably tight for six people. There are only three bedrooms. Aside from the fair-sized *matrimoniale* room for me and Peter, there is one with bunk beds (that Peter organised) for Jannie and Artie, then another very small room with twin singles pressed against the walls, which Sunday and Lewis will share. As well, there is a narrow walk-through lounge with strange white modular vinyl chairs under a beautiful sky-blue frescoed ceiling, and a really tiny galley kitchen. But the apartment is bright and light and the marble floors are spotlessly clean, and it is in the most perfect position. Downstairs are cafes and restaurants and clothes shops, and groups of tourists on walking food-tours. A hundred metres down from us is the oldest university in Europe, our host informs us. And then, of course, there is the view.

Across from the long glass dining table are wall-to-wall windows that look over the entirety of Piazza Maggiore. From our vantage point on the first floor, we can see across to the main council building (the *commune*) with the round clock on the spire. If we swivel our tired eyes even slightly to the left, they feast upon the imposing Basilica Di San Petronio, Bologna's main church, with its two-toned brown and cream edifice and army guards standing watch. The vista alone makes us forget any other shortcomings of our accommodation. Below are puffer-clad locals crossing the stone piazza, weaving on bikes among passing buses or simply sitting on the long steps that tier down from the church, seeking the fragile warmth of the low winter sun. It is so beautiful. It is so *alive*. It is so foreign. It is stunning.

We start to unpack, and soon realise that our apartment does not have cupboard space for all our clothing. Even with as little as we have packed, we are in an apartment that is designed for a week's stay – not several months – so we leave our summer clothes in their cases and slide them under our beds. We are all slightly addled with jet lag, the time difference and the realisation that, after all these months, we are finally *here*. Also, we don't even really know where *here* is, but food is always grounding, so the six of us head around the corner and stop at the first bar we see. We order coffees and crusty rolls with prosciutto and cheese, and are momentarily flummoxed when the waiter behind the counter asks us if we want them *caldo* or *freddo* – two options that confuse us because *caldo* sounds like 'cold' but actually means 'hot'. Eventually, our untoasted sandwiches arrive, along with a celebratory spritz of cheery orange aperol for me and Peter, and we all squeeze around a tiny teetering table and munch our rolls, and watch the Italians wandering up and down the picturesque lane.

Everything is Hollywood-set, art-direction perfect. The bar we are at is called *Gran*, and though we feel like we have just discovered it, it is an institution in Bologna. Like so many places in the city centre, it is ancient and beautifully preserved. We are outside, sitting under heaters, with grey woollen blankets over our knees. Inside, under a giant stained glass skylight decorated with flowers and coloured panes, white-shirted waiters assemble drinks at a long marble-topped counter. They pour complimentary potato crisps and olives into white bowls and whisk them out to their customers, who are all around us, smoking and laughing and admiring their shopping purchases. Overhead, Via D'Azeglio is lit with strings of bulbs that take the shape of saxophones and guitars, and spell out words to the lyrics of a song by Lucio Dalla, who we will discover lived in this street, and is one of Bologna's most famous and revered musical inhabitants. There are buskers playing saxophone, couples holding hands, pixie-sized shops selling gloves and handbags and gelato and nipped-in suits for men, and a couple of dogs under neighbouring tables wearing winter vests. Underfoot the stone is brown and overhead the sky is blue, and we are around the corner from our new home.

As the waiter sets down our drinks, he curiously asks us where we are from; this ragtag assembly of six, who are devouring our paninis as though we have not eaten for days.

We are from Australia, we reply. He pulls a surprised face and marvels at how far we have travelled. Then he asks how long we are visiting his town. We all enjoy delivering our unexpected response. We tell him we now live in Italy. We have just arrived, and we will be here for a year.

It is the first time we have said it out loud. It is unbelievable. And yet it is true. We are the Lewis Family of Bologna.

It is simply miraculous.

5

BALONEY, BALONEY, WE ALL LOVE BALONEY

I often say my husband is like a glacier.

In much the way a frozen river seems like there's nothing happening on the surface, but underneath it is exerting enough force to move mountains, Peter Allan Lewis is always planning and organising. On the surface he is very laidback (his nickname among our friends is actually 'Lazy Pete') but this belies his constant momentum. With the same determined diligence he shows in running his nightclub business or our children's extracurricular activities back home – ferrying our daughter to swimming or schlepping boyos around to endless basketball or footy training – he has undertaken the bulk of the logistical grunt work in moving the six of us to the other side of the world. It is Peter who has made sense of the daunting mountain of visas and passports, consular appointments, photos and birth certificates, tickets and schedules, school entrance exams and enrolments. And he has also, the first morning we wake up in Italy, organised for us to meet with some people from what is to be our new school.

So on Sunday lunchtime, after a bleary family expedition to the nearest supermarket to stock up on kitchen basics (like the locals, we take our rollaway suitcases and backpacks to carry our groceries home), he takes the children to meet his contacts. Among them is Olivia, the coordinator at the International School of Bologna, where all four of our children will be studying. She is a beautiful and vivacious porcelain-skinned Irishwoman and she has arranged to meet our brood in the large park just outside the walls of the old city with her girls, one of whom is Lewis's age, and the other, who will be in the grade nine class with Sunday.

Also, and this is unexpected, there is another Australian family at the school, also having a gap year. It turns out they live less than five kilometres from us in Melbourne, and although we have never crossed paths with Dave and Rachel back home, we share mutual friends. Their son Sam is in Artie's year and apparently can't wait to meet some fellow Aussies. Rachel, his mum, will be a no-show though. She is still on crutches from a nasty scooter accident she had before Christmas, when she skidded on the treacherously slippery speckled-stone terrazzo that forms nearly every walkway under the porticoes – the covered archways for which Bologna is famous. After a week in an Italian hospital (where the food is good, apparently, but you have to bring your own hospital gown), and months at home not being able to move at all, she is only now upright, moving gingerly on crutches. Of course, the boys don't care about grown-ups. After our big travelling and unpacking days, they just want to go somewhere to have a kick of the footy we brought with us.

I am also excited; while the children will head off to their new school tomorrow (eleven-year-old Sam will pick us up in the morning and lead the way), my beloved producer Sacha is arriving to prepare things for our first international *Hughesy & Kate* radio show on Tuesday. When I first told Hughesy I was leaving the show we've been doing together for eighteen years to go to Italy for a year, I expected a few tears and a farewell party but he wasn't keen on either. He was determined that I continue to do the *Hughesy & Kate* show, even from abroad.

Sacha French, our tiny-in-stature but giant-in-spirit Kiwi friend, has been the producer of our radio show and the third pillar of our three-legged creative stool for eighteen years and she has also spent more time in Bologna than we have. Once Peter and I decided that Bologna would be our base, the radio station sent her over for a reccie to find a studio where I could broadcast our afternoon drive show back to Australia. She spent her days driving around with an Italian guide, Giuseppe, who punctuated their trips with random boasts about Bologna's historical and cultural achievements, as seemingly endless as they were impressive. 'Bologna – it has the oldest university in the world!' he would declare. Or 'Bologna! Is not just the home of Ferrari, we also make-a the famous Ducati motorcycle!'

One day, on the phone to me back in Australia, she reported that, as they drove past a sports stadium in the centre, Giuseppe uttered a most worrying sentence: 'Bologna!' he exclaimed proudly. 'They call it Basket City!' When Sacha looked puzzled at this, he explained. Apparently Bologna is the centre of basketball in Italy, the game the Italians simply call 'Basket'.

This is the first I had heard of this. I asked Peter about it, and he was vague. But it niggled at me. I was looking forward to leaving the endless litany of basketball training and matches behind when we left Melbourne.

After scouting and ruling out every local radio station in Bologna – most of which are technically decades behind what we are used to in Australia – Sacha, via an Australian journalist contact in Rome, has come up with an alternative: an office down by the train station. It is used by filmmakers who, in the course of their work, shift large animation files, and it boasts the best wi-fi in Bologna. She has sublet a room and actually built a makeshift studio which I have yet to see. (Sacha is also going to be moving into our house back home in St Kilda with her teenage son Milo. It was too much to pack up our lives and put everything into storage for only a year. It is easier – and a bonus rent-free year for Sach as well – to have her move into our place.) But right now, I am so happy she is with us for the first couple of weeks. Not only will it be lovely to share the fledgling experience of our new home with her, but she and our Australian radio tech Andrea will be there every morning to make sure the initial broadcasts run smoothly.

The technical aspect of this is a big deal, by the way. Huge. Even in this digital age, our radio connection is via physical cables that run under the oceans that separate us. Each link is called a 'hop', and while Melbourne to Los Angeles is one hop, to connect Melbourne to Italy is an enormous five. Each hop can incur a slight delay, and though our technicians back in Australia have worked tirelessly to ensure the setup is seamless, we are slightly nervous about how the technology will stand up. To have delays in a conversation broadcast to millions of people every day would be a disaster. So I will be joining our radio show from the other side of the world, even though this has never been done before. (Little do we know at this point that working remotely will be the way of the future – who could possibly anticipate that?)

Sacha's arrival that afternoon, calling out to me from the piazza under our window, is simply glorious. Though it is less than a week since we farewelled each other in Australia, we are now literally a world away, and our reunion is joyous. She marvels at the view from our apartment and we have cups of tea while she gives the children hugs, teasing them about our enforced family togetherness. That night after we have made the children dinner, we realise one of the benefits of inner-city life; she and Peter and I leave them to get themselves ready for bed, while we wander around the streets below, stopping for glasses of wine and aperitivo (cocktail hour) snacks.

At one point we meander out of a fancy arcade and find it has started to snow. Under the fall of crystal flakes, we crunch our way down a cobblestoned laneway into a tiny, candlelit restaurant, where – though at seven thirty it is early for dinner – they welcome us like travelling saints. We eat an unforgettable Bolognese meal: tortellini in *brodo* – tiny belly-button pasta in broth, plump tortelloni stuffed with ricotta and served in a puddle of melted butter and sage. Slices of steak with crispy cubes of potato. Green lasagne made with spinach-infused pasta sheets. Our glasses are filled with sparkling Lambrusco – the local red wine that is a joke in Australia, but is delicious here – and then another vino rosso, the local Sangiovese. By the time we leave, the restaurant has somehow filled around us; a cavern of warmth. We gratefully farewell our hosts. Then, with snow still falling, we don our coats and walk back up the silent, shrouded-white laneway to our doorway. Through the arched entrance to the magnificent Piazza Maggiore, we can see it is carpeted in snow, glittering silver under the winter moon. It is a magical evening.

We spend the next few days in a fusion of work that somehow also feels like a holiday. Buoyed by how well our technology is working, we fall into a routine that, though it is tiring, is fun and harmonious. None of us wants to think about what will happen when Sacha leaves. Every morning, in the shroud of early-morning darkness, I pick her up from her hotel in the car she has booked for me. We turn into Via Guido Zucchini – the name of which never fails to make us smile – and go up the stairs to our tiny office–studio where Jacopo, a member of the crew our filmmaker hosts employ, is waiting. He has turned the lights on, and connected us via computer to the studio in Australia.

Jacopo (with the 'J' pronounced as a 'Y' like my son Jannie's name) is a twenty-something beardie of very few words, particularly at what is an obscenely early-morning hour for an Italian. He speaks so little, Sacha and I privately dub him 'Silent Jacopo'. While we catch up on-screen with Hughesy and our anchor Jack, and beloved assistant producer Darcie, with a spirited mixture of gossip and show-planning, Jacopo makes us coffee from the jar of instant that Sacha has left in the rudimentary kitchen. We soon find out he has never encountered instant coffee before, and have to instruct him how to make it. One morning he says to me in his shy English, 'You like this powder American coffee?' I explain that we use it because it is quick, and he looks slightly puzzled by the fact that we would prioritise convenience over quality, asking if we would mind if he instead made us espresso. Of course we don't mind. So, from then on, he brings in a proper moka pot, which he meticulously packs with ground coffee and boils on a portable stove. While we prep the show, Jacopo delivers two steaming cups he has laid out on a wooden board with tiny sugared biscuits, presented on a paper lace doily. Even at 5 am, we learn, the Italian way is to make things beautiful.

After the show every morning, which is cracklingly energised, and in which (along with our regular segments) I share with listeners and Hughesy our initiation into our new town, Sacha and I walk the two kilometres back to our apartment, enjoying seeing the centre come to life, and having those random encounters that seem to only happen when you are travelling. We wander past shops opening their doors, and greet storekeepers arranging tables, heaters and cushioned chairs outside, or sweeping their portion of terrazzo under the porticoes. We pass a local pot shop and venture upstairs, marvelling at the array of marijuana products and edibles on sale. Cannabis is legal here but apparently still a little frowned upon. Also, as the friendly shopgirl informs us, the active ingredient – the THC (the chemical that makes you stoned) – is capped. (This means you are unlikely to see people smacked around the head with their high, like you famously do in Amsterdam, and where my girlfriend's sister once collapsed, hideously tourist-stoned, on the tram tracks.) In her efforts to explain just how muted her products are, the shopgirl points to a Chupa-Chup-like display of lollipops. 'These ones are so mild-a,' she says, in her lyrical English, 'you can give-a to your children!' Sach and I obviously look a little shocked at the suggestion. The pot-girl clocks our response and laughs, throwing her hands up in the air. 'Of course, you don't 'ave to!' she adds, helpfully.

One morning, in a light fall of rain, we find ourselves waiting at the lights to cross to the large piazza where there is an open-air market. When we look down, we notice the half-dozen or so locals around us are all wearing formal office attire, but with Ugg boots.

These are considered extremely cool here, as are the Tasmanian-made work boots, Blundstones, that we will later see in several high-end boutiques for two hundred euros a pair: almost four hundred Australian dollars.

After the show we often meet Peter, who has walked the children to school, for breakfast. The Italians have a powerful early morning sweet tooth and don't really do savoury breakfasts. We soon tire of frequenting cafes for a sugary brioche or the standard Nutella and custard-filled croissants, and instead start going to the local deli in our laneway. Here, I order two hundred grams of mortadella to eat on warm, crispy flat rolls we have bought from the bakery around the corner. This is the start of a love affair that takes all of us by surprise.

Mortadella is one of the specialties of Bologna (which is also known as the city of fat). It is a roll of pink processed pork meat, though apparently during the war it was often made from horse, and you can still find this specialty in certain parts in the north of the country. Suffice to say, we are more than happy with the piggy version; studded with chunks of white lard, and sometimes pistachios and peppercorns, its description belies how utterly delicious it is. In Australia, it would be the equivalent of me falling in love with luncheon sausage (in fact, it is from here the Americans get their sliced meat 'baloney') but it is not congealed or stodgy. Fresh-sliced and carefully wrapped in paper and foil, it is perfection, and I can't get enough of it. So much so, that I have mastered the simple phrase in Italian: *Vorrei due etti mortadella, per favore?* (Could I have two hundred grams of mortadella please?)

The man who serves us at the deli Simoni becomes a morning highlight. He is shaven-headed bald, with a golden tan (even in winter) that looks even deeper against his crisp white lab coat. One day, obviously surprised that we are still here after the standard two-day tourist sweep of Bologna, he asks how long we are visiting. I tell him that we are actually living in his city, in one of the apartments overhead. He conveys the news to the others in the shop, who clearly share his amazement (it is funny to realise you have clearly been the subject of discussion), and after that, he goes out of his way to look after us. He has always addressed me in cheerful, fragmented English, but the next day, when I first make my mortadella request in Italian, he roars with delighted approval.

'*Due etti mortadella?*' he repeats, beaming. ('Two hundred grams?') Then he rattles off something in Italian that I realise is praise for my halting attempt at speaking his language. It makes my cheeks flame like a child's, in pleasure and embarrassment.

Although every butcher and corner store here seems to sell small-goods, the concept of pre-slicing doesn't seem to exist here – a far cry, I think, from my first job at the Coles deli counter, where we would have piles of round chicken loaf and square shoulder ham ready to go for our customers (by the way, whatever happened to shoulder ham?). Here, the procurement of daily groceries takes time. Around us, shoppers enter and chat with the storekeepers; an endless exchange of local gossip small-talk and food big-talk. I cannot help but think about Australia, where I am so busy and rushed, and how there I would place my order, then duck into the adjoining shops to grab some other needed items. I never see anyone do this here, so I learn to wait and smile. My deli-man also sees this as an opportunity to school me about food. Often, while I am waiting for my mortadella, which he carefully selects from an array of a dozen or so, he teaches me the names of fruit and vegetables in Italian, or hands over other treats: a thin sliver of prosciutto he tells me has just arrived from a village near Parma; a wedge of fragrant salami that he decrees is the best in town.

One day, during our Skype show-prep, Hughesy asks Sacha if she has met any Italian men yet, and when she replies in the negative, he is filled with mock outrage. Sacha's chequered romantic life has been a recurring subplot on our show, and it seems crazy, he says, that she is in the land of lovers and has not seen what is on offer. He tells her she has to go on a Tinder date. Sacha semi-reluctantly agrees. It is a daunting prospect but she is always up for an adventure so we select a photo of her (not too pretty; not too plain!), and she posts her profile on the Italian version of the app. At Hughesy's behest, she also adds a New Zealand flag – 'Men like different!' he maintains, and it seems he is right. The next morning, when Sacha checks her phone, she has been inundated with over one hundred expressions of interest. She is astounded by the response; in Australia, she says, a forty-something woman would generate very few swipes. Here, she is a hot commodity.

Throughout the show, Sasha scrolls through the contenders, flipping her phone at me and Hughesy as we discuss the merits of each one. Some of them are too complicated for a travelling encounter; we rule them out if they speak no English, or if they are too young or old. My vetting is tinged with empathy, while the thought of Sacha hooking up with a 21-year-old Italian with no English delights Hughesy – 'You'll speak the international language of love!' he says, cackling – Sach and I are more particular. After much scrolling, she alights on a picture of a man; shaven-headed and with a trimmed beard. He is riding a bike, and in the background are mountains.

'What about him?' she asks. There is something pleasing about his rugged features, and we are thrilled that his profile says he enjoys cooking and good food. Also, he is clearly a bike rider, as is Peter, and they are often, in my experience, reliable and competent. At the very least, we say, giggling, my husband can date him.

So Sacha swipes right on her prospective Italian beau. Perfectly, his name is Giovanni.

By the time the show is over, Giovanni has arranged to pick her up for dinner that night.

The next morning when I swing by Sacha's hotel in the pre-dawn darkness she is not waiting outside as she usually is. I am not worried about her; the night before, on her date, we were in phone contact, texting as she was swept from bar to bar, and then on to dinner with Giovanni and a couple of his friends. I know she was having a great, albeit late, night.

I go to message her, and just then she appears at the door of the car. She looks a little dishevelled but is beaming.

'Good night?' I ask her as I take her backpack and she climbs into the back seat with me. She grins in response.

'It was fantastic,' she says. 'We went bar-hopping, and then to this brilliant restaurant, and we ate such delicious food, and we drank amazing wine, and he was so lovely and I met lots of his friends, and then he drove me back to the hotel.'

She is flushed with happiness. Still, there is something about her glow, and her unkempt ponytail, that makes me press further.

'What time did you finish up?' I ask.

Sacha hesitates, suddenly coy. Then she bursts out laughing.

'About an hour ago,' she says.

I look at my phone – it is 5.10 am. I start laughing too.

Giovanni, it transpires, is still asleep . . . in Sacha's hotel room.

It would appear it was a very, very, very good night.

And how utterly stunning. In this country famous for romance, my little New Zealand friend – my *amica* – has found her very own Italian lover. As we joke later, on-air, it seems Sacha French has found her own purveyor of mortadella.

Though I think she may have got more than two hundred grams.

6

CELEBRATION OF THE ART

It is Artie's birthday weekend. Our beloved third child – our studious, diligent, sweet boy (more Lewis than Langbroek) – is turning twelve, and in honour of our first family birthday here, Peter has gone through the ordeal of booking a rental car big enough for all of us to go away for the weekend. Sacha is coming with us, even though Giovanni, with whom she has now been on a couple of dates, is keen for her to spend the time with him. Her Italian paramour will be busy though, since it turns out he has his own restaurant, ten minutes outside the old city walls. Anyway, Sacha is exhausted from the combination of early-morning work and her giddy nocturnal activities. She needs a circuit breaker from her holiday romance, and it will be nice, she says, to see something of the Italian countryside.

We are heading to a rural town about fifty minutes away called Castel San Pietro Terme. It is near where we rented the hilltop villa last year on our reconnaissance mission to scout our future home, and is full of natural springs and swimming pools. Last summer, we discovered it was impossible to get wet without a booking (something we are poor at) and so while the vast array of turquoise pools and water slides cascading down the hillside beckoned us during 40 degrees of searing Italian heat, we had to settle for driving past while the children eyeballed the resorts longingly.

Off-season winter seems a perfect time to avail ourselves of the hot springs.

Peter has left the apartment before us so he can complete the complicated process of renting our vehicle. This takes another solid hour or more of paperwork, punctuated with the standard Italian pastime of waiting, then carefully examining the vehicle to ensure you are not charged for imaginary 'damage' on its return – a scam that empties many travellers' wallets here.

Sacha has turned up at our apartment on time but is pale and shabby-shanks. In fact, she has a crushing hangover, a side effect of another late-night assignation with Giovanni. I am just tired, as are the children, so by the time we have walked to the other end of town and found Peter, who is also slightly harried, and piled into the rental van, everyone is grouchy. The children bicker; the adults are uncharacteristically silent. Sacha climbs meekly into the back with the younger boys and a travel pillow, and the seven of us set off on our weekend adventure.

This is Sacha's first time travelling on an Italian freeway, and she soon reminds us of how terrifying a first encounter with the autostrada can be. She conveys that fear from the back seat, in a series of yelps and 'oh my gawds' and 'this can't be rights' and – unforgettably – a truly panicked, high-pitched, 'This is fucking INSANE! . . . Sorry, kids,' as we forge our way into traffic flying along at 140 kilometres, and more, per hour.

Driving on the wrong side of the road in a manual vehicle would be challenge enough, but the exercise is rendered even hairier by the extremely short merging lanes which funnel you smack-bang into the speeding fray. Peter, though normally pretty calm, is always stressed by the freeway entrances, and then by the fact that there is not a lane in which to maintain a comfortable cruising speed. In Australia, you could stay in the left-hand lane but here that is not an option. For starters, the 'slow lane' (here, the right lane) is already filled with trucks, laden with produce bound to, and from, all parts of Europe. They are actually not allowed to travel in any of the other lanes. This, incidentally, is a brilliant initiative, but it's not comfortable to be sandwiched between massive eighteen-wheelers when you're in a passenger vehicle. Plus, drivers here handle their cars differently to us. Foreigners often refer to the 'mad' driving of the Italians, but this is misleading. They are, in fact, brilliant drivers, but where we find a place in the flow of traffic and hold it, they see a gap and have a seemingly genetic urge to fill it. They are constantly zipping in and out of lanes at speeds that would land us in jail back in Australia. Italians, as Lewis comments, all drive like they are in a grand prix. More than once we have been impatiently tailgated and then overtaken by a white-haired 'nonna', flying past at 150 kilometres per hour.

The freedom to speed is one of my favourite things about our new home, and it is undoubtedly exhilarating, but it is still somewhat of a relief when we exit the autostrada to stop in a town we have earmarked for lunch. Dozza is tiny, a medieval village basically comprised of a single laneway flanked by buildings painted by street artists. The muralled lane wends around the only eateries in town and leads to a picturesque castle. There is a small *bar* (what we would call a cafe) and across the street an *osteria* – an eatery with more rustic, simple food than a *ristorante*. (Traditionally, you could take your own food to an *osteria*, and go there just to buy alcohol but these days most provide meals.)

We, of course, haven't booked, and the owner, after greeting us with customary concern, and doing a headcount, shows us to a table. He tells us we had better eat early; it is the weekend, and the restaurant will soon be full. We accept his advice, and his proffered table, gratefully. We have often been caught out by the rigid opening hours of restaurants here, which open by noon or 1 pm, but are firmly shut by 3.30 pm, when the afternoon butts up against the sacred and mysterious 'resting time'. Then, nothing opens again until 7.30 pm. In between, you are left with few eating options, and we don't want to miss lunch, as we have in the past. Hunger, we have discovered, is a poor travelling companion.

The *osteria* doesn't exploit its monopoly with mediocrity; our meals are simply stunning. Food in Italy is so specifically regional that, although we are only half an hour from Bologna, the pasta here is different, as is their ragu – the sauce we call bolognese. (The making of this staple, by the way, is hugely political, from one end of the country to the other: garlic or no garlic? Fresh tomatoes or a dash of concentrate? Meat cooked in milk to soften it, or simply wine? Wars could be fought over this in Italy.)

The children are brought bowls of steaming pasta topped with the much less controversial pomodoro sauce. Like locals, they smother the brightness of the tomatoes under a snowfall of shaved parmesan. I order gnocchi, home-made and generously crowned with shaved truffles, to celebrate the end of the season. Pasta is an entree dish here – the *primi* – so when we think we have finished, we are actually brought more food: plates of steak and roast vegetables. Sacha, Peter and I rinse the last of our bleariness away with a carafe of local wine, and everyone shares several cans of restorative Coca-Cola – 'the black doctor' we call it in our family, so profound are its healing properties. Then, after short and silky espresso coffees, we pile back into the car and start the second phase of our magical mystery weekend.

We are now so pleasingly full-bellied and fortified we have a singalong in the car as winter-Italy flashes by. We pass picture-book farms with bare-leafed fruit trees biding their time. There are freshly turned paddocks and immaculate green-shuttered stone farmhouses emitting the occasional tendril of smoke. Otherwise, there is a sense of travelling in a capsule through a deserted winterscape; an impression compounded by the settling fog.

By the time we enter the town of Castel San Pietro Terme, it is wreathed in mist. We spy a clutch of old men, caps on heads and cigarettes dangling from mouths, chatting as they perch on a low stone wall. They are taking turns to fill up bottles from a roadside spring, and seem to be the only sign of life. The resorts we remembered from last summer as welcoming, green and manicured, are all closed: outdoor umbrellas tightly furled; window rollers bolted, like resolutely shut eyes. After doing a couple of laps of the town, we head back to the only hotel that has a sign saying *aperto*, open. It is a bleak-looking six-storey bunker, with two or three other cars parked on the paving at the rear, and when we tentatively enter, it seems completely deserted.

Eventually, an older man shuffles out and takes his place behind the reception desk, where we are all assembled. When we explain that we would like to book rooms for the night, he seems completely bamboozled, shaking his head. We attempt our request from Google Translate. Again, no. Eventually, we do what we have learned to do here: we wait. And, as is often the case, things start to happen. In this instance, 'things' is another man appearing. He is a comparative young gun in his sixties, blue-capped and translucently pale. When he addresses us, he speaks with an accent we recognise – ah, an Englishman! It turns out he is bilingual, and translates our request to the other fellow, with whom he seems very familiar.

Eventually, rooms are assigned. Peter and I have a double on the fifth floor. Lewis, Artie and Jannie will share a triple-bedder on the floor below us. There is such a weird vibe here – when the old man was checking us in, I mouthed '*The Shining*' at my husband and Sacha, and while this reference to the Jack Nicholson horror-hotel movie made us giggle, the truth is none of us wants to spend the night here sleeping alone. Sacha opts to share a room with Sunday.

Our English-speaking friend is helpful in a way that is unsettling. As it turns out, this is more of a reflection of us than him. His name is John, he tells us, and he is staying here through the off-season as a guest of the owner. He offers to help us with our bags and, though we have barely any, insists on escorting us to the car. On the way, he asks me what phone I use. I'm not sure what he means. I explain I have an iPhone, and am, impractically, still on my Australian phone plan. John embarks on a lecture about the dangers of the impending 5G network. It is obviously his pet subject. He is twelve minutes deep into a TED Talk about mobile towers, radiation levels and electromagnetic energy when Petie comes out and says we need to get to the pools before they close. Sach and I race upstairs to get changed, exchanging relieved eyerolls as we make our escape. Whatever happens, we vow, we are not staying here for dinner.

Everything in Italy, it seems, is complicated. When we get to the pool complex, the water slides and outside areas are closed. These, of course, are for summer. There is one pool open, but when we try to buy tickets, the female attendant tells us we can't without our passports. Peter walks back to the hotel and returns with them, and we watch as she painstakingly notes down all the numbers in a ledger. Then she tells us we cannot swim without appropriate head coverings. I am sorry, she says, but in Italia you need cloth bathing caps. We explain we are happy to buy them; she tells us she has none for sale. Now we are at an impasse. Eventually, I think because of the children's obvious disappointment, and our blank and helpless stares, she is moved to action. She tsks loudly and disappears to a back room. Several minutes later, she reappears and presents us all with disposable plastic shower caps. We must wear these to swim, she tells us firmly.

Finally, we get wet. The pool is magnificent. The twenty or so Italians already swimming and lolling in the warmth regard us curiously as we enter. We look decidedly half-baked with our plastic shower caps on but that is soon forgotten as we splash and duck under the clear vinyl strip-curtain that takes us through to the outside pool. The water is warm – almost hot – but our flushed faces are soon freezing from the winter air and we are so invigorated by it, the children start chasing each other; racing and wrestling. Sunday, like a porpoise, swims sleek laps. Lewis, with the cockiness of a young lion, stalks me and Sacha, repeatedly picking us up and dunking us, immune to our pleas for mercy. Sach, laughing helplessly, is clutching at her bikini top, as Peter murmurs drily, 'I think Lewis is enjoying Aunty Sach a little too much,' which is funny, because Sacha has known him since before he was a baby, but is also possibly true.

I swim over and shoo Lewis away, and discreetly relay Petie's observation. Sacha, as she always does, recognises both the humour and the oddness of the situation, and the pair of us pull into a quick mother-huddle while I tell her what I found in Lewis's room when

I was packing this morning. It was a framed photo of a pretty girl we have never met, in her Australian school uniform. On the back was scrawled a romantic message. Sacha digests the revelation thoughtfully. We may have physically brought Lewis to Italy, she says, but his heart may be back in Australia with his secret romance. I hope not, but it would explain his odd resistance to our new home. Lewis is normally sunny and open; lately he has been a bit flat and remote; grumpy, even.

But today we are all having fun, and by the time we head back to the hotel we are pleasingly water-logged. When we check the time in the foyer, we realise it is too late to get changed and head into town for dinner. Our English 5G friend, enjoying an *aperitivo* glass of wine outside the empty dining room, waves us over and tells us the owner has a table waiting for us in the restaurant.

It is so gracious, we can't refuse, but we are also wary. Eating at a deserted hotel in the midst of the off-season sounds, at the least, depressing, and at the most, like a recipe for disaster. 'Whatever you do, don't order seafood,' Sach instructs us all firmly as we take our places at a large round table. 'We can't afford to get food poisoning.'

On cue, a middle-aged lady emerges from the kitchen, flushed and cook-faced. She places a generous platter of sliced meats and cheeses in front of us, then tells us she has spent the afternoon making fresh pasta. Would we like some?

The answer, not surprisingly, is a resounding yes. What is more surprising, is the ensuing feast that emerges from her kitchen, and that a young boy is our waiter. He is about ten or eleven, and it turns out he is the cook's son and has been working with her in the *cucina*, the two of them preparing our food. The son brings out baskets of bread, which he shyly places on the table then reappears with plates of steaming creamy-sauced, silken tagliatelle, strewn with wild mushrooms and veal. The pasta is beyond delicious. We wolf it down and then, as we are wiping our plates clean with a torn piece of bread ('the little boot' as the Italians call it), mamma brings out an enormous platter of golden-fried morsels.

There is zucchini tangled with batons of eggplant and carrot, but mainly, the dish is from the ocean. White-fleshed fish. Prawns and calamari. Some tiny fresh sardines. They are all tumbled together and deep-fried in a light batter. Delivered, as it is, on the heels of Sacha's hissed 'no seafood' warning, we all burst into laughter. It is way too good to resist; crispy and salty and sea-fresh. It is so delicious, accompanied with crispy cubes of roast potato, that when our cook pops her head out of the kitchen, we give her a round of spontaneous applause. She blushes, then ducks back into the kitchen, reappearing with a long platter of chocolate-sprinkled tiramisu, adorned with a candle, which she places in front of Artie.

The seven of us sing 'Happy Birthday' in English, and then Peter asks our hosts how we say this in Italian and they tell us, so we haltingly sing '*Tanti auguri a te*', and the sprinkling of other guests join in. We take turns to go around the table and say words of love to our birthday boy. A bottle of summer-bright, sticky-sweet limoncello appears on the table with tiny coffees. We give Artie his present, a woollen scarf with the Bologna football team logo, and he is shining – like a blessed twelve-year-old Aussie boyo, not like a horror movie. We are all so happy. We are also secretly chastened about the mean thoughts we harboured about this one open hotel in the middle of nowhere.

To not judge by appearances is a lesson we will learn repeatedly in Italy.

We are reminded of it again when we go upstairs to our rooms, which, though they are basic, are warm and spotlessly clean. And again, when we climb into our beds, which are freshly made with immaculate Italian sheets.

That night, we sleep the exhausted, deep and dreamless sleep of people who have had a beautiful adventure in a strange land.

It is already more than we deserve.

7

THE AMBASSADOR AND THE SHOWGIRL

We quickly discover that living in Bologna is like living in a large village. Being expats in a foreign community also means we are part of a distinctive but very small club.

The Australian Ambassador to Rome has sent me an invitation to the opening night performance of an Australian play, *When the Rain Stops Falling*, in Bologna's main theatre. Also, would we like to meet the ambassador before for pre-show drinks? The answer is *naturalmente*. Of course we would!

The night in question is cold and rainy. It is a weeknight so, after donning our finery (for me, a sequinned cream dress I have brought from Australia; for Peter, a blue woven jacket he bought last year from a market stall in Lake Garda), we leave the children with Lewis in charge and walk down to the theatre. It is, like everything in the centre, around the corner from our apartment but we are running late and by the time we arrive, my feet (in uncustomary high heels) are throbbing from bolting over stone cobbles. The theatre itself is a handsome, refurbished building on the wide, main boulevard Via Indipendenza (Independence Street). We are to meet our hosts at the hotel across the road.

When we enter, we are greeted by a smiling, flop-haired Englishman who, deliciously, has the air of a man who breaks up long days with a stiff drink. He introduces himself as Paul, the Australian embassy researcher who emailed me the invitation for tonight. The ambassador, Greg French, is a neatly attired man who greets us warmly with handshakes and European cheek kisses. He asks how we are settling in Bologna and is happy to hear, despite our current challenges of trying to open a foreign bank account and lease our own car, that all is going well. He tells us his own posting (five years in Rome with his wife and children) has seen them all fall in love with Italy.

Despite his impressive international resume, the ambassador has a boyish streak of Australian playfulness. He is a widely respected international lawyer but also plays the guitar and has a knowledgeable conversation with Peter about pub music. The playwright, Andrew Bovell (who wrote one of my favourite Australian films, the brilliant *Lantana*), joins in. Despite it being his big night, he is not as sharply dressed as the ambassador. He is, in fact, artistically dishevelled. It turns out he has flown in from Greece for the occasion and is rapt, but modestly bemused, by the honour of having his work translated and performed here. Over drinks, we speculate about how we will all go, watching a play performed in a foreign tongue. Andrew will have a distinct advantage, we reckon. He, at least, knows his own work but Peter and I speak barely any Italian.

Embassy Paul checks the time and we head across the road to the upstairs foyer of the theatre where, after an address from the regional mayor, Greg is introduced to the thirty or so assembled guests. His speech, delivered in impressively fluent Italian, is all Greek to us, but is clearly well received; there is laughter at points, and nodding of heads. I scan the room. Everyone here has some sort of association with our home country but there seem to be very few actual Australians in Bologna. We meet an imposingly large fellow, a professor at the university, who is accompanied by his Italian wife (a scientist) and grown-up son, who has spent time in Sydney but now studies in Edinburgh. The professor has lived in Italy, he tells us, for nearly thirty years, but when he speaks his Aussie drawl is unmistakable.

After the speech, and having downed a glass of wine and some large chunks of parmesan and salami (most theatregoers will eat after the play, which will be too late for us at 11 pm), we head downstairs. The theatre is full; there is an evident first-night hum as we find our seats in the audience. Navigating an Italian cloakroom to check my large fur coat is too daunting, so I lay it over the chair, and snuggle into its warmth. Peter, next to me, does the same with his padded jacket. Then I discreetly slip off my shoes. (I would hate for any nearby Italians to see me do this; they are impeccably stylish and would be horrified to see my stockinged feet.) I am now completely happy. To be warmed by wine and cheese, and cocooned in my comfortable seat after my 4 am start is actual bliss.

The houselights dim. There is a murmur of excitement. The curtain rises.

There is a lone man, centrestage. He talks for a bit, and then – plop! – a large fish drops from above and lands at his feet. The actor picks it up and stands there holding it, laid out across his open palms as though on a platter, and resumes his monologue. I don't understand a word, except for the oft-repeated '*pesce*' which, unhelpfully, means 'fish'. After the excitement of the fish falling, it is a long monologue. Very, very long. The character is worked up about something. He holds the fish and talks and talks. Sometimes he sounds angry; sometimes he is reflective, sentimental, even.

I feel myself becoming heavy-eyed. I try to follow the words being uttered onstage, to single out some I recognise, but the actor's rapid-fire cadence makes it very difficult. Around us, there is an occasional collective intake of breath or ripple of laughter. The audience is clearly enthralled. I am swaddled deeply and firmly in my seat. I am the opposite of a *pesce*, I think. A fish is cold and wet, but I am warm. So warm, in the darkness. So cosy. So heavy-headed.

Peter nudges me. I wake with a start. Oh dear. I seem to have nodded off. I open my leaden eyes wide – really wide – and try to focus.

Onstage, there are more characters. They appear to be arguing. There is a younger man who seems to be the son of the first man who originally picked up the big fish. Now there is also a woman pacing agitatedly around a kitchen table. She uses another word I latch onto: '*zuppa*'. She speaks about it impassionedly; almost bitterly. I don't know why she is talking so fiercely about soup but it really means a lot to her. I think she is planning to make soup from the fish. That would be it. *Zuppa di pesce.* Fish soup. That's a thing. I ordered it the other day at the seafood restaurant around the corner in the student district. It was delicious. A thinner broth than I was expecting. Salty. I remember dunking my bread in it. I could probably make it at home. We have two local fishmongers down the lane from us. They are historical, I think, because the name of the street they are on is Via Pescaria, which actually means fish street. Or is it called Via Drapperie? Anyway, you always see the walking food-tours there, gathering to watch the white-jacketed men haul tubs of fish on and off trolleys. They will do anything for you in the shop; scale and fillet. I wonder if they would peel prawns. Even if they peel them, but don't devein them, that would be something. I think you use prawn shells in fish soup. Of course you do. And fish heads. Ergh. That reminds me of a creepy story my mother tells about when she was growing up in Brooklyn. She and her brother would fight over who would get to eat the fish eyes. They're chewy, she reckons. I suppose that makes sense because the eye is a muscle. No wonder they get so very, very tired . . .

Bang, bang! Again, I wake with a jolt. Onstage, the actress is slapping the dining table. Bowls are rattling.

Oh no. Things have clearly escalated. The actress has slumped into a wooden-backed chair. Her eye-muscles are weeping. She is really upset. I think I understand what is happening. She *doesn't* want to make fish soup! Now she is clutching her head. She is really wailing. No one seems to be comforting her. This all seems to be a bit unfair. I don't think she should have to make fish soup if she doesn't want to. Not everyone likes fish *zuppa*. Though it is a satisfying word . . . *zuppa. Zoo-pa.*

An hour or so later, I am woken by the sounds of applause. The play, it turns out, has been a great success. I am initially startled, but then, refreshed by my unexpected slumber, I join the clapping enthusiastically. Peter, who is also applauding, looks at me and rolls his eyes.

'You obviously enjoyed the play,' he says, grinning. He leans over and murmurs in my ear, 'You were *snoring*.'

Afterwards, we see Andrew, the playwright, accepting accolades and congratulatory handshakes in the foyer. I am a little bit embarrassed but he looks over at me and laughs.

I wonder if he fell asleep, too.

A few weeks later, we are in another theatre. This time, we are at the children's school for an afternoon concert put on by Jannie's junior classmates. We are in the original part of the building, which the international school occasionally gets to borrow from the Italian school, San Luigi. The two schools share premises and sometimes, to get to different classrooms, we wander through their gleaming terrazzo hallways, gazing in wonder at the stained-glass windows and soaring ceilings, walls lined with wooden bookcases and oil paintings of former students. There is a small room with fossils in glass cases and marble statues. It is incredible.

The school theatre is breathtaking. It has ornately painted ceilings and walls, and gold leaf-work on intricate plaster cornices. There are heavy crimson velvet drapes which frame the small stage. It apparently dates from the 1500s and, as fellow parent and our friend English Sophie observes, it is like something out of Harry Potter. We pass on this comment to another parent, Monica, who has come rushing in from work to join us in the darkened theatre. Her husband Riccardo, himself having ducked out of work, hands her a paper bag with lunch from his restaurant. They are both Italian and, like many others, send their son Robbie to the international school so he can better learn English. They smile indulgently as we marvel at our surrounds. Age and ornateness are no surprise to them, of course. Living in Italy is like living in a museum. And yet the Italians have somehow learned to meld the past with the present.

When the children – Italian, American, South American, Swedish, French, British and Indian – take the stage, they are in various costumes, dressed as artists in white smocks with berets (hello, Jannie!) or wrapped in sheets like ancient Romans. Some of them dance around; famous artworks come to life. There is the *Mona Lisa*! There is the star-jumping, sepia-man from the Leonardo da Vinci drawing! Some are playing instruments; the rest are singing in their reedy, piping, child-voices. It is simply beautiful.

But the barn-storming act is performed by the youngest class, the six-year-olds. The daughter of our new friends, the Australians Dave and Rachel, is among them; Nellie, our littlest, loveliest Australian. The children file onstage, some shyly, some strutting. They are decked out in overalls, crowned with homemade green and red hats that wobble as they shuffle to their places. They are, of course, the Super Mario brothers; a dozen tiny Marios and Luigis. Some of them are wearing giant black cardboard moustaches that come unstuck, dangling lopsidedly as they start to sing.

The crowd erupts with laughter and applause.

Unexpectedly, I have tears in my eyes.

Oh, Italy. I love you.

8

BOO HOO, POOR LUCKY ME

I remember reading somewhere that only in Western culture do we treat happiness as a destination. Most other cultures prize duty: to family, religious practice or tradition and, through that service, believe a satisfying life can be lived. We, however (I guess spoiled with plentiful food and labour-saving innovations), have become obsessed with happiness as an end unto itself. It is as though we are all hunting for a magic ticket that enables us to get off the despair bus so we can spend the rest of our days in some idyllic euphoria. Once we are there, we will probably spend all our time taking snapshots so others can see how happy we are. Ironically, this focus on happiness seems to make many of us chronically unhappy.

We have been in Bologna for several weeks now and I am mired in these thoughts as I walk home from work. It is not enough for me that there are moments of pure magic in our move to Italy – I greedily want the whole thing to be endless ecstasy, like the crest of a wave that never crashes. I want to have the joy without the hard work. Which is ridiculous, because I have never done anything in my life – that was worth doing – that *wasn't* hard work. Not my job; not having babies. Nothing.

Normally, my wander home is punctuated with neighbourhood sights that spark joy; today, my heavy-footed trudging echoes my mood. There is the con-artist on the corner who looks as though he is painstakingly carving a sleeping dog out of sand on the footpath but we have realised is just silica glued onto a plastic mould. Here is the altar to the blessed Santa Maria, the Virgin Mary, set into a plaster recess outside a bar, where someone always places fresh flowers. Up ahead is the African guy, a permanent fixture outside the mini-market where he touts for change. He is always well-dressed and early, apparently part of a southern mafia-run outfit of beggars who hit up tourists. He is so used to seeing me that we now exchange polite '*Buongiornos*' and, if I am dressed nicely, he whisks off his cap and greets me with a gravelly '*Ciao, bella*'. Not this morning; I am too leaden. I cross the street so I will not have to pass him.

I walk past the empty Piazza 20 Settembre, where the huge outdoor market happens towards the end of every week. Sometimes I take a few moments to sit on the imposing sweep of steps that lead to the huge statue overlooking the square – a bronze victor standing triumphantly over a fallen enemy – but this morning I barely look up. I do not know what happened on 20 September, or even what year, or century, this battle happened. How could I? I am not Italian. There is so much history in this place; so much language. So many different words and customs and traditions.

Even the turn into the bustling Via Clavature – the home straight that leads to our apartment – doesn't buoy my spirits. The laneway is lined with restaurants and cheerfully set outside tables and chairs. There is a centuries-old church, an optometrist and a food arcade. There are shoe shops, a randomly placed fresh orange juice booth, stylish boutiques and jewellers, and there is always a clash between the outside diners and the delivery trucks trying to make their way down the narrow street. Normally, it is the most glorious, simple entertainment, watching people scramble off seats and press themselves against historic walls, and old men suddenly officiously shouting directions at the drivers as they squeeze their way through unfazed pedestrians and bike riders. Today, I barely notice the chaos.

I am so glum. So tired.

I am tired of having to walk everywhere because we don't have a car; tired of endless, aching flights of stairs; tired of talking like a toddler in a foreign tongue. Peter and I enrolled at the Academya Lingue, the beautiful Italian school around the corner, but our lessons have only reinforced how difficult Italian is to master. In English, 'I run', 'you run', 'we run' and 'they run'; here, you cannot make a sentence without the correct ending to the verb. It is I *run-o*, you *run-i*, we *run-iamo*, they *run-ono*. But the rules are not fixed; different verbs have different endings. And even fixed nouns are – inexplicably – male or female; a bottle is a girl; a table is a boy. It is hopeless.

Tellingly, one of the first words I learned in class was '*stanca*' – I am tired. We notice Italians hardly ever say this of themselves; the same is not true of me.

I am tired of the time difference that means I have to speak-*o* to friends back home at the end of the day or first thing in the morning. I am tired of all of us having to squeeze-*iamo* into our tiny apartment. Basically, although Italy is incredible, I am exhausted by it. I am overwhelmed. The bitter truth of it is, I am sick of myself. Sick of being overwhelmed. Sick of some strange self-consciousness that stops me going into a shop to buy new knickers. I am sick of my own limitations, which I seem to encounter in a new form every day.

Also, I am hungry.

This is the real crux of my dilemma. I want some mortadella.

The best and most delicious is in the picture-postcard delicatessen Simoni, only fifty metres from our apartment, but that would involve a whole negotiation that, today, I am not equipped for. It would mean having to say hello to my shaven-headed friend behind the counter. I would have to summon the energy to engage with his cheerful banter. I would have to stand there, waiting, waiting, while he slices the sausage. I would be asked by the taciturn man who oversees the fruit and veg if I would like something from his part of the store, but he – a stern counterpart to his smallgoods-purveying colleague – would not find it at all charming when I couldn't remember the word for cucumber. Or celery. I would be embarrassed. Ashamed that my language is still so faltering. Then I would have to wait to pay the lady in the corner, whose job it is to exclusively handle the money. She would pick up the receipt from where it has been jabbed onto the spike next to her and rattle off the amount-owing in Italian. I would have to ask her to repeat it slowly (*piano, piano, per favore*), and then I would fumble around in my wallet, trying to find the right notes, the correct coins. All while some fancy Bologna matron would be waiting impatiently behind me, her haughty gaze boring into me, radiating disapproval at my morning uniform of leggings and fur-lined hoodie. No, no. The thought of it is too much.

Instead, I will double back to the little supermarket further down the lane. Their mortadella is horrible: sold in plastic packets and kind of speckled with pink freckles, but at least there is a degree of anonymity there. I can enter, select the vac-pack from the refrigerated shelves, pay and leave. It will be a straightforward transaction, devoid of any intimacy. No one wants to chat in the supermarket. Even in Italy. Especially not at a small, shabby Pam supermarket in the middle of glorious, world-famous produce stalls, laden with fresh flowers and gleaming towers of vegetables and fruit. The supermarket is designed for the weary, the tired, the busy, the desperate, the soulless. At this very moment, it is designed for me.

I am thinking all these thoughts; the despondent, emotional flat-lining of a stranger in a strange land, when suddenly, walking up the laneway past the lovely store I am too exhausted to enter, I hear a persistent knocking.

It is the sound of a knuckle rapping against glass and, when I look over, I see it is smiling Simoni making the sound. He is leaning into the front window of his delicatessen, reaching over primary-colour painted tins of Sicilian sardines and hillocks of black and green glistening olives, to carefully replace a leg of prosciutto. He has found himself here, looking out onto the narrow street, at the very moment that I am walking past.

He smiles when he sees he has caught my eye. His familiar grin is ear-splitting.

'*Ecco lei!*' he yells through the glass. ('Here she is!')

His delight at seeing me takes me completely by surprise. I wave a tentative hand in response.

He laughs and bobs his head in a mock bow. Then he calls out again: '*Due Etti! Due Etti!* How are you today?'

He delivers the greeting with staccato, faintly American-accented deliberation; like he has learned it in English class decades ago. It is so funny, and his enthusiasm so infectious, that I, too, start to laugh. My cheerful deli friend – for it is only a friend who greets you with such happiness – has somehow cut through my misery and self-indulgence.

Also, I appear to have gained my first Italian nickname.

I am no longer Katie from Australia. I am not the foreigner, or the mother of four.

I am a weight and a measure. I am, officially, from this day forth, Two Hundred Grams. I am *Due Etti*.

And everyone knows, once you have been given a nickname, you are no longer a stranger.

When you change your mood, it seems, you change everything. Ten minutes later I arrive home, climbing up the worn marble stairs to the door of our apartment. I have a slim, paper-wrapped package of mortadella in my hands, a tub of milky, tender burrata from Puglia, some new-season tomatoes and flat bread rolls that are still radiating warmth in their paper bag. Peter is at the dining table, his computer open in front of him.

He looks up at me and smiles.

'Surprise!' he says. 'I'm booking flights for us to Amsterdam. Just you and me.'

And then – as if that is not enough – he tells me that one of our favourite American comedians, Bill Burr, is playing at an arena in Amsterdam on Saturday night and that is the reason for our whirlwind trip. I am so completely, utterly surprised, I am speechless. I stand behind him and reach down over his shoulders to hug him. He briefly catches my fingers, engrossed in his online calendar, and explains what we have coming up; a family photo shoot for the cover of the magazine I used to write a weekly column for, *Stellar* magazine. As well, we have my parents arriving, and the first stage of the *Giro d'Italia*, the Italian equivalent of the Tour de France, which this year will start in Bologna – outside our front door. To sandwich in an escape for the two of us is an impressive logistical feat.

'We will have to find a babysitter,' he says, brow furrowed.

'I can do that,' I say, suddenly renewed.

I put the kettle on and make rolls with fresh mortadella on them, and slice the tiny red tomatoes. Sprinkle them with salt. I place the fresh, creamy burrata on a little saucer, and anoint it with olive oil and some sprigs of basil from a pot growing in the kitchen window, next to our jar of Vegemite – a gift from Peter's brother Paul and his wife Anna. Then we sit down with cups of tea, my husband and me, to plan a trip that is so perfectly European it seems surreal: a weekend jaunt to the capital of Holland. I send a message through to my WhatsApp group of school mothers, asking if anyone knows a good babysitter for an upcoming weekend. There is an instant response from one of the Italians; her niece Veronica would be perfect, she says. She sends through her number.

I take a greedy bite of my mortadella panini. Actually, I correct myself, smugly, it is a *panino* – it is singular. Regardless of the syntax, the roll is a heavenly combination; salty, crisp and chewy. I have made it Italian-style, without butter, and it is perfect. Through the bank of windows behind Peter, I look out over our now-familiar vista – the unapologetic, proud beauty of Piazza Maggiore. As we sit, church bells chime the hour. Dong. Dong. Eleven times they bell, marking the time, as they have for hundreds of years. As they will for hundreds more.

My goodness, I think. I am lucky to be here. I am so, so happy.

9

THE FIRST OF MANY

Everything we do is a first time.

After our first few weeks in Bologna, the children know the way to school across the piazza and over the picturesque cobbles of Via D'Azeglio for several blocks, though Petie accompanies them every morning when I am at work, and together we go to pick them up in the afternoons. We are on an English curriculum at the international school, which means we keep a schedule similar to the 9 am to 3.30 pm school hours we have in Australia. (This is markedly different to the local Italian schools. There, the children have two choices: either school five days a week from 8 am till 1.30 pm, or six days a week, including Saturdays, comprised of even shorter days. The expectation that 'la mamma' will be at home has not caught up with the reality of modern life, and we often wonder what working parents do to fill that gap in the afternoon. The answer, we gather, is grandparents.)

The children are making friends, as I knew they would. Like learning a language, making friends seems to be easier the younger you are, and Jannie is delighted with his grade four teacher, English Mister David, and the kids in his class. Artie, of course, has his Australian mate Sam, and the friendship network he has already forged, while Sunday and Lewis, who have been adjusted down a class (her to grade nine; him to grade ten) until the European mid-year end-of-year, are a little slower off the mark. Peter organises for Sunday to go to swim squad every Friday with a French girl in her class, accompanied by her mother. I find her an art class she starts to attend once a week with a lovely local artist, Elena. Lewis plays some basketball with a group of senior boys. One day the teenagers have a posse of friends turn up in the piazza, calling out to them from below, and, after a conversation yelled out the windows, they wander down to join them. It is not easy, and the transition stretches all of us, but life here is undoubtedly interesting. Everything is new; every person, every teacher, every landmark, every shopfront, every name. And our surrounds are stimulating. Beauty abounds. Everywhere there are statues and historic buildings and evidence of the rich history of Italy. The age of the buildings is astounding to us. 'We don't have to go to the museum,' I often say to Peter (who loves such pursuits), 'we live in the museum.'

One of the sweetest, simplest gifts is that I don't have to make school lunches here; the children have a hot meal every day – three courses, comprised of pasta, followed by meat and vegetables, with bread and cheese, served in the *mensa*, the school cafeteria. We soon discover this is the subject of much dissatisfied discussion among the Italian parents (of course!), who are constantly complaining about the food. But to us, it is heaven. In the evenings, we have an early dinner (the Italians would be puzzled by the thought of us eating our main meal at 6 pm) and discuss what has happened over the course of the day, what we have done, and what we have coming up. For Lewis, there is a school trip to Berlin that Peter will accompany him on, since we were not here for the official booking cut-off but have been invited to tag along independently. For Sunday and Artie, there is a looming spring school camp, the destination of which makes us laugh delightedly. In Australia, school camps are normally in damp church-owned properties only available in the off-season, this one is to a modest hotel (but still – a hotel!) in Cinque Terre, the five seaside villages that are a Mecca for tourists from around the world.

And we also have a family break coming up – what the Italians call 'White Week', where schools have a week off and everyone heads to the snow. In Australia, snow-sports are predominantly a pastime for the wealthy. In Europe, most people can ski before they can walk. Peter discusses with other school and basketball parents the best villages for skiing, and where we may still be able to book accommodation.

In the meantime, my husband wants to fulfil his dream of buying an Italian road bike so he can get pedalling. When Sacha was still here, he mentioned it on one of our nights out with Giovanni, and our new Italian friend has insisted on taking Petie to his friend's bike shop, where he assures us his mate will look after us.

True to his word, Giovanni comes to pick us up after my work one morning. We pile into his small silver van and set off on the *bici* odyssey. Our destination, it transpires, is well out of Bologna. We drive for forty minutes on the freeway, hurtling past winter farms and bare paddocks, before pulling up at a huge bike warehouse, seemingly in the middle of nowhere. Giovanni and Peter go inside. I initially accompany them, but it is slow business, drinking coffee and perusing the cycles, while discussing the merits of each one with Giovanni's meticulous and deliberate bike-friend, who doesn't speak any English. Giovanni is a willing interpreter, but when the men start to discuss different braking systems and colour options, I feel incredibly weary. I go outside to the car, lie down in the back seat and, wrapped in my winter coat, have a nap.

When the men return, I am refreshed, and Peter is on a high. His bike has been ordered; a beautiful Cinelli that he has requested in metallic Italian blue – a gorgeous grey-toned hue we have both always loved. It will take three weeks to be made. In the meantime, Giovanni, as always, is thinking of food. We roar off to a neighbouring town where he knows there is a restaurant run by a mother and daughter, who are brilliant cooks.

'Also,' he says, grinning at the thought of lunch, 'this one is not expensive! You can't believe it!'

He is correct. The restaurant itself, in a fairly muted, empty-looking town, is nearly invisible from the street; we would never have found it if we weren't with someone with local knowledge.

There, pinned under a sheet of glass outside, and affixed to the unmarked doorway, is a handwritten menu: gnocchi, and spaghetti with various toppings – tomato, of course, but also zucchini and pancetta. There is a pasta called *garganelli* with prosciutto and cream, as well as a few mains: fillets of grilled beef with eggplant, crumbed schnitzels of chicken and sliced steak with porcini mushrooms, and, of course, meatballs. All of the dishes are five or six euros. The steak, the most expensive dish, is eight euros. And the food is magnificent. Giovanni, who loves to take charge at the table, orders for us and chats to the mother–daughter combo, who appear at the table, gleaming with their kitchen exertions. When they depart, he informs us, giggling, that the food is so reasonably priced because they don't pay rent. We never get to the bottom of this; we are too busy getting to the bottom of the platters that rattle out of the kitchen. The food is plentiful and so delicious. It is incredible that two people have made it all.

Giovanni drives us back to Bologna, taking the back roads this time, because of the wine we have had with lunch. Peter and I will pick up the children from school, and after that will head off to meet with our potential new landlord, to try and secure our 'permanent' home; an apartment in a huge old palazzo (a palace), around the corner from our serviced apartment.

Like Giovanni with his bike-shop friend, everything in Italy seems to happen through connections, and our tip on this apartment has come through a friend back home, who knows Australian Rachel, who put us onto American Denise, who already lives in a large apartment in the building with her husband and four children. I had emailed Denise from Australia, introducing us, and she had, also via email, introduced us to Ferdinando, the owner of the building. After a month or so of back and forths, we had been invited to see the apartment for ourselves. What a thrill it was when Ferdinando came downstairs and opened the giant arched wooden doors that admitted us into the front courtyard. And how beautiful the old palace is, its four storeys divided now into many family and rented apartments, but still grand and spacious. The apartment we are looking at is huge, a far cry from our current cramped quarters. It was Ferdi's former law offices; he is in the process of joining the four or five enormous rooms, with their soaring medieval ceilings, to what was his family apartment on the same floor. Now he has retired and his children are grown, he has moved to a smaller flat at the top of the building opposite.

The renovation is massive; Ferdi tells us he has been working on it for three years, but it is clearly still far from complete. Still, I believe it is worth waiting for. Peter is less convinced – not that the apartment is not stunning, but it is hard to see how it will be ready for us before the end of the year. Unwilling to put all our accommodation eggs in one basket, my husband has taken me to look at another apartment in Bologna *centro*. This one presents its own problems – it would be rented unfurnished and without a kitchen (Italians often take their kitchens with them when they move). It is too complicated for us to try and furnish a place, I argue. At this stage, we don't even have a car. And Ferdi's place, he assures us, will be rented furnished. In fact, it is crammed with furniture. Inside, covered with plastic sheeting, is a labyrinth of old wooden chairs and dining tables, ornate paintings, and in the middle of the clutter is a huge lamp – a black cherub atop a wooden plinth, holding a flaming torch. It is stunningly beautiful, even through the patina of dust and debris, and I have faith it will be ours. The only question is when.

One day Ferdi says to me: 'Please, come by whenever you like to see the progress.' Then he adds, 'In Italy, we have a saying, "Only the farmer can fatten the pig".' It takes me a while to work this out. Then I realise he is encouraging me to monitor the renovation so the tradies will complete it more swiftly. He wants me to be the farmer that will fatten the pig? This surely is madness. As anyone who has ever shared a table with me will attest, in this scenario, I am much better placed to play the role of the pig.

Nonetheless, we fall into the pattern of dropping in once or twice a week to check on the progress of the building works. These are often impeded by historical checks – the discovery of old frescos on the ceiling that must be preserved; or a small secret room revealed behind old panels above a staircase. I sometimes drop by to hang out with Ferdi and chat with him as the two workmen – who seem to be a permanent fixture – go about their work at a sawhorse in the marble-floored ballroom. One day, when he is asking what furniture we would need, he tells me has more at his 'country house'. He never stays there, he tells me, but was left it by his godfather, who adopted him, and gave him the second part of his hyphenated surname.

It is such a strange story, because I know he had his own parents – I have seen portraits of them hanging in what will be (I hope) our entranceway. I smile when Ferdi tells me of the godfather adoption, and I say to him: 'You must have been very cute.' He stares at me, puzzled, and I explain my thought.

'You must have been very cute for your godfather to adopt you,' I say.

He now looks positively confused.

'I was thirty-eight,' he says.

It is too Italian for me to understand. But gosh it makes me laugh.

That afternoon, Ferdi tells me if we want the apartment, it is ours. He will not let it to anyone else. I am surprised; I didn't know he was thinking of renting it to anyone else.

Still it is a small note of certainty. I just hope it will be finished this year, in time for us to move in before we leave.

Two days later, Jannie comes running in to tell us we need to look at the piazza. We go to our front windows and take in the sight of the public square covered with sunglasses and spectacles. When we go downstairs, there are thousands and thousands of them, each laid out neatly on the ground, an artistic display to highlight blindness and sight issues in more impoverished parts of the world. It is, I think, executed by a version of our own Fred Hollows Foundation in Australia, but it is also confusing. The display is, punnily, quite spectacular, but there is nowhere to donate to the charity or NGO that has organised it, only black-clad young people painstakingly straightening the rows of frames on the ground.

The following day, the glasses are gone, replaced instead by a circuit of physical challenges: skipping ropes and witches hats laying out a running track, small seesaws and a couple of basketball hoops, as well as a giant chess set, which Artie and Jannie race over to play.

Peter and I tell the boys we will be at our favourite cafe Gran, and when they are finished their game, they can meet us there. We walk around the edge of the piazza, through the throng of Saturday people doing Saturday things; shopping and eating. Riding bikes. Pushing strollers. Bathing in the winter sun. As we make our way across the square, the bells chime from the church tower.

I stop and turn to face Peter.

'I don't think I'll be ready to go home at the end of the year,' I say.

He looks at me. We hug. To passersby, we must look like Italian lovers.

'Neither will I,' he murmurs into my hair.

10

HAMSTERDAM: NEAR CANAL; FAR CANAL

Amsterdam was so much fun. Since we had only three precious days to enjoy it, Petie and I abandoned any notion of financial practicality and lived large. We booked a hotel my dad had told us about that was perfectly, magnificently grand, but also cosy and welcoming. Our room had been upgraded to a suite overlooking the water. There was a bottle of champagne waiting in an ice bucket and, through a frame of navy velvet drapes, we looked out onto a scene of canal boats, their decks dotted with tubs of winter flowers. Below, the streets were lit with lamps smudging Rembrandt light against the afternoon grey and, a bridge over, were cyclists – so many cyclists – pedalling their way past the majestic Rijksmuseum. It was glorious.

The weather was freezing – so Dutch, so damp – and after an arrival nap (one of my favourite things) we donned the sheepskin coats we bought in the sales from the ritzy boutique under our apartment in Bologna and headed out to eat. Peter wanted a schnitzel, and the tall and handsome concierge at reception said he knew of a place nearby.

'Somtimes afftter verk, I am going here myselff for schnitzel,' he said, drawing it for us on a map. (Gosh, I love my father's people, who are, by the way, also the tallest people in the world.)

We wandered to the restaurant, which was studenty and cheerful, and ate delicious crumbed chicken Dutch-style, with apple sauce. We drank giant glass mugs of beer – even me, who normally finds it too bitter – and then, as we were leaving, we turned to take a different route back to our hotel, and right next to us, surrounded by steep and narrow canal houses, was a coffee shop.

OMG-for-ganja. An Amsterdam 'coffee shop'.

We could smell it before we saw it; the herbal, unmistakable aroma of marijuana. Mary Jane. Pot. The chronic. Dope. The old stinkweed. And here we were, without children for the first time in months, off the leash and giddy with freedom, so I grabbed Petie's arm and, without even discussing it, we went inside. The young Lebanese guy running the joint (pun noted but not intended) was obviously familiar with wide-eyed tourists venturing into his establishment. He was cute and friendly, and after a chat about Australia, he talked us through the menu – an actual menu – of what was on offer. There were descriptions of flavour and THC counts, and the various strains had names like Heavenly Haze or Bent Buddha or, more alarmingly, Amster-Damnesia or Thai Trainwreck. While we were talking, a man popped in to pick up some takeaway – a small bag of weed and some smoking papers.

It was all amazing. I asked our hemp-host if he had something mild that would make us happy and giggly. He made a selection for us, and handed over a long conical joint in a narrow plastic tube with a stopper, explaining that when we'd had enough we could put it back in its case and save it for later. It was five euros, not even eight dollars in Aussie money. We ordered a pot of tea (no alcohol allowed in coffee shops) and filled glasses of water, then went inside and found a table in the corner. Through the haze of cloying smoke, we studied our fellow stoners. The place had a distinct loungeroom vibe, with a mix of a dozen or so people – some old, some young – playing dominoes, scrolling through their phones or lying back on cushions and watching music videos on the wall-mounted TV. Intriguingly, everyone seemed to be drinking Chocomel, the Dutch chocolate milk.

And then we got blazed.

It didn't take much. And it was so bizarre and fun to sit and get wok-eyed with my husband after months and months of being so responsible and adult. I can't even remember what we talked about but I do recall that after about an hour I was suddenly desperate – DESPERATE – for a chocolate milk.

On the way home, we stopped in the middle of a bridge over a canal and peered down to see if any bicycles had been thrown in the water, apparently the most prevalent Dutch crime. Then we tried to take a selfie that included every element: us, the water, the bridge, our beautiful hotel, the moon – and of course it was impossible. Every photo turned out blurry, and then we realised it was actually us who was out of focus, with our hoods up and our puffy, rose-tinted eyeballs. Peter said, 'You'd better not put this on *Amstagram*, the children might see it,' and I said, in a faux-dramatic way, 'Those *parasites*!', and we laughed so hard we nearly toppled into the canal.

The next morning, we woke up late, and starving. A little sheepishly, we called to check in with our beloved parasites. They, of course, were innocently oblivious to the thought that their parents might be frequenting foreign drug dens. In fact, they showed barely any interest in us at all. We could tell from their distracted air that Veronica must have granted them screen time. They weren't missing us one bit.

Responsibility fulfilled, Peter and I gleefully got dressed and ventured out. We walked along the canal to the littlest pancake restaurant in Amsterdam; a tiny room with four tables up a staircase so wonky and narrow you had to walk up single file and sideways. There, we ordered *pannekoeken* with cheese, another with lemon and powdered sugar and Peter had a Dutch classic, with apple and cinnamon. The guy making the pancakes was squeezed in at a bench next to us; a couple of round hotplates in front of him, like a DJ at the decks. He was Indonesian, it turned out, and was excited when he found out, that – like so many Australians but relatively few Europeans – we had been to Bali. Though we were full, he insisted on making us a final pancake with the last of his batter. We shared it; forking mouthfuls of our gifted crepe with crispy smoked bacon and *siroop*, the treacly Dutch syrup. It was so, so good.

That evening, we caught a taxi to the outskirts of the city to see Bill Burr's stand-up show, only to encounter a massive, unmoving queue of people waiting to enter the stadium. A couple of things made this remarkable: we had finally found something poorly organised in Holland, a nation renowned for its smooth running and peerless engineering prowess. (I mean, really, the whole country is literally built on a seabed.)

Secondly, it was astounding that an American comedian could command such a huge audience in a non-English-speaking country. Understanding a foreign language with a degree of fluency is difficult enough; to appreciate comedy in a non-native tongue requires another level of comprehension altogether. I know this, partly because I had recently, ahem, made my first simple joke in Italian. The proprietor of a cabin we had rented at a farmstay outside Bologna spied a massive lemon I had bought, resting like an emu egg on top of our other groceries. With an Italian's unerring eye for food provenance, he complimented me on it, and identified it as a lemon from Sorrento, in the south. I remarked that the fruit was so huge, it was not merely a *limoni* it was a *meloni-limoni*. (Like I said, a simple joke. But how thrilled I was when the farmer roared with laughter.)

The reason for the impressive English the Dutch speak is also simple but fascinating. You see, the Dutch don't dub. In Italy and Spain and France, every English-language TV show or film is dubbed by local actors, who revoice the dialogue to match the onscreen action. The practice is so prevalent that the actors who regularly do the voiceovers end up with their own fan clubs – there is an Italian 'Brad Pitt' and an Italian 'George Clooney', both of whom, apparently, are wildly popular. (In our Italian class, our teacher told us that when the Italian actor who dubbed Homer's voice in *The Simpsons* died, the country was so bereft they didn't screen any new episodes for several seasons.)

The Netherlands, like many of the Nordic countries, uses subtitles rather than dubbing. It means from infancy, when they watch TV, they are hearing English; when they are old enough, they begin reading the corresponding words in Dutch. They effectively spend their recreational viewing time in English class and, as a result, their mastery of the language is incredible. This is why Bill Burr, a visiting American, can fill an arena with four thousand Dutch men and women who not only follow, but love, his comedy.

At the moment, though, the size of the audience is more a curse than a reason for rejoicing. After ten minutes of waiting futilely to enter the venue's main doors, I shove my cold hands deep in my coat pockets, and find treasure. It is the joint left over from last night, nestled in its plastic casing. I ask Petie if we should light it. We are momentarily uncertain; in Australia, of course, this would be highly illegal, and here, we are not sure of the rules. As if to allay our doubts, a man from a group bunched in front of us casually lights his own joint and starts passing it around. That settles it. I pull the long roach from its tube and we spark it up.

By the time we pass security and bag checks and are finally admitted into the foyer of the stadium, the scene is one of disarray. We join the nearest bar queue, buy a couple of giant beers in plastic cups and enter the auditorium.

Inside, there is no one to help us find our places; not a single usher.

We peer at the numbers on our printed tickets and try to get our bearings in the vast room. Eventually, I work out our seats are near the front of the tiered section, at the end of a full row of punters. It is unusual that I take charge of any situation involving navigation but Peter has become strangely passive and confused so I lead the way. It is a disaster. We are climbing over strangers in the darkness, balancing beers. Also, we are stoned by now and somehow, in our shuffle-sorry, shuffle-sorry squeeze through the crowd, I manage to catch the strap of my handbag over an armrest, which pulls me up short, causing me to tip beer into my boot. It is ludicrous. And my reactions are all wrong. I should be mortified but instead become convulsed with laughter. Peter, butting up behind me, is less amused. He nudges me to keep making my way along the row, but I cannot move. I am so weak and overcome at our stupid predicament I can only stand there, hunched, my shoulders heaving with sobs of laughter. Eventually, the Dutchman whose lap I am apologetically slumped over, kindly untangles me. Showing amazing restraint, he gently propels me down the row, where we finally collapse into our allocated seats.

The show was brilliant, by the way. I don't remember much specifically, but at one point I was laughing so hard, I was slapping Peter on the thigh. I mean, that's a huge compliment to a comedian, when you find yourself slapping *someone else's* thigh. As we overheard a happy Dutchman remark, filing our way out of the theatre: 'Dat Bill Burr, ja? He iss as funny as fock!'

11

BASKET CITY

We are soon in a blur of work and home life and visitors and language classes and basketball.

Yes. Basketball.

Before we even arrived in Bologna, Peter, the sly super-organiser, had organised for Jannie and Artie to do tryouts for the local basketball team, Virtus, even though it was mid-season here and the squads were already filled. I guess he was right to be confident of their abilities because they were both accepted into their age-group teams. Now, on top of everything else, we are committed to getting the boys to three individual training sessions a week and to matches on the weekend. We still don't have a car and I still get lost on my way home from work sometimes when I try to walk a different route. Also, I am still getting up at dawn to do my radio show, then shopping and cooking for and feeding six people, so I am a reluctant (some might say 'sulky') participant in the whole process. Often training times are only announced the night before, making it impossible to plan anything else. When I am there, I can't communicate with anyone. And because this is Italy and everything happens in the evening, sometimes the boys don't get home till 11 pm. One night they came home hungry and I had to cook. It was nearly midnight, and my alarm was set for 4 am the next morning. So when Peter presents me with a bus pass he has purchased from the local *tabaccheria* (the slightly shady tobacco stores that supply everything from morning coffees to shots of liquor and postcards) so that I can regularly get Jannie to his Tuesday night practice, while Peter is ferrying

Artie to his, I don't even feign gratitude. I grimly remember Sacha's guide, Giuseppe, and his proclamation that Bologna is 'Basket City', and I realise that I have been played.

See, part of my fantasy about our family moving overseas was that I would get to free myself from the ludicrous sporting schedules we maintained back home, with three sporting boys and an early-morning swim-squad daughter. And it seems naive now, but I vaguely imagined Italy (when I had time) as a blurry pastiche of long lunches, siestas and wandering through cobbled laneways clutching a loaf of crusty bread and a bottle of wine, Sophia Loren style, while handsome men called out '*Ciao, bella!*'. Even though I couldn't project exactly what form our life here would take, I know I longed for an escape from the grind of responsibility and hectic scheduling of extracurricular activities that brutalised us (and so many other parents) in Australia. But, really, who the hell did I think I was? I might be on the other side of the world, but I am still *me*. I am still a wife of one, and a mother of four. And though I sometimes glance with envy at celebrity mothers who seem so good at prioritising their own pleasures and pastimes (is there a more tiresome mantra than *self-love-self-care* – especially from people who we know outsource all of life's grunt work?) I cannot bring myself to do it. Even though I have the desire to be selfish, I just don't know how to fully commit to it. And I certainly wouldn't be encouraged to do so by following the lead of my selfless husband. So Italian basketball it is.

Anyway, the boys seem to love the game and it is undoubtedly compelling. Basketball is vigorous here – more physical than even back home – and there are nuanced differences that make it interesting. After a match, for instance, the Italian boys, even the littlest ones, have hot showers, then don dressing-gowns they have packed and painstakingly blow-dry their hair. (My Aussie rough-and-tumble sons, for whom an elective sport is avoiding any shower-time at all, find this amazing.) On court, when a player is hurt in the game – whether genuinely injured, or simply taking an embarrassed dive after missing a shot – and gets back up on his feet, the parents from both sides applaud and call out '*Bravo!*'. It is a clever and sweet strategy, for who doesn't like having their bravery acknowledged? (I would actually like that chorus of approval when I drag myself out of bed every morning.) But the biggest change from Australia, where parents are discouraged from being too vocal, is that the Italian *mammas* and *papas* are passionate barrackers and sideline coaches.

The other basket parents we have met so far are simply lovely, on and off the sidelines of battle. Also, they are *real* Italians (even if some of them are not strictly Italian) – our shorthand for indicating they are not from the generally wealthy microcosm of the International School of Bologna. They are, without exception, friendly and welcoming and, because we are such a novelty, deeply curious about us. Despite the fact that we barely speak their language, and only a few of them speak English, they open up a world of local friendship to us, sharing rides to games, and inviting us to backyard barbecues and post-match dinners where we all squeeze into local pizza restaurants.

A few of them are standouts from the start: cheerful Albanian Speranza and her Italian husband Daniele, who videos all the games; William and his ever-smiling Spanish wife Begoña, who, unusually, also have a son called Luis. The parents of team superstar Baiocchi are a good-looking, chain-vaping, motorbike-riding couple who are deaf; and there is peach-faced Francesca, who actually speaks near-perfect English, since, intriguingly, she works as a translator of romance novels. (One day, when we are bored watching practice, she tells me all the euphemisms she is allowed to use for a fictional hero's tockley. Even in Italian, I learn, no reader seeking romance wants to read about a man's 'penis'. We would, apparently, much rather hear about him 'unsheathing his love-sword' or his 'swollen manhood'. These expressions, which Francesca whispers to me in Italian, make us laugh till we weep.)

There is only one couple that exists in our Venn diagram crossover of basketball and the international school: tall, dark Riccardo and his platinum blonde, pixie-haired wife Monica. They have a boy Jannie's age, Robbie, who on the first day of school greeted our youngest son with a million-watt grin. Robbie has been tight with Jannie ever since, a friendship cemented by their taking to the court together. Robbie's parents are an interesting duo. Riccardo, who manages his family's Hotel Portici, has also built up his own business – a small chain of restaurants selling Bolognese food as 'fast food'. Bottega Portici is a brilliant idea, featuring takeaway pasta meticulously made fresh in the window of his main, midtown eatery, and local wines with platters of cheese and mortadella. Monica works in fashion for a company started by her uncle but which now supplies boutiques worldwide. Both of them love their jobs and work longer and harder than anyone else we know. When we express amazement at their long hours, they modestly explain this makes them novelties even among their fellow Italians. We have to join the dots on this; Italians are notorious for prizing leisure time over work.

The first tournament I have to take Artie to by myself is being played in Bologna but is against opponents from Milan. The fashion capital of Italy is only just over an hour or so away on the fast train but half-a-day's travel by bus, and when the team turns up, it is clear they mean business. The parents are religiously decked out in their team colours. And they have brought *drums*. Not Matthew-McConaughey-is-lit-again bongoes, but giant bass drums, like you would see in a marching band. This is to a 'friendly' match played between twelve-year-olds. A couple of the dads strap the instruments onto their shoulders, and when the game begins, there is a cacophony of sound that fills the small stadium. BOOM go the drums. BOOM! BOOM! BOOM! The other Milano parents blow horns and sing. Some have brought giant flags, which they sweep through the air. The Bolognese parents return fire with giant banners and their own clapping and hooting. Everyone from our side yells '*Virtus! Virtus!*' till we are hoarse, and then the singsong chant that quickly becomes my favourite: '*Noi vogliamo cinque lione!*' (We want five lions!). It is madness – glorious, unimaginable chaos. At one point it is so loud and cramped in the basement arena that I think we will surely be evicted for safety reasons, but everyone around me is having a great time. Well, nearly everyone.

Our head coach, our short but highly impassioned mentor, is nearly bursting with frustration. He gets into a furious fight with one of the umpires, arms raised and wildly gesticulating, then, moments later, heads over to us at the sidelines and lets loose on one of the Bologna mums. It turns out she has upset him with her vocal courtside coaching. I am astounded that he can even hear her over the din – everyone is heckling and yelling so loudly. The mum argues back. The parents around me watch the fight unfold with an air of philosophical detachment. I can't believe what I'm seeing. Everyone is doubly entertained it seems – firstly by the argument itself, then by my amazement at the spectacle. They don't seem surprised by any of it; they are more concerned with the decimation our boys are facing on court.

We were clearly outclassed by the Milanese team. Their twelve-year-olds looked like men: tall and strong. The scoreboard reflected their superiority; it showed a routing. And then our wild-eyed coach, in what I can only imagine was a last-gasp act of despair, subbed on his newest player: the little sandy-blond curiosity from Australia. Artie. I had been watching him from across the court, sitting alone on the players' bench like an unread book, while his teammates excitedly jabbered on either side of him, and I had a despairing pang of 'What have I done?' It suddenly seemed too much, to have brought him here to the other side of the world, to make him play a game with wild foreigners with whom he shared not even a common tongue.

Artie trotted obediently onto the court. I could see with my mother eyes that his breath was high in his chest. He was nervous. And then, after an inauspicious start, which saw his talented opponent casually steal the ball from him and streak past him to score, something inside him clicked. I saw him take a ragged breath and don his battle-face and suddenly, my modest, team-playing son – who always passes, rather than seek glory for himself – became possessed with the spirit of one who has nothing to lose. Off court, he could barely communicate with his teammates, and yet, here he was, playing point guard like a leader. He bolted up and down the court like a dervish. He played defence and offence. He scored a couple of lay-ups that made our home side roar. He was red-faced and fast and fierce. It was incredible. We were still getting beaten but now there was no shame in it. The other parents noticed. And then something else happened that I will never forget.

Towards the end of the match, with the scoreboard now reflecting our phoenix-from-the-ashes rally, the parents took up a new chant – one I had not heard before. One that took me a while to understand. Then I realised what they were saying. 'Art-ee! Art-ee!' they were chorusing. The whole side, this company of strangers, was cheering on my son. When the game was over, they flocked around, patting him on the shoulder, and congratulating me for being his mother. I saw Artie, flushed and proud, while the coaches and parents – angst forgotten – tousled his hair, brought him drinks, and cupped his face and ear in that quintessentially gentle, Italian gesture. It was like something from an underdog-makes-good movie. Except it was real and beautiful.

12

BE CAREFUL WHAT YOU WISH FOR...

Once again, everything feels so hard.

I am so tired.

And once again, I keep thinking: I did not move to Italy to feel like this.

Every day I get picked up at 5 am to go to work at the studio-office Sacha has set up for me near the train station to do my radio afternoon drive-show back to Australia with Hughesy. While we are organising the show via our computer link, I moan to him and Sacha about how much I miss her; how exhausted I am; how I am washing and cooking for six people; how I am sick of being squeezed into one three-bedroom apartment; how many strange and foreign systems there are.

My troubles are big and small. I still get lost sometimes walking home from my downtown 'studio'. I made someone annoyed in the supermarket because I forgot to weigh and price my fruit and vegetables *before* I got to the checkout. I can't even peel a potato because I can't find a normal veggie peeler. Or spring-tongs. The ones here are just a fork and spoon joined together.

As well, there is the friction of apartment life, with half-a-dozen people living on top of each other. Sunday and Lewis had a physical fight in their tiny room because Sunday wanted to open the windows. Lewis didn't want to because there is a bar directly underneath them and their room fills with cigarette smoke and noise. Their room is so hot because our whole apartment is madly overheated. It is illegal to

Our first hour in Bologna, the city Peter and I chose as our base in Italy. The guy who brought our cocktails gestured to my hair clips and sunglasses and said '*Fantastica!*'

Just a day in our piazza in Bologna. You can see our apartment windows behind us.

The view from our apartment window onto Piazza Maggiore: ringside seats for every fiesta.

Toasting our new home, the city of red. While the name supposedly refers to Bologna's political leanings as a university town, it also applies literally. Every building in the city is shades of terracotta and rossa. It is beautiful.

The courtyard of our palazzo ...

One day I walked out of our apartment to this.

Heading home on Valentine's Day with a guitar for Peter. Bologna's famous Fountain of Neptune in the background.

Saturday morning flower market in the piazza.

Photo shoot of the family in Bologna for *Stellar* magazine – the kids liked the ice-cream but were disgusted with their outfits.

We might have groaned about our tiny kitchen but we never got tired of this view from our dinner table.
PS. Italians would be horrified at my wrinkled tablecloth.

Pit stop before school pick up in Bologna.

Jannie and his friend Robbie, who on the first day of school greeted our youngest son with a million-watt grin. Their friendship was cemented by basketball. And me taking the scenic route to pick up our car for yet another basketball date.

La Traviata, my father's favourite opera, and the name of our friend Manuela's restaurant, dangerously placed on our walk to school.

When I couldn't decide between two pasta dishes at Manuela's restaurant she brought them both to me on this plate.

Petie's riding friend, Simone, came over to teach him how to make pasta using the pasta machine his Nonna used forty years ago.

With Peter's parents Maree and Bryan outside our apartment in Bologna. Peter's dad said to my mother-in-law: 'There's just one thing I don't understand, Maree: Why don't they speak English?'

With beloved mother-in-law Maree and son Lewis in our Italian kitchen.

Lewis learned to cook with Maree in Italy. Fried chicken.

At a little farmhouse we stayed in outside Bologna. I was still working on the Hughesy & Kate radio show so Peter got up at 4 am every morning and drove me into Bolo to do the show. Then we came back to swim and laze.

The von Trapps of Italia.

Our friend Kane flew over from London and joined us at our villa in the hills outside Bologna.

My mother-in-law Maree and our daughter Sunday at beautiful Lake Garda.

Golden Italian Days. Artie, Jannie, Lewis and Sunday.

With my in-laws Bryan and Maree, friends Monica and Riccardo and their son Robbie. We love a long table.

An idyllic Easter break in beautiful Tuscany. Peter's hand is bandaged from a bad bike fall.

I dress for aperitivo. My friend Hughesy says Italians are the original hipsters, with their slow food and obsession with coffee. Here is proof.

Parking Italian style. It's an art form.

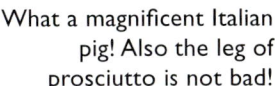

A little mortadella.

What a magnificent Italian pig! Also the leg of prosciutto is not bad!

Strolling at dusk through Bologna's main shopping street, Via dell'Indipendenza, closed to traffic on the weekends.

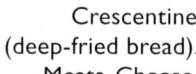

Crescentine (deep-fried bread). Meats. Cheese.

Sunday and Lewis – cat and dog sharing a room.

Italians are madly into Easter or *Pasqua* and the hugest, most ornately decorated eggs and window displays.

Sister-in-law Anna with all the classic Australian favourites the kids were missing.

Six take Italy – but take very few photos all together.

turn the heating off before 15 April (just as it is illegal to turn it *on* before 15 November), and we don't have control over the settings, even though the company who runs the serviced apartments insists that we do. All winter we have had to leave windows open, even when it is snowing or raining.

We are waiting to move into our new, bigger apartment but every week, the date we can move in gets pushed back. First March. Then April. Now, of course, May. Every visit to the site we watch what seems like the same two tradesmen, shrouded in a fog of dust, sawing and sanding. It is a job that looks like it would take ten men a year to complete.

My moans are endless: I can't ask for what I want in a shop and I can't go to Italian class to learn because I am working. We still don't have a car so I have to walk everywhere, often schlepping groceries. I ache from trudging over hard stone and stairs, endless stairs. Also, our bathroom stinks. I mean, really rotten, like something died in there, and no amount of open windows and scouring seems to make a difference. As Peter wryly observes to me, the ancient Romans famously invented indoor plumbing but modern Italians seem to have lost the art of it. Our shower is always blocked, often flooding the floor.

As he listens to my litany of complaints, Hughesy laughs. A little cruelly.

'You're living the dream,' he says, and it makes me laugh back. A little bitterly.

Because that is also frustrating; every time I speak to friends or family back in Australia, they seem to think I am gorging on pasta under sun-dappled trees before quaffing a bottle of wine and enjoying a siesta. I'm doing my best with the pasta and the wine, but the truth is, I have never worked harder in my life. Everything is foreign. And I know I wanted that – in fact, I fought for it – which makes me feel like a double loser when I have pangs for the simplicity of our Australian life.

I miss basic things, like having a babysitter or being able to buy sour cream. A rubbish collection. Here we have to sort bottles from plastic from aluminium from paper, and carry dripping bags of organic kitchen waste a block away to the nearest communal bins. Our tiny kitchen is constantly crammed with sorted bags of trash waiting to be taken down, by children who never think of it. I miss my car. I miss being able to put a plug into a power socket and not having the wrong type. (Some of them take three prongs, and some of them take two. Why, Italy, why?) I miss having the privacy of even a tiny space to get away from the tumble of five others. The other day I was trying on a new pair of boots in front of the full-length mirror behind our door, when Lewis suddenly appeared in the hallway behind me with a mate from school. 'Mum, this is Alessandro,' he said, seemingly oblivious to the fact that I was wearing nothing but a singlet and knickers (and the boots, of course).

I miss being able to be understood. Here, when my mental elves open my mind-drawers, which are normally stuffed full of words, they are pitifully empty. All I can say is '*Si*' and '*Grazie*', and I often leave a market stall with something I didn't mean to buy because I am too embarrassed to admit I was wrong and start the negotiation again.

As well, there is endless paperwork needed for us to stay in the country. We have to go to the post office, and then to the *questura* – the police who handle all citizenship and passports – and in between getting fingerprinted and awaiting identity cards, we are instructed to prepare for a home visit at any time. The boys required a full physical at a sports doctor (including an ECG) before they were allowed to play basketball. (They are nine and twelve.)

The bureaucracy at every level is next level. Papers get lost, and no wonder. Every government office you enter has towering piles of paper and documents stuffed in plastic dividers with a weary public servant about to be swamped by them, like Moses holding back the Red Sea. The reliance on paperwork is like the 1950s. Everything goes through a dizzying maze of triple- or quadruple-handling. When Peter finally sets up our Italian bank account, he has to pick up the pin number from the local tabaccheria. In between making coffees, the guy who works there hands him a slip of paper with his top-secret-never-share-this-number-with-anyone scrawled on it. Our citizen cards finally arrive but mine is issued with the wrong birthdate, meaning we have to start the mind-numbing process again.

As well as the bureaucratic loop de loop, there are unavoidable inconveniences simply from living in the city centre. We need to lease a car, but have nowhere to park and have to find a parking garage four hundred metres away. Every day, they have to enter our registration on a central system so we don't incur more fines for driving into the old city. We enlist the help of a local paralegal, Madalina, who is sunny and cheerful and meets us at the Statue of Neptune with a baby on her hip, to help us navigate our way through the jumble of requirements. Even though she is experienced and determined (and speaks five languages, including her native Romanian), meeting the demands of the various government departments and rental agreements is like untangling strands of overcooked spaghetti.

I have learnt another word: *schiava*. It means 'slave', and I am slaving for my family. At night, we are so exhausted, Peter and I don't even fall asleep; we pass out, shrouded in tobacco fumes, to the din of revellers in the street below us. At 3 am, the street cleaners come, their clanking metal brushes and glass-bottle collecting making such a racket, ricocheting around the stone laneway below, we often wake, hearts pounding, before lapsing back into precious unconsciousness.

Even though I am exhausted and overwhelmed, I am determined to maintain some family traditions. One of these is what we refer to in our household as a Saturday morning 'pancake party'. We have been doing this for years, and it involves me making an enormous pile of thin pancakes (Dutch style), which we have with cheese, maple syrup with bacon, or lemon and sugar. When the family was smaller, this was not so much work but now that there are so many of us (and frequent guests) a pancake party means I have had to transition to using two or three frypans. (Had I known then what I know now, I would have started making fat American pancakes and saved myself a lot of time and energy, but tradition is tradition so crepes it is.)

Anyway, today Marshall is coming over to join us.

He is Lewis's friend from the international school – an Australian sixteen-year-old who lives in a little apartment in the centre. He is studying to be a pilot, and because he also has an Italian–Australian father, has based himself in Europe, where there are lots of air routes. When we first arrived, we couldn't believe this grade eleven boy from the Mornington Peninsula in Victoria lived here on his own, eking out his allowance with 2-euro pizzas from the supermarket, so we began inviting him over for meals. He is clever and diligent – I find him amazing, and a lesson to us in how resourceful and independent a teenager can be. Marshall has been living in Bologna for eight months already, and spends his downtime finding cheap flights all over Europe. On weekends he will go to Prague, for instance, on a 7-euro ticket, often travelling on buses overnight to avoid spending money on accommodation. He is also no stranger to the wormhole of Italian systems, and tells us the tale of how the questura lost his birth certificate, and he had to get another certified and sent from Australia. Following their instructions, he travelled to Milan with his passport to present the new document, *the original of which they had lost*, only to be in a kerfuffle involving half-a-dozen officials and a half-day wait. Eventually he was told no one could accept his birth certificate from him because he was under eighteen. His dad ended up flying out from Australia to lodge a single form.

Anyway, the reason for Marshall joining us for this morning's pancake party is twofold: as well as feeding our Australian 'orphan', he has invited Lewis to join him on a six-day adventure over Easter to Split in Croatia, then to Liechtenstein, Montenegro and Kosovo (where Marshall wants to collect a passport stamp before it obtains official nation status). Lewis's grandparents back in Australia are horrified at the idea (as is Hughesy), but I can't help but think the very reason we are in Europe is to have adventures like this. The boys are going to talk us through their plans this morning. Then

Peter and I will decide if Lewis, at fifteen, can make this trek with his mate through Eastern Europe, while we meet other friends from Australia for a welcome, but less adventurous, Easter break at a villa in Tuscany.

The rest of the family is just stirring awake and I am, heavy-headed, setting the table and slicing lemons and juggling pancake batter with stupid sticking frypans on the tiny, even stupider induction stovetop in our tiny kitchen, when the doorbell rings. I open it to a handsome, twenty-something Italian. He lets forth a stream of words, of which I only understand 'Marco' – clearly his name – and the word *bagno*. Ah! A plumber! Here for the second time this week to try and unclog (and hopefully unstink) our troublesome shower. I show him in; by the time I make it back to the stovetop from the bathroom, my pancakes are burnt.

This is the final straw. I scrape off the charred crepes, burning my hand in the process. I finally get everything to the table as Lewis emerges, yawning. He gives me a sleepy hug, and then looks at the table, set with a lace cloth and covered stacks of steaming pancakes; the glorious church and square of Piazza Maggiore framed through the windows behind, and he says: 'Wow. This is like magic'.

And for some reason (see all of the above), his use of the word 'magic' releases the pressure cooker of my exhausted rage.

'Oh yes!' I hiss at him. 'It's *magic*! Nothing here required any effort!' I gesture wildly at the table, my anger gaining momentum. 'Look! Everything has just magicked its way to the table! It must be the magical fucking kitchen elves!' I bang the frypans into the sink to punctuate my fury.

Lewis is still reeling from my unexpected response as the other members of the family, alerted by the noise, come out to see what is going on. They look at me uncertainly as I continue to unload, my anger peaking irrationally at the sight of my well-slept, tousle-haired children. Peter, clearly alarmed, tries to take over the kettle I am boiling, but I fend him off furiously, and slam a pot of tea on the table.

'And here's a MAGIC TEAPOT!' I exclaim.

'Come on, everybody! Let's sit down and enjoy a MAGIC fucking BREAKFAST!'

I have now been yelling so loudly, and so madly, everyone just obediently takes their places. There is an awkward, confused silence.

'Well, go on!' I say.

Rage finally spent, I plonk myself down at the table, breathing heavily, as the children – though not with much joy – cautiously start to serve themselves.

Behind us, the silence is broken by a polite clearing of the throat.

It is Marco, the plumber. I had forgotten he was here.

He has heard everything. My ranting. My swearing. My yelling.

Head down, he nods towards the bathroom.

'I finish,' he says, simply. Then, still without meeting my eyes, he adds: *'Buona giornata.'* And he lets himself out.

Have a lovely day, he said. I am mortified.

Two weeks later, Lewis sets off with Marshall on his Eastern European odyssey, catching the train south to Ancona and then the overnight ferry to Split.

The rest of us head to Tuscany with our friends Jojo and Noddy and their flaxen-haired son Ambrose, the eight of us in our new leased van. We eventually find our villa by bumping our way over, as the Italian directions say, a 'dirty old road', and the house is perfect. It is two storeys of Tuscan gold, set in grounds of soaring trees and stone walls, looking across a hillside of grapevines to a village church. The elderly caretaker couple who are waiting to meet us have put the heating on: for the children, they say.

Our break is idyllic. We sleep in, eat giant Fiorentine steaks several fingers thick, T-bones with the tenderloin still attached – a specialty of the region. We drive up hills to sweet villages and swing on the garden swing, and walk around the local town and eat gelati and drink wine. Jojo and I have a girls' outing; we take Sunday and spend a morning at the local Prada outlet, where she finds some colourful runners and I buy a pair of white leather boots and a matching handbag. Back at the villa, our friends present us with the most magnificent gifts: a packet of plastic vegetable peelers from Australia, a Melbourne tea towel printed with pictures of trams, and two pairs of aluminium spring-tongs. They are more precious than jewels.

On Easter Sunday, we wake to messages and photos from Lewis – alive and happy in Montenegro – and eat Australian chocolate eggs the Easter Bunny has brought. Noddy has built a roaring fire in the grate.

I make pancakes. They are delicious.

In fact, everything is magic. Italian, Australian, magic.

13

I BELIEVE IN MIRACLES

Before we left for our overseas odyssey, some girlfriends and I had a farewell party where, in between dancing and general revelry, we ended up having hilarious conversations in which we imagined me meeting their Italian counterparts. Who would become my people in Italy? Who would be my Alice, my Miranda, my Georgie, Carla or Moomies? Who would fill that void of nourishing companionship, that wellspring of humour and solace that female friends provide?

In Italy, I think of those conversations often because the truth is, several months in, I have not found 'my people'. I am not even slightly sad about it but it is apparent that, at the international school, where there is a diverse group of nationalities, the Italian women seem to be the least friendly – at least to the other foreigners. I had thought initially it was just me but it seems to be a pattern clocked by the other women at the school also, some of whom have been there for years. It is hard to know why this is: it may be a language thing, since many of the Italians are understandably not comfortable with English, the default language of most other Europeans who, like the Dutch, often grow up hearing it on the television. It may be that we live in the wealthier north, where people are known for being more reserved, although this is not the case with the other open-armed Italians we meet through basket. Whatever the case, when we go to school pickup, there is a clutch of expats – Americans Kristie, Patricia and Trisha, Indian Vineetha, Swedish Johanna, English 'top-bird' Sophie, South American Caroline, Indo-Dutch Diah, and fellow Australian Rachel. These are women who are always convivial and warm, and I gravitate towards them.

There are Italian exceptions, of course, but they are notable for their rarity. There is lovely, stylish Carlotta, my friend Monica, and a graceful and gracious beauty called Antonella. But the divide is never more obvious than when I drop by for the weekly lunches organised by my soon-to-be neighbour, Denise, an American mother-of-four who runs a casual lunch group and WhatsApp group that proves to be an invaluable resource. Of this group, we can ask anything, big or small: from whether or not to drink the Bolognese water (with its distinctive smell and calcium deposits) to where to find a doctor or dentist. With the pool of knowledge from these women from around the world, you can work out where to find a parking garage, when the next public holiday is, how the children are travelling at school or where to buy marshmallows.

The lunches are held on a Wednesday and as I have been busy working for our first six months in Bologna I have attended very few of them. This week, I have resolved to be more social (and also *lunch*) so I put my name down on the bookings list. On the day, Rachel comes by our apartment (limping still, from the terrible scooter accident that left her couchbound for five months) and we wander, slowly, down to the mandated Greek restaurant together.

Something happens at lunch that day that ends up being a life lesson to me: don't look for *your* people; just open yourself up, and you will find *people*.

The little restaurant is in the middle of the town centre near a church where there is a fabled embalmed saint, and when we are seated and discussing this centuries-old holy relic, Rachel says, 'We have an Australian saint now, too, Sister Mary MacKillop.'

Antonella nods knowingly, and in the slight pause that follows, I find myself piping up: 'We have had a brush with Mary MacKillop in our family.'

And, before I can even begin to think about it, I start to share the story of Lewis.

I do not know what prompts me to do this. It is an enormous tale, for starters, but it is also a deeply private one that we rarely recount, and one of the liberating things about being in a foreign country is that no one knows of it. So when I hear myself, on the other side of the world, suddenly speaking aloud this most sacred family travail, I am astounded. It is almost as though I am outside myself.

As soon as I start talking about Lewis's leukaemia diagnosis at the table, it is like I have thrown an intimacy mantle over Rachel and Antonella. The three of us lean in to each other, the hubbub of the restaurant falling away, as I recount my family's frightening excursion into the underworld of children's cancer.

Six months into his gruelling treatment, when Lewis was supposed to be in remission, he went blind in one eye. This was bad. Very, very bad. The obvious conclusion from our team at the hospital was that he had relapsed; that the leukaemia had prevailed over the pummelling regimen of lumbar punctures and radiation and chemotherapy. We now had to explore bone marrow transplant. In the meantime, the hospital had to find a surgeon who would perform a biopsy on Lewis's eye, to see if, as suspected, there were leukaemia cells lurking in his optic fluid.

Our friends, though winded, as we were, by this terrible blow, rose once more. Friends of Mum and Dad's brought back a bottle of myrrh oil from Jerusalem, and I would rub it into Lewis's feet, clawed by one of his chemo drugs. Our girlfriend Priscilla's then-husband, Anthony, a devout Catholic, started a fasting meditation for Lewis, praying every day with an elderly nun he had known as a child, in between his long stints as a motorbike courier. The nun gave him a bookmark with Mary MacKillop to pass on to us. I had – somewhat hollow with fear and overwhelmedness, stuck the bookmark in one of the Harry Potter books we read to Lewis at the long, long hospital sessions as we moved from MRI to day-chemo to brain scans to surgery at the Royal Victorian Eye and Ear hospital; between various departments all trying to discover which of our shrinking treatment options we should next explore.

We were back at the cancer clinic at The Children's Hospital, waiting to see our oncologist Dr Heath, a reserved and seemingly conservative doctor I had engaged with previously – and somewhat bitterly – about seeking out alternative treatments. He, like most of his colleagues, made it clear he took a dim view of anything other than traditional mainstream treatment, and was reluctant even to request a vitamin D test for our son, even though, as I argued, Lewis was already having blood drawn for myriad tests measuring T-cell and platelet counts.

It was a terrible day in a terrible, terror-filled time. I was mired in despair and exhaustion. Lewis's body was shrunken but swollen with steroids. He was down to eighteen kilos, and had a nasal feeding tube. His eye was still blind, and was bandaged from the surgery. There was to be no good news, and as we shuffled into the doctor's office, me full of dread, but trying to be calm and push away the stomach-dropping nausea that came with fear, and keep upright and strong for my boy, my love, my firstborn, my prize, my heart song, my frightened and weakened little bald badger, I faltered. In between holding Lewis's hand and half-carrying him into the consulting room, I dropped our hospital bag, and the contents spilled out onto the floor.

Doctor Heath bent to pick up the book. He retrieved the bookmark from his feet, looked at it and said, 'What is this?'

I was so sick at heart, I didn't want to tell him. I was flushed with the shame of a mother daring to hope for a miracle, in front of a medical practitioner who believed only in the miracle of science. Eventually I said, 'It's Sister Mary MacKillop. A Catholic friend gave it to Lewis.'

Doctor Heath paused for a moment, and surveyed the picture in his hand. He studied the image of the nun with her humble country face. He carefully read the writing on the back, and all the while I was watching him, expecting him to scoff, or subtly roll his eyes. Instead, he said, 'You know to be canonised a saint you have to have performed two miracles?'

Did I know? I don't think so. I nodded dumbly.

'Well,' he continued, 'one of Mary MacKillop's two miracles was performed in this very hospital.'

He slid the bookmark back into the book, and handed it gently to Lewis.

I was so weakly, meekly grateful, my eyes filled with tears.

That Saturday, another of our oncology consultants, Dr Francoise, called us at home: the call we were expecting with the results from Lewis's biopsy. I remember pouncing on the phone and racing outside onto the porch – not because I was keen to take the call, but because I couldn't bear to hear the bad news in front of the other children. And through the crackle of the phone, made even more indistinct because of her French accent, Doctor Francoise said, 'I 'ave good news. There is no trace of leukaemic cells in Lewis's optic fluid'.

I couldn't believe my ears. I called for Peter so she could tell us again, both of us at once. Then we asked her to repeat it once more. And outside, in the morning light, at our front door, we clutched each other and wept and called our parents to share the news. Together, we shed tears of weak-kneed relief; of reprieve; of joy; of unbelievable blessedness.

I thought then, especially, of Sister Mary MacKillop. Our Australian saint. Who had performed a miracle before at the Royal Children's Hospital. And who maybe had again.

So here I am, eight years later. My son Lewis is a tall, healthy teenager. Strangely, I am recounting this story – his story – in the middle of a Greek restaurant in Bologna, to a new Australian friend who knew something of our past, but also to Antonella, an Italian from a land *filled* with saints, and to whom this unexpected conversational detour, though moving, must seem oddly random.

And then, as the three of us dabbed away tears, Antonella took my hand, looked me in the eyes and said quietly, 'I actually know this Saint Mary MacKillop very well. I have written a book about her.'

That, my friends, is how you find your people.

And when it happens, it feels like what it is: a miracle.

14

I CAN SMELL FREEDOM

Summer is coming, and so are my friends from Australia. I am so excited.

It is hard to imagine, but in a week's time, I will be reunited with Hughesy, who is arriving to visit me in Bologna. In our eighteen-year partnership, I have never gone this long without seeing him. Pleasingly, the *Hughesy & Kate* show, with me broadcasting from Italy, has been a huge success. To mark the end of my six months here, our off-air team has organised a celebratory event: twenty listeners will win a trip to Europe, in itself an incredible prize. But there is more. First, they will fly to London to see the Spice Girls reunion concert at Wembley stadium with the hosts of our sister-show *Carrie & Tommy*, then everyone will travel on to Bologna. Here, we have activities planned that will culminate in a glorious dinner and party in the hills overlooking my new hometown. (At a meeting to think of a name that fully sums up this round-the-world odyssey, the irrepressible Tommy Little suggests The Spicy Meatball Tour. The name is so silly, it makes us all laugh, so of course it sticks.)

And I can't wait for The Spicy Meatball Tour. Mainly because I will get to see my beloved colleagues and friends but also because it marks the end of my work on the radio show while we're in Italy. After our final show, I get the rest of the year off. Peter and I have already made plans for a summer of freedom and adventure, where we will get to fully embrace the Europe-ness of our new life: our friends Lawrence and Lou's wedding in Positano; a trip to Sicily. My girlfriend Georgie is booked to visit from Sydney and we are, madly, going to a music festival near Switzerland to see Midnight Oil play. Though they are titans of Australian music, I have never seen them perform live, and it will be fun to watch them with a bunch of Euros. As well, Peter and I have booked a chateau in Provence for a family holiday in the middle of the unbelievably long twelve-week school break. (A chateau, of course, is simply a house, but it sounds so decadent in French, I insist on referring to it this way, much to the annoyance of the children.) But first, in keeping with my blossoming jet-set life, I have to go to London, to interview Madonna.

I am to fly to Ol' Blighty the day before my parents leave Bologna, where they have been visiting for three weeks. Originally, the plan was that they would stay with us in our new apartment but that, of course, is still not ready. Ferdi, our gracious future landlord, with whom we have now spent *a lot* of time, felt bad, I think, that the original schedule had not been met. In that Italian way of magicking a solution, he has put Mum and Dad up in a lovely apartment, which he also rents out as an Airbnb, in the palazzo. It is a two-room cosy attic nook, directly above our holy-grail home, with a loft and windows that look over the red roofs of Bologna. Mum and Dad have become so embedded that they are now part of the extended family; they have been invited to Ferdi's grandson's christening, to be held in the downstairs, wisteria-covered courtyard. It has been a beautiful visit. The children have fallen into the easy habit of stopping at the attic apartment on their walk home from school for a game of Connect 4 or a quick hand of cards and a snack. The attic is so sweet and perfectly located, Sacha has booked it for her own accommodation when she arrives next week. Everyone, it seems, will be moving into the palazzo before we do.

Anyway, my parents' visit is significant for a couple of reasons. It has been lovely for them to see our new life – to have dinner at our friends Riccardo and Monica's home, to pootle about the shops and myriad churches or take daytrips into the countryside. Because Dad has an uncooperative knee, he is not overly mobile so we take things slowly, and the Italian schedule of daily rest has been restorative for them both. But mainly, given their initial fierce resistance to the idea of us moving overseas, it is heartening to see they have accepted our decision and, despite themselves, can see the beauty of our choice. The mountain, if you like, has come to Mohammed. And the mountain really likes Italian food.

We farewell them at our favourite restaurant around the corner, a comfortable and homey trattoria called La Traviata, where we have become friends with the owner and head cook, the dimpled and charming Manuela. Her restaurant, set back under the porticoes on our walk to pick the children up from school, has become a weekly treat. We often drop in there for a plate of pasta, which Manuela makes fresh, just the way her mum – whose photos adorn the walls – did before she passed away. Like her mother, she is a *sfoglina*, a master pasta maker, and everything we eat there is beyond delicious. As well, she and her staff, a mix of family, are now so familiar with us, the only decision I have to make is what filling I would like in my tortelloni. The offerings are plentiful – artichoke or prosciutto or in-season pear or figs – but I find it hard to deviate from the classic: the silken twists of pasta simply filled with ricotta, and served in melted butter with sage. Peter, who mixes thing up with a Bolognese-style green lasagne or molten, cheese-topped, crumbed cotoletta, is entrusted with the biggest decision: whether we will have a full or half-bottle of bubbly Lambrusco to accompany our meal.

The farewell lunch, though bittersweet, is perfect. The food is sublime, the pasta tender and succulent. (When they'd first arrived, Mum and Dad, much to our mortification, had picked the equivalent of a fight at the tiny restaurant next to their apartment. They sent their pasta back twice, saying it was too hard. It is true, the Italians like hard pasta cooked with a strong bite to it. But still, in Italy, certain things are simply not done. Like putting cheese on a seafood dish or having milk in your coffee after 11 am. And overcooking pasta, just to please a couple of tourists? *Non!*)

Today there is no such scandal. Sunday sits near her opa, showering him with granddaughterly love. She is holding his hand and kissing his bald head, while Jannie, Art and Lewis are engrossed in a joke-telling competition with my mum. We finish our meal with bowls of fresh strawberries and mascarpone, a deceptively simple dessert that Manuela makes stunningly – 'the best in Bologna', as a local friend told us. Then, while we are having coffee and liqueurs, a man from an adjacent table approaches.

It seems he has been watching our table of eight while eating his own lunch. He shakes hands with Peter, and asks if we are with his parents. No, I say, this is my mum and dad. From Australia. The man places his hand over his heart, and says something in Italian that Manuela hastens over to translate. 'What a beautiful family,' the stranger says. 'Your hearts, like your bellies, must be full.'

It is, of course, the ultimate Italian blessing.

And then, reaching over the table, he kisses my mother's hand.

15

IN BED WITH MADONNA

My three-day stint in London is not as exotic as it sounds.

I have not been to this city since I was a teenager travelling with my parents, and as much as I'd like to explore, I spend most of my time prepping in my hotel room. Because there is a lot to learn about Madonna. Her body of work spans decades, but I am determined that when I finally meet her, I will be able to converse with her Madge-esty without notes or clipboards. So many celebrity interviews look like police interrogations, I think.

England time is an hour earlier than Italy, so the first morning there I wake up blearily and head to Virgin Radio, gloriously placed next to London Bridge, to broadcast back to Australia.

Aside from the hour, it is fun to see the hub of English radio, and even more brilliant that my former boss in Oz, Mike Cass, is now back in his homeland, running the place. It is actually double happiness because his right hand is another friend – our beloved Nicklebob – who, with his equally cherished BF, Kanye, had moved to London from Melbourne three years before. They had stopped for a couple of glory days with us in our rented Tuscan villa, when our dream of moving to Italy was barely formed. Such joy, then, to see my old *amici* now in London. Such a lot of exhausting *BIG* conversation after being in a country where I can barely utter a sentence.

Carrie Bickmore and Tommy Little are also here, and also in full work mode like me; filming behind-the-scenes vids and preparing for their Spice Girls extravaganza. Unlike me, they are doing all of this while also recovering from jet lag. Still, we manage to sneak an evening at the hotel bar, where we toast the glorious reality that we are in London, and on the cusp of a spectacular adventure.

Carrie, who is staying with all three of her children and her partner Chris in the one room, is not as exuberant as footloose Tommy, whose main responsibility seems to be exploring London's dating scene. She, by contrast, is tired – so exhausted that she has barely had time to celebrate just having been awarded an Order of Australia. My long-time colleague is now Carrie Bickmore, OAM: the honour bestowed in acknowledgement of her extraordinary fundraising work for brain cancer research. A decade ago brain cancer cruelly claimed her husband, Greg Lange. Carrie, with her young son Ollie, was mired in this grim reality at the same time my six-year-old son Lewis was diagnosed with leukaemia. Both of us have been brushed with the demon-breath of cancer. But my hard-working friend also loves to cut loose. She knows the lyrics to every pop song, and on the dance floor – though she denies it – can do an unrivalled, spectacular move called a 'slut-drop'. Basically, I can't wait for our party in Bologna.

But first, Madonna.

Accompanied by a producer from our radio network, I was to meet the legendary superstar the next night, in a private members' club about forty minutes away. The building was classic posh English, an elegant Edwardian mansion with glossy black doors and enormous lion's-head brass knockers. When we arrived the front door was cautiously chinked open by a plain-suited security guard and we had to utter the secret password we had been issued to gain admittance. This was such top shelf, cold war spy stuff, I loved it. But I couldn't get over the fact that the password we were given was 'Madonna'.

We were ushered into a smallish front foyer and, after filling out embargo forms (promising we wouldn't leak a track from her new album), we were shown to the initial waiting room: a glass conservatory, green with foliage, that looked out over a large garden bar. Then, another room – inside, this time, and hung with opulent tapestries. We went from one room to the next for the next two hours or so, as we, and an assortment of other press and music industry writers from around the world, waited for our allocated interview slots. In the final antechamber, there were platters of food and a long bar serving drinks. Everywhere, it seemed, was a coterie of Madonna's staff, vibrating at a level of anxiety that only people who work with famous people seem to exude. They were polite and efficient, and thoughtful and manic; everyone trying to anticipate what their queen might need that they had not thought of. It imbued the whole atmosphere with a weird, slightly jagged energy.

When my time came – predictably, an hour-and-a-half or so behind schedule – I was shown into the filming room; an overheated den crammed with cameras and lights. It was searingly hot and bright, and there, in an oversized lounge chair, with her legs propped over its padded arm, was Madonna.

She was tiny and perfect, alabaster-skinned in green-and-black Dolce & Gabbana. In between takes, she was attempting to peel off a pair of long PVC gloves to get some fresh air. She riffed a little with the camera crew as they reset their equipment, and clocked me. She was undoubtedly regal but also kind of coquettish and, though her evening had been long, seemed to be in good spirits, cracking jokes and mugging playfully as her makeup was touched up. ('I'm staaaaarving, when do we get to eat?' she asked, at one point of no one in particular. Someone, of course, scurried over with the answer.) Her whole demeanour was intriguing: oddly shy yet highly alert. So quick and clever. She was also wearing an eyepatch; ironically her 'vision' for the character of her new album, *Madame X*. It left her with only one green eye exposed, a gimlet gaze that was both unnerving and transfixing. Like Cyclops, she could see everything through that single eye.

Afterwards, in the car heading back to the hotel, I couldn't remember a word of our actual conversation. All I knew was that it seemed to pass so quickly, I was shocked when I got the wind-up signal from the keeping-time assistant. When we wrapped, Madonna moved to the fireplace behind her, arms spread along the mantel in a tension-relieving stretch. I was gathering up my bag when she said, in her bell-clear voice, 'Kate! Come and get a photograph,' which kind of took me by surprise because we had expressly been told not to ask for a photo with her. Also, I was so addled, I had forgotten about the concept of 'photographs'.

The whole thing – the lateness, the weirdness, the hotness, my intense prep – had taken a toll. I felt physically ill. I was so sure the interview had been a dud: discordant, stilted, awkward. Despondent, I sent a sad message to Hughesy and then to Jack, our anchor, who would be doing the edit for our radio show. I told him to be prepared to cut it to the bone. 'Don't be ashamed of me,' I said to him. So feeble; so humbled. Because of the time difference, I didn't hear back from either of them that night.

The next morning, I woke up, stomach clenched with dread, to a message from Jack.

'Just listened to the whole interview. I honestly don't know what you were worried about. It's actually brilliant. There is nothing to cut out. In fact, we're going to run the whole thing in three parts.'

Then he said, which made me laugh, 'And I'm not just blowing smoke up ya bum.'

Jack, it turned out, was right. When the interview went to air, there was a stream of positive feedback. I was astounded. Hughesy, always my champion, claimed to have known all along it would be a 'triumph'. There are, it will not surprise you, a lot of passionate Madonna super-stans, and they all seemed to listen, avidly and critically, from South America to Japan to Europe to Australasia. And they were happy. So, apparently, was Madonna's manager, a droll New Yorker who had briefed me before the interview, and now sent a lovely message thanking me.

All of which just goes to show, you never know.

But wow. I am tired, I think, as I board the plane to fly back to Bologna. So spent. I really need a holiday. As someone I know once sang: *It would be so nice.*

Luckily, a holiday is just around the corner.

16

I AM, YOU ARE, WE ARE ITALIAN

I am driving to the airport to pick up Hughesy.

For the last couple of days, members of our off-air team have been arriving in Bologna. Today Hughesy flies in via London, where he has performed a sold-out stand-up gig for expats. He will be arriving with a posse: the radio station's Spicy Meatball Tour winners; Carrie and her on-and-off-air partners, Chris and Tommy; and their radio producer, the tiny but fierce beauty, Annabelle. Sacha is already here and has hit the ground running; a lot of work, mixed, Italian-style, with pleasure. She sits beside me now in the front of our vehicle, looking slightly frazzled after having watched me navigate my way out of the car park near our apartment.

Last night we met Giovanni at his favourite bar, a standing-only arrangement in a single, warm room lined with bottles. Antica Drogheria Calzolari is a local haunt in a former pharmacy in the student district, a miniaturised, Italian version of the TV classic *Cheers*, where everybody knows your name. Ironically, its own name is such a mouthful, we never learn it properly; to us, it is simply 'Giovanni's mate's bar'. We often drink there, standing, surrounded by wines of the region, and (in that random Italian manner) jars of jam and Nutella, and packets of handmade pasta. Last night, we had several drinks, a pit stop before heading to dinner together. I was so hungry, I was more interested in emptying the complimentary bowls of peanuts and dry bread twists – the ubiquitous *taralli* – placed on the counter for aperitivo.

At the bar, we were greeted with undisguised amusement by 'Giovanni's mate' Stefano, the older, twinkly-eyed man who owns the bar. He has known Giovanni for years and is now used to the sight of Peter and me at his establishment but was clearly intrigued to see the return of Sacha, the international love-interest. He stood in his customary position, in front of the No Smoking sign stuck to the mirrored glass behind him, chatting and polishing glasses. He was, of course, smoking, the cigarette dangling from his lip as he urged us to try one local wine after another. (On a previous visit there, when I asked for a glass of the sparkling white wine *pignoletto*, he and his crew give me a scolding, insisting instead that I drink a prosecco deemed more worthy.) By the time we left to make our way to the restaurant a couple of blocks away we were glowingly tipsy.

The whole evening was bathed in the joy of reunion, but had another unexpected layer. Over the past seven months, Peter and I have spent so much time with Giovanni, it is like Sacha is now having a holiday romance with *our* friend. We were happy, then, to see their reuniting marked by the ease of familiarity and an undeniable dose of *amore*. Giovanni is a man of very few words but I noticed he had been cranking up the kilometres with Peter on their bike rides for the last four weeks or so, obviously wanting to get in top nick for when his little New Zealand love-song blew back into town. And when we sat down at our restaurant table, he couldn't keep the smile off his face. Actually, none of us could. Why should we? We were outside, under the fabled porticoes of Bologna, eating glorious food and drinking wine with beloved friends, under ancient stars. I noticed, too, how Giovanni sat with his arm spread out along the back of Sacha's seat, tenderly stroking the back of her neck. It seemed the most natural thing in the world.

Despite being a little seedy today, Sach is rapt to be back here; she has been dreaming of Bologna, she says. Last time she was here though, it was January and snowing; now it is hot – humidly, oppressively hot – and Italian summer is upon us. 'It's like a different city,' she keeps remarking.

By the time we get to the airport, with me negotiating the traffic through the maze-like back streets, we are dripping with perspiration.

There are no car parks outside the terminal, of course, just vehicles jammed up against each other, doing laps until they find a space. As though the parking gods are looking after me, a car reverses out of a gap in front of me. *Perfetto!* Sacha points out that my glee is misplaced – it is not a legitimate park, she says, it is the walkway to a (faded) pedestrian crossing. I ignore her naysaying. I have to nab the vacancy quickly before someone else does, and I slightly mount the kerb to squeeze our van into the snug space. I execute these manoeuvres with a satisfying thump, and turn off the engine. The children scramble out of the back of the vehicle, tussling over the enormous 'welcome' banner painted on an old sheet, which they have brought to unfurl in the arrivals hall. Sacha, next to me, is still. I turn to see her looking at me, her eyebrows raised.

'What?' I ask.

'Oh my god,' she says, shaking her head. 'You are so Italian.'

The deluge of summer visitors is like an adrenaline shot. There is so much to do and see; so much to explain. Every morning, we convene at our tiny office-studio, which is now crowded and steamy, with me and Hughesy, Jack and Sach in the small room. Our talented videographer Kasey is there as well, planning escapades for the day ahead that he will film for our audience in Australia, who are following the trip online. Jacopo, still smiling, but even more silent in the presence of the boisterous foreigners he has previously only seen on Skype, sets up the computers, as he always does. Then he makes us all coffees; painstakingly, one by one, until Hughesy, who burns through three or four caffeine hits a morning, hands over a 100-euro note and says that maybe it is easier to buy them from the corner cafe. Always generous, Hughesy instructs him to keep the change.

Jacopo is clearly shocked at the largesse, for two reasons. Firstly, an espresso coffee here only costs eighty cents; it is one of the extremely cheap commodities, like bottled water (and is regarded as equally essential). Secondly, for a lot of Italians, money is not plentiful. The economy here is sluggish, particularly for young people, and many get by living with their parents and grandparents – even into their forties, when they have a family of their own. Italian families have also, in the space of a generation or two, shrunk rapidly; far from the big, shambolic tribes of children for which they are famous, Italians now mainly have one child – which has led to the country having the lowest birthrate in Europe, and the oldest population. Money is tight here; easy to forget in the face of Italian generosity and style. I recall when Jacopo stopped smoking tailormade cigarettes because they went up forty cents a packet back in March (to around seven dollars Australian). When I told him how much a pack costs in Australia – nearly fifty bucks – he was dumbfounded. The hundred euros Hughesy has gifted him, then, is a small fortune, and he accepts it appreciatively. Tonight, he will take his girlfriend out to dinner, he says.

After the show, our own adventures await. The first port of call is, of course, dinner at Giovanni's restaurant, Lambrusco. We sit in the front paved area, while Giovanni (a little nervous, I think, to meet our radio *famiglia* patriarch) bustles around, tending to his other guests, before finally sitting down with us to share his customary glass of wine. Afterwards, Hughesy gives Sacha's summer romance his nod of approval. It doesn't really matter of course whether or not he approves, but it is lovely that he does, and Sach, though a little embarrassed by all the attention on her love life, is beaming.

The next day Hughesy and I take a quirky route around the city, hiring tiny vintage Fiat 500s (Bambinos, as they are known in Australia) and following each other up the road that winds out of town. We whiz up the snaking route to the Sanctuary of the Madonna di San Luca, a seventeenth-century domed church that stands sentry over Bologna. On the way Hughesy marvels at the porticoes that line the four-kilometre walkway up the hill. Bizarrely, there are 666 arches, a most unholy number considering they were designed to protect religious pilgrims from the elements on their way to the sanctuary.

We speed up country lanes, past glorious summer greenery, only stopping again when we get to one of my favourite places: a park with horses and a villa at the end of a long driveway. Here we replenish ourselves with iced aperol spritz and beers, and plates of bread, cheese and sliced meats from the couple who run the summer canteen. Hughesy, who doesn't drink alcohol, has a fizzy *aranciata*, orange juice, and as he sips, marvels repeatedly at the beauty of Bologna. 'It's so pretty,' he says. I feel a little swell of pride, as though I can somehow take credit for the marvel that is Italy.

My funny friend, by the way, not only doesn't drink, he also doesn't smoke and doesn't eat meat. Given these are celebrated pillars of pleasure here, Hughesy enjoys what is left to him: driving. He takes to the wheel with his customary sense of adventure. There is the thrilling unsanctioned freedom to speed, of course, but also the roads themselves, some of them with built-in chicanes, designed purely for road-handling and challenging the skills of the driver. One day he and some of the Spicy Meatball Tour winners head out to the Lamborghini factory, where – aside from marvelling at its pristine cleanliness (their boast is 'You can eat off the floor!') – he ends up behind the wheel of one of the precious Lambos. When we watch the video later, it is insane. There he is, in a gleaming, half-a-million-dollar prestige car, with two wheels off the surfaced road, skidding through the unsealed gravel in his efforts not to drift to the wrong side of the road. When he alights from the vehicle, he is giddy with endorphins, and the valuable car is covered in dirt. His hosts seem to take it in their stride, with customary, head-shaking amusement. The Italians say, of driving (and life): 'You watch your front; let everyone else watch your back', and Hughesy, kicking up dust, seems to have taken it to heart.

Finally, there is our much-anticipated party for the Spicy Meatball Tour winners. In planning the party, we made a surprising, and somewhat disappointing, discovery about Bologna. There are apparently no restaurants in the hills immediately surrounding the city where you can look down onto its red roofs. When we ask

Riccardo, Bologna born-and-bred, even he shakes his head. 'No,' he says. 'There is no place like this.' Undeterred, the brilliant leader of our off-air team, Harriet, has found a private villa usually hired out for weddings and has rented it for the night.

We arrive in a succession of cars, making our way down a sweeping driveway lined with tall European pines to a marble columned entrance, where we are greeted with suited waiters and trays of cocktails. Then we are shown through to the outside grounds, a lush green garden set with potted summer flowers. Resplendent on the lawn is a long, white-clothed table for thirty, immaculately laid out with elegant crockery and glassware, and more flowers. And there, spread out beneath us, is the prize. In the shimmering haze of Italian evening light, is the city where I now live, Bologna: The City of Fat; The City of Red. I catch my breath as I wander to the edge of the lawn. From here, I can see the landmark *Due Torre*, the Two Towers. I can see our piazza, our apartment. Our home.

The trip winners cannot believe what they see. The opulence, the hospitality, the postcard-perfect vista is beyond amazing. Also the temperature is sublime. (I never cease to marvel at how you can step out into an Italian summer evening and not need a wrap or cardigan. The air kisses your bare shoulders. It is as though it has been designed by angels for maximum human pleasure.)

After glasses of prosecco, and much toasting, we all sit down to a stunning meal of Bolognese specialties: lasagne and tagliatelle with ragu, bread and olive oil, mortadella and pecorino, and roast meats and vegetables. Tommy sends one of the drivers to buy bottles of local liqueurs and, after dinner, we swig them and try to guess what flavour they are: everything from coffee to artichoke – which no one gets right. A DJ plays Italian classics (which sound as though they are all from 1984) and we all end up with our shoes off, dancing on the grass.

Because we are Aussies – and never more so than when we are away from home – one of the trip winners plugs their phone into the DJ console and we have a rousing finale singalong to our national anthem: Farnsey's 'You're the Voice'. It is riotous and glorious and wild. Italians love any kind of festivity, and the villa staff look on with smiling but muted approval. They are, I can tell, a little shocked at our Australian drunkenness, which is on a scale we never seem to encounter amongst our local friends. (Away on basketball tournaments, Petie and I often send each other photos of how a table of a dozen parents will only order one or two bottles of wine, barely a small glass each. Their cultural restraint is astounding to us – back home, the table would be littered with bottles and stubbies, most of them drained.)

In keeping with our party-hard ethos, then, our work is not yet done. After bidding farewell and issuing *molto 'molto grazie*'s we take our cars back down the hill to kick on in town. Sacha and I share the same driver who brought us here, who is now, disconcertingly, groaning aloud, saying he must go to the hospital for stabbing kidney pains. He moans all the way down the winding road, at one stage making such primal sounds of agony, we offer to get out and take a taxi. He refuses. 'Maybe I don't drink enough water today,' he says. It is very dramatic; very Italian. Down on the flat, in the walled *centro*, a group of us heads to the wild Bebe bar around the corner from our apartment, where the revelry continues. At two in the morning, at least one of our party (who shall go unnamed) is throwing up in the piazza.

Out of respect for their old-world surroundings, however, and because they are not new-world barbarians, they make sure to vomit in a bin.

17

THE HOST WITH A GHOST

I begin to wake from my post-show, post-party siesta the next afternoon and, distantly, in my dream, I hear Hughesy's distinctive voice floating up from the narrow street below.

'Famous! Famous in Australia!' he is saying, in the fractured English we somehow all resort to here in an effort to make ourselves understood. It takes me a while to drag myself up from the ocean floor of sleep and realise it is no dream. My friend is downstairs in the closet-sized cafe in the laneway under our apartment. Kasey and Jack are there filming, while Hughesy, brandishing his phone where he has googled himself for proof, tries to explain to the cafe owner that he is on the radio. He is a celebrity back in Australia. It is ridiculous. Bra-clad and disturbed from slumber, I fling open the shutters and, like a 1950s mamma, stick my bed-head out the window and, in Italian, yell at Hughesy to go away. Thank goodness, I think, that I am leaving the immediate neighbourhood soon. Or am I?

We are still waiting to move into our new apartment in the grand old palazzo around the corner. Sacha and Hughesy are keen to see it after hearing my constant and tedious updates about its renovation progress. We wander over with Giovanni and two other visiting friends, Davo and his Irish wife Tash, to meet our distinguished future landlord, Ferdi. We buzz one of the many buttons on the brass plate affixed to the wooden doorframe and the soaring arched wooden doors that appear impenetrable from the street swing open. We are admitted to the generous internal courtyard, where tenants' vehicles and mopeds are parked under tendrils of wild rose and wisteria. Ferdi, always gracious, comes down to meet us. He seems unfazed by our constant stream of guests; if he is now having second thoughts about renting his former family dwelling and law offices to us, he doesn't show it. ('You are artists,' he often says to me, nodding curiously; though every time he makes the pronouncement, I am reminded of our Italian friend, Liv, back in Australia. She snorted when she heard this, and retorted bluntly: 'This is not a compliment!' which made us all laugh. Still, she is from Milan, renowned for being a more stitched-up and formal city. Here in Bologna where there are so many university students our slightly vintage vibe seems to be, if not actually approved of, at least tolerated. The children tell us that the other parents at school describe us as 'hippies', which we also find amusing. In Australia, I am pretty sure we are normal. But I am also happy to be wrong.)

Peter and I show our friends up the private sweeping stairway that leads to the huge rooms of our unfinished dwelling. I am excited and see only the beauty of the place (the parquetry floors, the soaring medieval ceilings, the sixteenth-century Romeo and Juliet forged-iron balcony off the huge lounge), but Hughesy, in particular, sees the grim impracticality. We wander in and out of rooms filled with furniture and layers of century-old dust and sinks still unplumbed (there are seven bathrooms), past stairs with wooden risers missing, and the uninstalled kitchen, and it seems impossible that we will be moving in within the projected two weeks.

'You won't be in before September,' Hughesy remarks, pessimistically. I am annoyed to hear this; I tell him I want to be in residence by the time his adored Holly Wife (real name: Holly Ife) and their three children arrive from Australia in a fortnight. In the meantime, I distract myself from his negativity by chirpily continuing my tour.

In the long marble ballroom, through gilt embossed doors, there are three huge gold-framed mirrors mounted to the wall. They are spectacular: three metres tall and rich with age. They are impossible to move, and, as Ferdi tells us proudly, date from the 1700s. They are so old, I say to Tash (who shares my excitement about the apartment), that if you turned around really, really quickly, you would surely be able to see the past. She loves the thought, and laughing, we whip our heads around trying to catch our own reflections, before Peter takes a pic of us posing in front of the infinity mirror.

When we casually cluster round to examine the photo on my phone, we are shocked. There we are, both of us smiling. I am red-faced from heat and happiness and excitement; Tash is her impossibly lovely self: crystal-blue eyes and glossy dark hair. But it is not our laughing image that stuns us all into silence. It is what is behind us. There, reflected in the ancient mirror, is a hooded figure; a clearly discernible figure of a man. He is wearing a conical-shaped white hat, and has what looks like a crucifix around his neck. We are rattled. All of us are in the room together; there is no way it could be a prank, although it would be a brilliant one. We pass the phone around, all mystified.

Giovanni studies the picture and gives a strange grin. 'A *fantasma*,' he says. 'A ghost.' Then he pauses. 'Maybe you will not be alone in this apartment.'

Later, we show the photo to other Italian friends. They also peer, frowning at the image. Apparently, the ghost behind us, in our new old Italian apartment, is known to them, but not by name. It is, you see, a medieval spectre.

It is a plague doctor.

18

TWO TAKE THE AMALFI

Peter and I are on the train to Naples.

We have bought tickets on the fastest of the fast trains, and are speeding through the countryside and towns at nearly 400 kilometres an hour, chewing up the distance between Bologna and our destination on the Mediterranean sea. We are outwardly quiet; well, relatively quiet. I am reading a book about the many judges and journalists who died trying to bust the mafia stronghold in Sicily in the 1980s and 90s, and it is so amazing that I keep reading passages aloud to Peter, though he is immersed in his own book. He is reading about the formation of Italy which, incredibly, only became a united country in 1860 or so. This was achieved by a general called Garibaldi, whose revered name I know from Australia. It is a brand of salami.

We are both enjoying our downtime. We are beyond weary from the dizzying collision of our family life with the international visitors we have been entertaining. And though we are tired, we are also exultant – buoyed by the knowledge that we are now officially free and unencumbered. As the Italians say: 'To taste the sweet, you must first taste the bitter', and while we have not exactly suffered so far, to finally step into the lemon-scented, grapevine-strewn freedom of an Italian summer is intoxicating.

Our sense of liberation is twofold. I have officially finished work, and the rest of the year is mine. Or, I intend it to be. Before we left Bologna, where Hughesy was finally reunited with Holly and their children for the start of their own *Roman Holiday* (and where our apartment was still unfinished), my on-air comrade tried to convince me not to leave our radio show, but to return in October. I tried to explain how that would leave me with only three months of freedom from my hard-fought-for year overseas. Hughesy was, as always, determined and naggingly persuasive, even recruiting Lewis to his quest. (Lewis had been away with him and Sacha for a weekend in Cinque Terre, the centuries-old, five towns perched on the Riviera coastline, and after two days in the company of his adored 'Uncle Hughesy' he had returned as a loyal foot soldier fighting for his cause. 'Why don't you do it, Mum?' he said to me, at a breakfast where we were all gathered. 'You know you love it.') Unable to withstand the pressure, I did what every coward does: I bought time. I told Hughesy I would let him know my decision after the lengthy school holidays, which finish in September.

The other reason for our sense of newfound liberty: Peter's parents – my cherished in-laws, Bryan and Maree – have arrived from Australia. The reunion with Nanaree and Grandpa elicited much joy but also some low-level trepidation. We were always expecting Peter's mum to visit; Maree couldn't wait to see Bologna again. But the fact that Bryan, my 'classic Aussie' father-in-law, has also arrived is a huge surprise. He must have really missed us, we think, because prising him from his pleasures – his comfy lounge room, his weekly trips to the casino and his footy on Foxtel – would have required a superhuman force. 'Like lifting Thor's hammer,' Jannie helpfully contributes, when he hears us discussing the miracle. And it is true; only love could bring my meat-and-three-veg father-in-law, who doesn't eat pasta or pizza, to this country on the other side of the world, so far from what he is used to.

(It is not easy entertaining visitors who are not into Italian food. The Italians are so monocultural in their tastes, every restaurant offers the same dishes, or variations thereof. Being gluten-free is readily catered for, but if you don't actually like pizza or pasta, your options are limited. As they should be. In fact, what the hell are you doing in Italy in the first place? There are a few exceptions, like a couple of 'all you can eat' Asian restaurants, one of which is around the corner from us, and where Bryan, over a plate of fried rice, will later astoundingly declare: 'This is the best meal I've had since I've been here.')

The lack of spoken English outside of Italy's well-trodden tourist trail also makes things challenging. At the supermarket, where the eight of us have divided into smaller groups to speed up shopping for supplies, my father-in-law has one task. His job is to get two cartons of milk, but he becomes lost, overwhelmed. I understand that everything is foreign but, even so, it is not as though he has never been in a supermarket before. From the other side of the store, we hear Bryan, loudly and repeatedly muttering the word 'MILK'. His volume rises as he wanders around, his frustration clearly mounting, to the point where he is actually yelling. Alarmed, I pop out of the pasta aisle to see him accosting a hapless store attendant who, naturally, has no idea how to respond to this gruff foreigner and his desperate demands for 'MILK! MILK!'

Sunday appears before I can reach him, her own arms full of bread. 'It's called *latte* here, Grandpa,' she says gently, and together they head off to find the dairy section.

The next day Maree gives her husband a pretty blunt motivational talk. 'Things are not the same here, Bryan,' she says patiently. 'It's Italy! It's a different country. You need to be prepared for that.' Bryan, nodding, seems to take this on board. Then he says, 'There's just one thing I don't understand, Ree.' He pauses, genuinely puzzled. 'Why don't they speak English?'

Anyway, the pair of them are now in our apartment, looking after the children (or, as we joke, the children are looking after Grandpa) while we head south for an event we have been looking forward to since last year.

We are bound for Positano, where our comedian friend Lawrence Mooney is marrying the love of his life, Lou. She is, actually, already his wife – and the mother and step-mother of their adorable daughters Maggie and Lily – but they have, in their live-life-large manner, decided to renew their decade-long vows with a family and friends spectacular in Italy. Last year, at a surprise winter-night gathering in a restaurant in Melbourne, Lawrence got on one knee and proposed to his wife for the second time. 'This time, I want to do it properly,' he said, which, knowing his wild ways, made the whole room laugh. And now, the festivities are upon us. Peter and I are headed, for the first time, to the glorious Amalfi coast.

When we arrive at our small hotel in Naples, our euphoria is forgotten; replaced, instead, with a thumping headache and fever. Both of us are similarly, mysteriously afflicted. Ignoring the welcoming pool, the very reason we made the booking, we head straight to our room, where we crawl into bed and sleep for twenty-four hours. The malaise is a strange one, and takes precedence over the plans we had to tour Pompeii, the ancient city famously entombed in volcanic ash from Mount Vesuvius. The next evening, somewhat healed by our marathon sleep, but driven out by hunger, Peter steps out into the heat of night-time Naples, returning with a couple of boxed pizzas. They are thin and crispy, creamy mozzarella and *piccante* salami melted over a billowy base of wood-charred pastry. We consume them greedily in our room. They are the best pizzas we have ever eaten.

Late the following morning, over coffee and pastries on the tiled terrace outside the hotel reception (who have been very concerned by our poor health), I am surprised to hear my name called. There, having breakfast al fresco by the pool, under a crimson arch of bougainvillea, are two fellow Australians – journalist Wendy Squires, who we know, and her travelling companion, a nut-brown, smiling woman called Jane. Unlike Wendy, who is sheltering her creamy complexion under a large sunhat, her mate is bikini-clad, soaking up some rays. It is the greatest coincidence that we would have found each other here, in a tiny hotel in the third-biggest city in Italy. Even more incredibly, our Australian friends are both also bound for the Mooney wedding. The four of us cannot stop marvelling.

Peter and I spend the rest of our day doing our favourite thing: wandering. We turn up laneways steep and humid and buzzing with mopeds. We walk past humble kitchens that open directly onto the street, where old people sit outside on plastic chairs under clotheslines strung with a bunting of t-shirts and sheets, sharing gossip with others across the way. They stare at us as we pass. Naples is like a rustic village but damply tropical, with crumbling plaster on elegant buildings. It reminds me of Vietnam. We replenish ourselves with tiny iced glasses of lemon granita from street vendors, their brightly coloured wagons decorated with plastic vines and clusters of oranges and lemons. We eat crispy fried Neapolitan pastries: the delicious papery puffs of ricotta called *sfogliatella*.

I buy a ten-dollar hat from a street stall, woven yellow straw with a sweeping brim. In a nearby boutique, Peter buys his own headgear, a flat cap made of linen. He is also convinced by the owner of the store, through a mix of canny salesmanship and cultural ambassadorship, to forfeit his hot runners and socks for a pair of beige suede loafers. Our self-appointed Italian stylist leads my husband over to a full-length mirror, overcoming Peter's obvious reservations with effusive handshakes and back-clapping.

'Forget Bologna!' he says, grinning. 'Now you are like a Napolitano!'

19

WHEN THE MOONEY HITS YOUR EYE LIKE A BIG PIZZA PIE...

Positano is a dream: a blur of friends and food and rolling festivities.

We arrive at our hotel after an hour and a half of informal tour commentary from our driver, who has steered us from Naples and then up, up, up along the perilously narrow incline that is the only route into town. Our journey is slow, crammed with buses and beeping traffic. Tourists, rattan-hatted or draped with scarves to fend off the searing summer sun, seek out the shade of the tiny shops and restaurants that line the road. They are confined to a narrow walkway eked out against the stone barrier on the sea side of the road. Undeterred, they weave their way through impatiently idling vehicles, deliverymen wheeling trolleys and white-shirted waiters hot-footing it across the bitumen to bring drinks to thirsty customers.

Our hotel, like all the others, is built on a rocky clifftop hundreds of metres above the sweep of glittering turquoise. As we alight from our car, we peer over the stone barricade and, though the view is spectacular, we are somewhat dismayed to see the hundreds of cascading steps that lead to the ocean far below. They are, mercifully, punctuated a third of the way down by a stone-terraced pool, and there we spy our friend Lawrence. We call out to him, our Italian greeting sailing out over the water. He looks around, like a dog that has heard a whistle but can't quite place it. Then he spies us, waving up above. He lets out a bellow of joy and raises both arms in exultation before leaping into the pool. Below, we hear the squeals of outraged delight from his daughter, who he has just water-bombed.

Everything from now on is wreathed in Italian charm – *bellissimo*, as we have learned to say.

Weeks earlier, when we had gone to book our Positano accommodation – characteristically slow off the mark to organise ourselves – it turned out the entire hotel was already full. This was not surprising – there were dozens of Mooneys in the wedding party. We sent a follow-up query about an unreserved suite Peter had spotted on the website, mysteriously marked as 'unavailable'. Ah, we were informed, this one was being renovated. It is, sadly, not for booking. A few days later, we received another email: after checking the dates for our visit, it seemed the elusive suite *would* be ready. In fact, the reservations manager told us, we could be the first guests to stay there. He quoted the rate, and we didn't falter. We projected our future mood: a dual celebration – the end of work and a wedding with cherished friends – and a beautiful room in the thick of the festivities. Also, when we peered at the pictures on-screen, the suite already looked perfect – a giant bed, windows looking over the sea. How much better could it get? The answer is: very.

Now, when we are led up and down the maze-like configuration of travertine steps that lead to our room, we are astounded. It is glorious. Beyond glorious: it is royally, decadently, magnificent. There is a long entrance hall that leads to our spacious bedroom, an Italian blue-and-white-tiled masterpiece with a white linen lounge and matching patterned cushions and drapes. Bifold glass doors concertina onto a sweeping stone terrace that is so huge we can't stop laughing.

'This is bigger than our apartment in Bologna,' Peter remarks, and it is true. The outside area stretches the entire length of our temporary kingdom, and contains its own lemon grove: a minicluster of trees festooned with yellow citrus. The iron railings that corral the patio are topped with giant Sicilian ceramic heads; some white, some dark, full-lipped beauties that would be frowned upon in Australia (and probably destroyed in the statue-toppling climate in America, which has seen Black Lives Matter demonstrations sweep the major cities). Here, a physical and cultural world away, they are celebrated, filled with succulents and flowering plants – white and green and fuchsia-pink blooms that cascade over the railings against the backdrop of the sparkling Mediterranean.

To the right, overlooking the bustling port and town far below, are several reclining loungers, and a wrought-iron table and chairs. From there, you can access the enormous stone-tiled bathroom, with a double-headed shower as big as a walk-in closet, and a Roman bath so deep and long it is like a mini swimming pool. In fact, the whole bathroom smells of chlorine and the bath seems to be left permanently full – not surprising, since it would take a day just to fill it. More of a mystery is why the spa jets are constantly bubbling, or how we might turn them off. We cannot find a switch anywhere.

But that is not our immediate concern. Lou Mooney has sent us a welcome message that is also an invitation: she has booked three boats for a sunset cruise. It leaves in an hour or so.

At the jetty, we are reunited with more of the wedding party: Mooney's two brilliant brothers and sisters-in-law, and assorted high-spirited nieces and nephews. Our beloved mate Sam Pang is there, with his adored wife Adriana, who we refer to as Banana. There is Lehmo, another comedian from Australia, my funny friend Marty Sheargold and his lovely Ange. Just laying eyes on each other is magnificent. As we pull away from our mooring, cocktails in hands, it is difficult to imagine a more splendid introduction to our Italian *festa*.

When the boats pull up, in open waters clear of the harbour, our captain produces a platter of aperitivo snacks. There are more cocktails and then we leap off the boat into the water. Overhead, the sun is low on the horizon. We are caught in one of those dazzling 'I hope I remember this on my deathbed' moments: diamonds of sparkling water and the golden glow of sunset. There is only one bum note. Literally, a bum. It is Mooney's. He has whipped off his togs, and, as naked as the day he was born, does a triumphant tockley-swinging dance on the deck of our vessel before gleefully somersaulting into the sea.

Sometimes a bum note can hit the perfect pitch. It is joyous and wanton, and hilarious.

That night, Peter and I have a late dinner under the stars on the patio of the hotel restaurant. We drink wine. We eat seafood so fresh it simply requires a sprinkle of salt and olive oil. We are sun-kissed and glowing. We raise our glasses to our friends; to each other; to our amazing hotel room. We drink, as we always do, to Italy.

The next morning, we assemble at the port again. This time we are transported by speedboat, pluming our way through the crowded harbour waters amid myriad other vessels.

At a private beach club, under orange-and-white beach umbrellas, we feast and drink, and dance in the sand. Mooney, cigar in one hand, and – madly – a megaphone in the other, recites a poem to his already-wife-to-be. Lou, resort-chic in a bikini, open robe and platform slides, thanks us for joining them; though everything is so glorious, we should be thanking them. Our Italian hosts, a family of jovial, perma-tanned southerners, race over the scalding sand barefoot, seemingly impervious to the blistering heat. They ply us with food and drink, and then, more food. It is meltingly hot at our tables – even though they are shaded – and we all take to the ocean for some relief. At one stage, I am standing in the water, waist deep, communing with my husband and Marty Sheargold and our beloved Pangularay. A couple of the waiters come bounding down the beach. They are carrying an inflated li-lo, which they lower carefully into the water. Then they proceed, fully clothed, to wade it out to us. They are laughing and calling out to each other in Italian as the water creeps up their black pants and wets their shirts. When they finally reach us, we see they have brought us a gift.

In the pockets of the floating mattress, held upright in multiple circular recesses, our hosts have placed plastic glasses of aperol spritz. Delighted by our delight, they proceed to hand them out amidst cries of *Salute!* Here, impossibly, in the middle of the Amalfi sea, we have our own impromptu floating bar. We raise our glasses. *La vita*, we say: the life. Just then, I am hit from behind by a small wave, the wake from a passing speedboat. It knocks my knees out from under me and I take a tumble. Moments later I resurface, drenched but triumphant. My drink is unspilled, still gleaming orange in my raised hand. I have not lost a drop. This unglamorous, but highly entertaining feat, elicits group applause.

Later, the boys (and, impressively, Lou) are drunk and scramble up the cliff to jump into the water below.

Peter is anxious about it, but there is nothing to worry about, it seems. Crazy, joy-filled boys and girls have been jumping off those cliffs for thousands of years.

It is life-affirming, not life-ending. It is *la vita*.

The wedding day dawns bright and sparkling, and, like every day in Positano paradise, it is hot, hot, hot. I am too bleary from a raucous harbourside dinner the night before to venture down the thousand steps to the idyll of the ocean. I content myself with filming Petie, who has risen before me and, undeterred by the descent (and, more dauntingly, the long, baking, return ascent) is now a Morse-code dash swimming laps in the sea far below.

As anyone who works in comedy knows, timing is everything: I am actually videoing him when he unexpectedly stops short in the water, and thrashes about for a bit. Fifteen minutes later, when he makes his panting way up to our patio, where I have coffee waiting, he holds out his wrist. There is a series of ugly welts across it. Mid-swim, he was stung by a jellyfish. How delighted I am to present him with footage of the actual moment. (Of course, stings are nothing to worry about here; there are not tiny poisonous box jellyfish waiting to kill you, like there are in Far North Queensland. And though we once encountered a fettuccine-thin viper in a pool net in Tuscany, on land there are no tiger snakes, or red-bellied blacks or king browns. There are no white-tailed spiders waiting to rot your flesh. There are no folksongs about redbacks on the bidet seat. In the water, there are no man-eating sharks. The Italians often marvel at the fabled savagery of our wildlife back home and, while we have always enjoyed our wild oceans, there is an unexpected extra pleasure in swimming here. You never have to worry, in that imprinted-from-birth Aussie way, about what may lurk in the deep. Mostly, if something is coming to get you, it will be a handsome Italian. On a boat. Wearing a fedora.)

Anyway, we don our finery for the celebration ahead: for me, a neon-pink one-shouldered bodysuit and a flowing patterned green silk skirt. Peter buttons up a Dolce & Gabbana shirt, topped with his new flat cap, which he rakishly turns backwards. We assemble in the hotel foyer with the other fifty or so guests, an excited buzz of us, and take turns being bussed to the wedding venue. It is, not surprisingly, idyllic: a small farm and vineyard sandwiched between stone cliffs and olive groves, further up the hillside.

There, on a patio overlooking the sea, Lawrence is standing: a vision of a handsome, well-groomed groom, waiting for his bride. Marty Sheargold, his best man, is at his side. Both of my friends are uncharacteristically nervous – I have never seen them check their watches like this before, or huddle to whisper, or check notes they have written on crumpled pieces of paper they anxiously produce from their pockets. Mind you, I have never seen them in immaculate suits before, waiting to make and witness lifelong promises. I have never seen them do anything this serious, and it makes my heart swell.

When Lou arrives, she is breathtaking. An accompanying musician plucks the mandolin as her best friend Kath heralds her arrival with a famous soaring aria by the Italian master, Puccini, 'O *mio babbino caro*'. The song is a girl pleading with her father to marry her love: if she is denied, she will hurl herself into the river Arno. Her soprano voice is magnificent and it fills the hillside. There is no other music for this moment. Lou steps her way down the grapevine-covered pathway, a vision in a sheath of muted gold sequins. Three flower girls, cream-clad and sweet-faced, make their way to the front of the assembly led by Lawrence and Lou's daughter Maggie. The youngest Mooney daughter bossily choreographs her cohort while her older sister, lovely Lily, and her cousin are also brought forward to stand with the wedding party.

The vows are beautiful. They are tender and heartfelt and moving.

Mooney has tears in his eyes as he kisses his beautiful bride. So do we all.

And then we celebrate. We make our way inside the restaurant, to long wooden tables arranged under ancient rafters, covered with flowers and jugs of wine. Through a doorway next to us is the bustling kitchen, where the cooks can be heard laughing and yelling over the din of clanking pots and pans. The food is exquisite. There is pasta, of course, and meats grown and grazed on the terraced plots that surround us, and platters of homegrown vegetables. There is the wedding dessert; a tower of lemon-cream genoise cakes. There are speeches, where Marty is funny and touchingly sentimental, and Mooney, constantly interrupted by his excited youngest daughter, gives vent to his fatherly spleen. There are words of love – so much love – and there is dancing. A band comprised of older local men weaves their way into the room, serenading tables. We all join in. The party is so joyous and happy, the kitchen staff emerge to join the singalong, the *nonno* Luigi banging saucepan lids in raucous percussion. An aunty gets sent, drunk, back to the hotel. Mothers are thanked. Absent loved ones are remembered; voices choked; eyes are filled with tears. Little girls do a shy performance before being led away by grandmothers. We kiss and gossip and convene under the wisteria on the balcony where it is cooler, and where Wendy gives advice to a beautiful Mooney niece – about love, of course. What else is there, ever, to talk about?

The whole evening is utter, utter perfection. It is *amore*.

Back at the hotel, we make the most of our beautiful terrace, by hosting a high-spirited after-party party. We promise to not disturb the other guests (who are, actually, us) and the man on the overnight reception desk brings us beers – six at a time. Eventually he realises he cannot keep up with our Australian thirst, and sends two of his staff over with giant silver ice buckets crammed with stubbies of Peroni, the Sicilian beer Messina and bottles of limoncello. Mooney's nephew, a plumber, though initially confident, cannot for the life of him work out how to turn off our perma-bubbling spa bath. There is much laughter. Italy, Italy. Someone plugs in their phone. There is music. A bottle gets smashed on the stone. Peter and I dance in the moonlight. There is broken glass crunching beneath our feet; it is lucky he is wearing his new loafers. They are rubbing his feet, he says; the charlatan in the shop in Naples sold him the wrong size. We laugh, bathed in the heady fragrance of lemon blossom, mixed with chlorine. The moon, like our hearts, is full. Maybe it is waning. Whatever. We live in Italy. Next year, we vow, we will all meet again. This time, our friends will come to us, to our home in Bologna.

Like I said: perfection.

20

THE FIRST TIME I CRY

At a farewell party at our house in St Kilda in the Australian summer before we embarked on our overseas adventure, my beloved girlfriend (and Sunday's godmother) Alice speculated about how long it would be, in my new country, before I cried for the first time. Obviously she didn't mean happy tears but the moment when I would find myself overwhelmed. Homesick maybe. Lonely. It is an interesting notion, and one that has sprung to mind often here when times have been challenging. Yet, I have, so far, remained dry-eyed.

And my eye drought is unlikely to break now, even as the six of us make our way through the crawl of European holiday traffic, heading to the French alps. We are on a 600-kilometre journey to a house Peter has booked in Aix-en-Provence in the South of France, and we are breaking up our road trip with a stay in a bed and breakfast in the Italian north before crossing the border. It was a big decision, working out where to spend this summer break, but we eventually whittled down our choices on the basis of two criteria. The first of these is somewhere we can drive in our leased van and make the most of our prepaid annual mileage allowance. Second, and most importantly, we want to go where we will get to eat butter. The Cote d'Azur in France, where Peter and the children have never been before but I have (years ago I attended the famous Cannes Film Festival), gets two ticks on this short imaginary checklist. As we always say, we can't do anything wrong. All of Europe is new to us; wherever we end up will be an adventure.

Along the way, when Peter mutinies against my DJ'ing (which, despite my best intentions, always seems to end up a mix of Beyoncé and *Les Misérables*), we play family road games. There is 'spot the country', featuring the profusion of licence plates we see around us, and their countries of origin: Romania, Albania, Poland and Germany. Is 'N' for Norway or Netherlands? As well, we gamble: we have a fat nylon bag of coins we have accumulated all year, and I run a book on how much the tolls at the various autostrada booths will lighten our sack. This game is surprisingly interesting: road tolls here are levied according to a logic that escapes us, so you don't know if your stretch of road is going to cost two euros or ten. We could, of course, have registered for a Telepass, a digital account that would allow us to sail through the emptiest queues at the tollbooths but, like most Italians, we prefer to pay cash. Consequently we spend a lot of engine-idling time watching those around us emerge from their vehicles to smoke (Italians or Eastern Europeans) or simply stretch their legs (every other country) as they wait for the endless lines of traffic to move. The winner of toll-lotto (the one with the closest guess without going over) gets a chocolate bar of their choosing at our next roadside stop. This will be after a lunch of roast spatchcock with crispy potatoes, sliced steak and pasta, or tomato and mozzarella salad with bread and wine. That we can eat like kings at a service station (in Australia, our choice would be between a bucket of chips or a fried dimmy) is a thrill we never tire of.

Actually, Peter and I never tire of it. After all this time in foreign surrounds, Lewis and the other children are missing home. They have taken to fantasising about Australia, taking turns to announce what food they will eat when we return. (Back in Bologna, one afternoon, I overheard Lewis and Marshall discussing Burger Rings and which supermarket sells multipacks of Wizz Fizz sherbet. Lewis let out a heavy sigh. 'I miss Woolworths,' he said, wistfully. It was so ridiculous, it made us all laugh.) Every time – like now – when the children casually reminisce about their most-missed foods and people, I feel a small clench of anxiety in my stomach. I sneak a furtive look at Peter, who determinedly has his eyes fixed on the road ahead. The pair of us are harbouring a parental secret: we have decided to extend our stay in Italy for another year. And on this trip, somewhere, we are going to break the news to the children. At night, in bed, our only time alone, we discuss it. Sunday, with her weekly art classes and her coven of school friends, will be pleased, and the little boyos are happy wherever we are. But Lewis, we fear – with his secret paramour back home fuelling his stubborn resistance to Italy – will not take it so well. (Despite the fact that we know of his Australian girlfriend, he has never formally told us about her, but he is often tired in the mornings from having kept down-under hours with her and more than once he has fallen asleep with her on Facetime, tucked under his pillow.)

But we do not need to worry about speaking of future plans yet. We are in the beautiful Italian alps in an unremarkable town where our accommodation is remarkable. It is an old farmhouse on a plateau overlooking, as always, a church on a distant hill. Our room is quaint and beautiful: lace-covered windows and a flowered, embroidered quilt covering a crisp-sheeted, springy, old iron bed. At the other end of the long main building, the children have been shown by our farm-girl hostess to their own domain. It is a series of intersecting attic rooms, with cosy beds tucked under dormer windows, and – in a tiny nook – a made-up wooden cot for guests with toddlers, which Jannie and Artie immediately resolve to sleep in. They squeeze their too-long bodies into the wooden-framed recess, a giggling yin and yang, till we order them out.

If our whole holiday was here, it would be more than enough. Outside are tables and chairs overlooking a spill of vineyard that disappears into the valley below. There is an orchard, with trees hung with summer fruit – flat peaches and round, two-toned tiny pears – and a sweep of vegetable patch along a flowered path that leads to the large pool. We spend a couple of idyllic days, the boys frolicking and wrestling, bouncing balls on the basket court. Sunday swims laps and lies in the sun, her tan deepening in front of us. There is only one other family in residence, a tall, blond Dutch foursome, who – in the manner of their people – are orderly and quiet and neat-casual. At breakfast, over plates of sliced cheese and meat and chocolate-filled pastries, Peter talks to the father about their own travels. They have come to Italy looking for sunshine and good food, rarities in their native Holland, the father says dryly. In the mornings, Artie and I wander through the damp grass of the orchard, filling our pockets with pilfered ripe peaches (he is a sucker for sweet stone fruit), until the dogs at the adjacent farm – huge white Maremmanos guarding the neighbour's chickens – frighten us away with their loud barks.

Then we are on the road again. We drive through one of the longest tunnels in the world; the fabled Mont Blanc – eleven kilometres of engineering prowess bored through the base of the mountain. At sixty euros, it is expensive (a big dent in our collection of coins) and when we pop out at the other end we are, magically, in France.

Another day of driving takes us along the coast and then to the energy-sapping hunt for our chateau. This is always the worst bit of a day's travel – the search for elusive coordinates that match the directions we have been sent in a ream of WhatsApp messaging. As we wind our way along a snaking rural road – looking, looking – I spy some ornate wrought-iron gates set between sandstone pillars. Through the greenery is a long tree-lined drive. It is so beautiful, so French, I long for what lies at the end of it. 'I wish that was our house,' I say wistfully, as we drive past. Five minutes later, after Peter has made a 'help us' phone call to our French hosts, we do a U-turn. 'Guess what?' he says, grinning. The wrought-iron gates are ours.

At the bottom of the driveway we crunch over gravel to an unexpected conclusion: a Mexican-looking hacienda. It is two storeys of tan-coloured stucco covered with vines, and a dog comes out to bark a tail-wagging greeting. As we spill out of the car we are greeted by a lovely tall girl, brown and tattooed and somehow – even in miniskirt and singlet – stylish, in the French manner. She greets us in shy English that, as seems to be the European custom, she apologises for. Then her mother appears, carrying a cleaning cloth for a last-minute sweep before our arrival. The women welcome us so warmly, the mum fussing over the children, plying them with icy poles, and offering Peter a welcome beer that is extremely welcome. It turns out to be the first time they have rented out their house and they are clearly pleased by our compliments as they show us around. And it is easy to marvel: the 1970s modular olive-green couch that smells faintly of cigars and good times; the open hearth and terracotta tiles; the large, well-used kitchen. It is perfect.

Then the daughter leads us outside. The yard is huge: a mix of soaring oaks and pines, gravel-planted succulents lining the pathway to a stoned terrace and the most spectacular shining, blue-bright pool. Adorably, there is an inflated unicorn tethered to the pool ladder. It is five feet tall with one drooping, wilted wing. 'I could not fill this one with air,' the daughter says in her lilting English. 'Maybe it was injured in a pool party.'

We spend our days there making our own pool party, where we realise that the unicorn most likely punctured its wing on the spiky cactuses planted inconveniently around the pool edge. At least once a day there is a desperate cry for 'Tweezers!' as Jannie and Artie end up spiked, and Peter spends half an hour patiently removing the fine needles from bronzed legs or arms. Despite this minor drawback, the pool is almost impossible to leave. We venture out for trips around the area; once, spectacularly, to a national park near us where we hike for two hours over sandstone to the sea. Another day we set off to the nearby port town of Marseilles, where we celebrate Lewis's and my joint birthdays (a day apart). It is Lewis's wish that we eat Vietnamese food – spring rolls, sweet crispy pork and the much-missed flavours of coriander and mint – and we do, at a table outside a cramped, no-frills restaurant that reminds us of Australia. My family presents me with my gift, a dress-ring in the shape of a flower with the petals enamelled in pink and blue. I had coveted it in a vintage shop back in Bologna when our friend Kelly Black was visiting and she had obviously relayed the message to Peter. After lunch, we wander past a French vintage shop, where Peter buys some old-new runners and vivid Hawaiian shirts for the boys. Later that evening, after a dinner by the sea (where stupidly and tiredly, we order pizza – French pizza is awful even if you've never lived in Italy), we walk back to our car with a scatter of other tourists. As we make our way up the hill to the council car park, an elderly woman standing on her front terrace in the cool of the evening air, hisses at the children and tells them to be quiet.

It may just be chance, of course, but it seems more like a taste of the fabled French indifference to, or intolerance of, children, and it makes me glad we chose Italy for our new home instead of its more sophisticated European frenemy. In eight months in Italy, our offspring have never been reprimanded once – except by us. Children are so understood and adored there, I am constantly amazed. Once, killing time in a hotel in Milan, I watched a group of children on a school trip irresistibly drawn to the grand piano in the foyer and plinking at the keys. A suited staff member left the reception desk and approached them. I braced myself for the inevitable reprimand. Instead, the concierge started playing 'Chopsticks' with the tiny humans, laughing and directing their fingers to the correct keys, while the other staff members watched on indulgently.

Even though we came to France on a quest for their magnificent food, and have had a couple of lunches out (one at a local pub that has a vending machine outside that dispenses freshly baked baguettes), the rest of the time we cook at home. It is such a joy to have a proper kitchen. Lewis has found a recipe for pot-roast chicken, first seared in butter on the stovetop and then baked. It is so good, we make it twice, with tiny potatoes and new season green beans. There is an outdoor market nearby that sets up twice a week in the town square where we buy locally grown greengage plums so delicious that we gorge on them till we all have tummy aches. We leave with jars of clear jelly made from gooseberries (whatever they are), lavender honey and a wedge of fresh-churned butter from the 'butter man', and every morning when Peter returns from his bike ride we smother them on the croissants or baguettes he has picked up from the local bakery. Even the supermarket is brilliant: cornfed chicken, rows of gleaming-eyed fresh seafood, ornate bottles of French cordials in every hue. The house, brilliantly (though the children don't think so), has no wi-fi so we spend our time mostly outside: reading, swimming, napping, eating.

It is such an idyllic regrouping of our family. Just the six of us, enjoying each other and our nothing-in-particular-but-everything time together. We are sad when it is time to leave, but we are on the move and our next stop is an antidote to our outdoor life. We are headed to Lyon, a picturesque riverside city. We have booked an apartment in the city centre around the corner from the main cathedral. It was impossibly cheap and we discover why when we arrive. Downstairs, in every direction surrounding the apartment block, the road is torn up, being resurfaced. The air is noisy with jackhammers and greasy with the smell of fresh tar. Still, five storeys up, we are not so perturbed. Our aspect is onto rooftops and into the windows of the elegant white stone apartments that surround us. Down below is a bustling met-stop, and the view from our bedroom is of a large public square, with statues and fountains. I could look out the windows all day but the children, oblivious to the French beauty around them, fall greedily on the wi-fi.

Their gaming and movie-watching leaves me and Peter with a chance to spend time together. One night we walk in the rain to a restaurant around the corner and have a meal that is so delicious and Gallic that it is as though time has stood still. We share pâté on crispy wafers of baguette, a salad of tender green leaves speckled with oil and vinaigrette, then scallops and a dumpling-puck of seafood served in a pink sauce so delicate and classic that I am sure Marie-Antoinette would have eaten similar. Next to us a pair of workmen, their hi-vis vests glistening with rain, enter and take a table by the window. They have a spirited five-minute discourse with the waiter about the menu before their own meals arrive and then they eat in total silence, savouring their three courses. No wine for them; only water. I cannot recall ever in Australia seeing burly workmen fine-dining after a day's work. So French.

The next day, after recovering from a sweltering excursion via bus and train to a secondhand market on the outskirts of the city, we make a booking at one of the textbook bistros around the corner. That night we will enjoy French fare in a setting so beautiful that we are sure to remember it forever. We are seated in rich, red leather banquettes, the table set with crisp linen napkins and fine china. When we are presented with the menu, Peter, swept away with his surrounds, boldly orders snails. Artie and Jannie select steaks from the children's menu – looking forward to, of course, the ubiquitous French fries that will accompany them. When the waiter has taken our order, Peter and I take a deep breath. We have something to tell you, we say to the children. After our Christmas holiday back in Australia, we will return to Italy. We have decided that we are going to stay in Bologna for another year.

There is a stunned silence at the table. Then Sunday's face breaks into a smile. Lewis does not speak. He looks down at the table, unmoving, and stays like this for several minutes. When he finally lifts his head, he is flushed with hot tears. Jannie, seeing his brother's anguish, also starts to cry. So does Artie. Then, her initial positive response forgotten, Sunday also succumbs to the mood at the table. By the time our meals arrive, the children are all in tears. The poor waiter. He maintains a professional demeanour but is clearly perturbed as he places the meals in front of our weeping family. Only Peter seems to have a grim appetite, determinedly forking snails into his mouth with a tiny fork, as his family sobs. For the rest of us, the exquisite food may as well be chaff in our mouths.

Lewis doesn't speak to me for the next three days, maintaining a hurt, angry silence. When he looks at me, it is with daggers. It is terrible.

The measure of any relationship, I think, is not how you are in good times, but how you handle the bad.

On our way back to Italy, we spend three nights in the French alps at a picture-book turreted castle with a swimming pool. We are in a narrow three-storey apartment in the repurposed stables where it is impossible to escape from each other. Here, Lewis continues to wage his cold war, muttering about me and his father to the other children; quietly enough that we can't make out his words but with enough volume for us to hear his tone. One morning, after returning from a bike ride, Peter decides he has had enough. He orders the younger boys to the pool, placing Sunday in charge. Then, in the tiny kitchen, we have a conversation with our eldest son.

It is an adult dialogue; painful and honest. As is so often the case, however, it is not words of anger that bring down the walls; it is gentleness. Peter is brilliant – kind but firm. He declares, firstly, our love for Lewis, and each other. Then he speaks about how hard I have worked; that I have sacrificed the first six months of my year away, so that we can all have this incredible experience. Even I am stunned at his words. So is Lewis. To hear his father, normally so measured, speak emotionally like this, is powerful. Tears course down my son's cheeks. And mine. When he is eighteen, Peter says, which is only two years away, Lewis can make his own decisions about where he lives, and with whom. Until then, we, as his parents, make the call about what is best for our family. And we wouldn't be staying in Italy if we didn't think it was the right thing to do.

Lewis, listening with his head bowed, nods. He loves us too, he says. He is sorry for how he has behaved. He was just so bitterly disappointed.

I understand, I say. Believe me, I understand disappointment. This makes us both laugh. I hug him, and he hugs me back.

And then, Peter and I present our ultimate peace offering. Lewis and Sunday can return to Australia for the last two weeks of school holidays. They can visit their grandparents and see friends – or 'friends'. But then, and there is no doubt this is an enterprise agreement, he will return with his sister to Italy, to a life he will commit to and strive to make a success of. Lewis nods soberly, face shining. It is a such a relief, this resolution. The three of us embrace.

Somehow, we are okay again.

21

DON'T GO CHANGING (WE CAN'T, YOU'VE LOST OUR SUITCASE...)

> *In European Heaven:*
> *The chefs are French,*
> *The police are English,*
> *The lovers are Italian,*
> *The mechanics are German,*
> *And the whole place is run by the Swiss.*
>
> *In European Hell:*
> *The chefs are English,*
> *The police are German,*
> *The lovers are Swiss,*
> *The mechanics are French,*
> *And the whole place is run by the Italians.*
>
> A poem pinned to the wall at the funicular in the
> Italian alps that made me and my mother-in-law laugh

Back in Bologna, the city is deserted. Everyone, it seems, has left the heat and humidity of the red city and decamped for the summer, as is traditional. The shops are closed. Only a sprinkling of restaurants remain open. During the long weeks of school holidays, and particularly in the searing month of August, two things happen. The children, whose parents are left with a staggering fourteen weeks of idle time to fill, during which they are mainly still required to work, are sent to grandparents, or to sporting or scholastic camps across the country and throughout Europe. The pin-board at school is full of A4 sheets advertising language camps in Denmark or Sweden, football camps in Germany, and art camps in Bilbao or Prague. Italians also make a mass migration during this time, vacating baking stone cities and cramped apartments for seaside family dwellings down south in Puglia or Sicily, or – the more intrepid – to Croatia or Greece or Portugal. It is almost anticlimactic then, when our landlord Ferdi tells us that, finally, our new apartment is ready.

The renovations are complete and we can leave our serviced apartment above the piazza. We have not met any of our intended KPIs – Hughesy and Holly have been and gone, as have so many visitors: Peter's eldest brother and sister-in-law; my gorgeous hairdresser Olga, who came with her son Alex for the huge international hair expo in Bologna; my parents; our friend Joey who was researching lasagne (in anticipation of starting his own brilliant catering business, 1800-LASAGNE, back in Melbourne). My in-laws are still here but when it is time to physically make the move we are all scattered by summer. The youngest boys are at basketball camps in the countryside with their mate Robbie. Lewis has left by train for a couple of days at the nearby beach-town of Rimini with some friends from school. And I am bound for adventure of my own. I am leaving for three days in Ibiza.

The invitation to visit the Spanish party island has come about unexpectedly. My friends Carla and Georgie Damm are headed there after escaping Melbourne winter for Mykonos. Peter and I, meanwhile, have just returned by train from our Midnight Oil music festival in France with my high-octane girlfriend Georgie Harrop. She has been travelling around Europe by rail and bus, spending work-time in London and Germany, and visiting an old school friend in Holland. And what an auspicious time to arrive. Georgie has been keeping track of our seemingly endless renovation the whole time I have been away, and instructs me to video her face when she finally gets to see it for the first time. I am so glad I did: her expression is properly, appropriately astounded. This is a palace, she says, mouth agape, and we both laugh because it is. It is also a hot box. Though the apartment has been deemed finished, the newly installed air-conditioners are not working. It is sweltering inside so, as stunning as it is, we can't stay here – in this glorious medieval oven in this baking, deserted town. When I present my girlfriend with two escape options – camping at Lake Garda with my extended family or Ryanairing our way to Ibiza – she chooses the latter.

This is twofold brilliant. Aside from getting to visit the fabled Spanish island party destination (a short flight away, like seemingly everywhere in Europe), in my absence Peter and his parents will shift our belongings to our new abode. We don't have a lot but, even so, there is always more than you think, and I am grateful to not have to drag our stuff around in 40-degree heat. My stoic in-laws are undaunted by the task. Plus, as Peter points out, we now have a car park downstairs in our very own courtyard. As long as it is not the weekend, they can pull up under our old apartment, load up our van and decant it in one or two trips.

What a beautiful husband he is. How brilliant. I leave for Ibiza with his blessing, to three days and nights of ridiculous fun. We meet Carla and her Georgie at the tiny terminal there, the happiness at our reunion tempered by a classic travel fail. Their luggage has been misplaced on the single direct flight from Greece. After waiting for another futile hour or so, we decide to head to the hotel with just the carry-ons my Georgie and I have brought. Because of Ryanair's notorious weight-gouging policy, we have measured and culled our 5 kilogram allowances to the gram (my adolescence spent behind the deli counter in Coles proving invaluable for weights and measures). The four of us will share clothes out of these tiny bags for the next few days.

Our Ibiza hotel has a distinct party vibe. We have two adjacent rooms overlooking the ocean boardwalk, a spectacularly wide pathway enjoyed by a cross-section of European sun-seekers: scantily clad hard-bodies, retirees, Segway riders and scooters. Ironically, the boardwalk is more attractive than the beach it promenades alongside, a somewhat underwhelming sweep of tarnished sand and flat sea. Compared to Australian beaches it is limp and plain, but it is enough for us. Anyway, most people come to this part of the island not for nature but for the pleasures of indoors: nightclubs and nightlife. At the very most, they spend their few daylight hours in recovery by a swimming pool, maybe not even venturing onto the sand. And we are no exception. The first night we are there, we head out for dinner, Spanish-style, at midnight. We take a taxi and head to the old city, where – led by Georgie D, whose food knowledge is incredible – we eat seafood in a laneway flanked by clothes stalls bulging with lace and sequinned dance clothes and bag-sellers flogging copy-designer goods of varying quality.

The next evening, after a lazy afternoon at the rooftop bar, with margaritas and bowls of melted Spanish cheese and tortilla chips, we watch Instagrammers pose for hours in the adjoining pool. Then we get ready for our own nocturnal activities. We dress from our communal wardrobe, and I do everyone's hair with our one shared curling tong and converter. Just getting ready to go out with girl-friends is a treat, a high-spirited slumber party, but the best is yet to come. When we head to the dance party, it is old-school happy house – a night called GlitterBox, organised by an Australian music-promoter friend of GD's. There, in a club crammed with thousands of revellers in a succession of rooms, we dance until we are dripping. We make new friends there, some Germans and cross-dressing Span-iards, and, unexpectedly, bump into the Australian actor Hugh Sheridan and his cute sister Zoe.

We leave the club at dawn and walk back to our hotel along the beach, drinking beers we have bought from a convenience store. Carla has to wee. She is in the clothes she has borrowed from me – wide-leg, frilled-mesh leggings – and with her balance already compromised by alcohol and a case of aching dance-thigh, she strug-gles to squat. GD and I watch her wince and wobble, warning her sternly about ruining our one precious, shared pair of pants. The laughter weakens Carla further. Mid-squat, she topples over in the sand, a helpless, weeing, legs-akimbo crab. It is so stupid and funny and light-hearted and fun. There, along the seawall, as the sun rises over Ibiza, we laugh until we nearly all wet ourselves.

Later that day, when we confirm our respective flights, my girlfriends are told their luggage has finally been found. They decide to leave it at the airport and pick it up tomorrow en route to their next destination, Barcelona. As a farewell gift, I sneak the wee-pants into Carla's handbag.

Back in Bologna in our huge, vacant apartment, my beloved Georgie soldiers on through what has become a summer flu, helping me make up beds for my absent family. We schlep and sweep and carry, tugging fitted sheets over six beds and climbing up the flimsy wooden ladder to make the little boys' top bunk (such a difficult task). It is exhausting work, let alone in the heat, and we wander to a nearby bar to replenish ourselves. On our way, a car with two local polizia slows down so that we can jaywalk in front of them, raising a lazy hand in acknowledgement of our thanks. We head to a secondhand shop around the corner, where I buy staples for our new apartment: saucepans, a couple of pretty platters, some wineglasses. Georgie buys a new bread knife as a housewarming gift, giving it to me with a coin for good luck. My always well-groomed friend has also found what she declares to be an essential – a magnifying mirror, with suction cups that attach to the wall. It is the first time I have looked at myself for months: the sight is unforgettable. I may feel beautiful and free and sunkissed but the image magnified is that of a crunchy face, swollen like one of the suns of Jupiter. Also, I seem to have grown a goatee. We lie on the couch in the baking lounge room, taking turns at examining our amplified, ravaged faces, shrieking with mirth.

'Forget the plague-doctor ghost,' Georgie says, wiping away tears of laughter. 'The true terror is in this mirror.'

Tomorrow, my beloved friend will leave for Florence to meet her brother, who is on a cycling trip with Australian mates. I will take the train to Lake Garda to reunite with my extended family. They are keen for my arrival: they do not realise they have a bridge-troll for their wife, their daughter-in-law, their mother. I am seedy but happy. How important it is to be with people who see you with eyes of love. People who only want the best for you. People who make you laugh.

At Lago di Garda my mother-in-law Maree and I will make meals in our neat adjoining cabins and the eight of us will eat outside under the shade of beech trees. My father-in-law Bryan will make jigsaws with Jannie, both of them master-puzzlers. Later, we will head to the giant pool and Grandpa will thrill everyone by shooting down the tubular waterslide. We will wander along the flower-lined paths that lead to the pretty town of Lazise for cones of afternoon gelati and I will buy a pair of pretty summer sandals (made in Italy, like nearly everything we buy here).

We will have dinner on the terrace of a local restaurant when a crazy summer storm hits, and watch market stall vendors try to pack up tables of goods before they are washed away in the sudden downpour. Sunday and I will share a bowl of strawberries and cream as big as our heads. The six of us, swimming in the crystal lake, will incur the wrath of a German holiday-maker, furious that we have climbed aboard a floating nylon buoy that has been bobbing enticingly in the open waters for two days. He will scream at us until he is red-faced, ignoring our apologies, our explanation that we thought the floating device belonged to the holiday park. He will curse, and when Peter asks him not to swear in front of the terrified children, will curl his hand menacingly into a fist. Then he will unwittingly provide a catchcry that will become a family favourite.

'I don't give a fock about your focking children!' he will yell, so rancid with rage he is actually spitting.

Our aforementioned children, now swimming at Olympic speed back to their grandparents waiting on the shore, will never forget it.

Ah, Europe. What a brilliant, amazing, glorious, mixed-bag of glittering treasure you are. You are priceless.

22

WHEN NOTHING IS EVERYTHING

Relieved of alarms, clocks and schedules, we roll into the greatest gift we have given ourselves: Italian summer. It is seemingly endless, a lazy yawn of blue skies and every glorious cliche of *la dolce vita*, the sweet life.

We are en route to Sicily with Artie and Jannie and there is so much room in our van, with Lewis and Sunday back in Australia. The fledgling eagles have landed, the journey having gone smoothly with Lewis in charge. The only hiccup, apparently, was at their transfer in Dubai, when Lewis – irritated by his sister and flexing his seasoned international-traveller muscle (thanks to his trip around Eastern Europe with his friend Marshall) – told Sunday he was going to leave her there and fly on solo. He was, of course, crying wolf; she was just crying. Anyway, the pair of them are now safely home down under, happily house-hopping between our house with Sacha and their two sets of grandparents.

Divested of the complexities of teenagers, the four of us remaining have embarked on two free-wheeling weeks driving down to the toe of the Italian boot. En route we stay in Calabria at a homestay run by a family with a small farm and an unexpectedly large swimming pool, planted between grapevines at the rear of the property. When we arrive after a long day's drive, the mother of the house, Emilia, is waiting to welcome us. She ushers us inside, where she has laid out a spread: glasses of her homemade limoncello, home-grown peppers in oil and chunks of cheese and bread. While we eat, her aged father, whose room is opposite ours on the second floor of the brick family compound, watches the boys intently. Like so many Italian grownups, he is seemingly enchanted by children, smiling and nodding and mumbling in dialect that, of course, none of us understand. At one point, Jannie, eating hungrily, drips olive oil on the plastic tablecloth and, slightly panicked, tries to wipe it up with his hand. The old man roars with delighted laughter, clapping, and tousles him proudly on the head, before producing a handkerchief from his dressing-gown pocket and wiping up the spill.

With the support of the voice function on Google Translate, our hostess asks us if we have come for the festa that is on tonight. We haven't but are happy to hear of it. Every town in Italy has festivals celebrating patron saints, of which there are seemingly hundreds. The pageants involve varying degrees of town decoration and sophistication, and all of them seem to culminate in a procession, where a statue of the local saint is carried through the town, followed by – of course – celebratory food and drink, and a concert. You could easily devote an entire year to just attending festivals, and we decide to head into town for the celebration. We ask Emilia if she is going. She shakes her head, as though the idea is ridiculous, and issues a rapid stream of Italian into her phone. The translated robot voice tells us no, she will stay here and make us a chocolate cake, for breakfast.

The festival has taken over the entire village. The winding streets are lined with archways of lights, twinkling blue and white, under which are an assortment of tables laden with a mix of shoes, clothes and religious trinkets. There are several food vans, most of which feature the same local delicacy, a strange cut of meat the locals are eating loaded on bread with various toppings: onions, braised fennel and tomatoes. We examine the meat curiously then realise it is cow's tongue, boiled pink and thin-sliced. It is an unappetising treat to us but heartily enjoyed by those around us. Artie and Jannie spy a carnie stall that takes their fancy and come rushing over to ask for five euros. We hand over the money and follow them back to the stand that has them so excited. It is a shooting gallery, run by a brusque and cheerful youngish woman who, disconcertingly, has one scarred and wounded eye. Here, our ten- and twelve-year-old boys are given rifles, actual proper rifles, to shoot at targets. They are giddy with adrenaline, even more so when they leave with the trinkets they win for being crack shots. Peter and I are more pleased they are leaving with two eyes. Apiece.

We wander through the streets to the local church, its edifice ablaze with cascading lights, and join the queue waiting to go inside. There, amid the cool archways and ancient wooden pews and stained glass, we light candles for those we love. It is a tradition I normally keep with Sunday. Tonight I light a taper for my blossoming daughter – with me, but far away from me – on the other side of the world.

Afterwards, in a brick-stepped piazza that descends to the community hall, we share a wooden picnic table with some elderly locals, who regard us with undisguised curiosity. We buy drinks and order pizzas from a van where three or four burly local lads are hard at work spinning dough, filling dockets, putting more wood in the fire of their homemade domed oven. We order our favourites: the traditional, simple basil-topped margherita, with its proud Italian colours of white, green and red; and a *diavolo* – devil – so named for the spicy, thin slices of salami that top the melted cheese. The pizzas, delivered to our table by one of the sweating cooks, are magnificent. The couple next to us smile approvingly as we devour the crusty slices, waving hands over our mouths at the spiciness of the salami. '*Calabrese,*' they say, nodding. '*Molto piccante. Molto buono.*' Very hot, and very good. We toast our new friends with plastic cups of wine.

There is music coming from up the hill. After we have eaten, we join the crowd watching the band. The whole town is there. There are children on the shoulders of fathers or a sturdy *nonno*, and women, blow-dried and tight-skirted, pushing prams in high heels. There are teenagers – silken-haired and wearing uniform fresh white runners – eyeing each other shyly or clustered in splinter groups along the raised stone walls. Always, always, there are family members in wheelchairs – sometimes incapacitated by age, sometimes young – being pushed over stone cobbles by the able-bodied.

Onstage, there is a smartly dressed grey-haired singer. This is a given at every festa we have attended; it is as though musicians from the 1980s are a renewable resource here. This singer is handsome in his tailored suit and hat, a tanned-leather silver fox. The crowd is familiar with his back catalogue, and when he announces what is clearly his greatest hit, there is a flurry of applause. Everyone joins in, even the little children, in a joyous, unselfconscious singalong. I look around the crowd. There's an occasional couple dancing together while young and old sing the same song.

The next morning at breakfast, everything is *cioccolato*. There are chocolate croissants in packets, chocolate chip biscuits, and a big box of chocolate flake cereal. There is bread – to be spread from a large jar of Nutella. Peter and I are brought cappuccinos, unusually sprinkled with cocoa, and the children are presented steaming mugs of hot chocolate. Then, of course, there is Emilia's chocolate cake, a rich, dark disk sprinkled with icing sugar. It is in pride of place at the table.

The hospitality is spectacular, generous and heart-warming, but I am not Italian enough to face a sweet breakfast. I doubt I will ever be. When the children, peaking on sugar, race outside to jump in the pool, I wrap slices of the cake in paper napkins, and place them carefully in my bag. We will enjoy them later, Australian-style, for morning tea, on our drive south.

We emerge from the forty-minute ferry trip that has taken us from the mainland to Sicily – to the port of Messina, a name we recognise from the gelato ice-cream shops in Australia. Back in our van, we forge our way onto oleander-lined roads and the crush of summer traffic. More crushing is the realisation that we have no accommodation booked. After a few futile attempts at finding a room, I put in a call to Giovanni in Bologna. A friend of a friend is a true friend in Italy and, after a corresponding phone call at his end, we are instructed to head to a seaside town called Taormina. There, we are met by Giovanni's friend, Giovanni, who roars up on his scooter. He shows us to our rooms, simple and perfect, in an airy two-storey stucco house up a steep driveway, run by his mum and dad. Here, he says, we are welcome to stay as long as we like.

We only intend to stay a night or two, but soon find a rhythm that sees us extend our visit, day by day, for over a week. We spend most of our time at the nearby beach. It is an idyllic crescent, breathtakingly lovely, but with a stony beach that means becoming familiar with the politics of beachside recliner rental. We must book our berths the day before, although we don't need to leave a deposit. 'If you no come-a, it no matter!' the animated man who runs the umbrella rentals explains to us. So we fall into a simple routine. We take three deckchairs (the boyos sharing), and read and snorkel and swim out to where the boats come in. In between, we entertain ourselves by watching people try to exit the water, sinking knee-deep in the stones that form the shore. There is no dignified way to do this. When you are lurching out of the water, sometimes reduced to crawling out on hands and knees, it is mortifying. Watching others do it, however, is highly amusing.

One day we get to the beach late and decide to save our chair money. Instead, we pick our way to the free part of the shore where we end up jammed in so tightly between families, greased brown bodies and even the occasional dog that when I attempt to lie back the lady sunbathing behind me has her foot in my hair. The squeeze is unbelievable. And yet we never hear a raised voice. There is no annoyance, even at people who set up folding chairs across the path that leads to the water. We watch in awe as the mother of the family next to us pulls out a bottle of olive oil, pouring it on herself and her husband – all the better to bask – while the four of us seek to protect our freckled Australian skin from the same sun, under a huddle of towels and sarongs. The Italians are such sunflowers, I think, and recall a story our neighbour Denise told me. She and her family of fair-skinned Pennsylvanians, sunblock-smeared and behatted, were asked by a Sicilian on the beach if he could get a photo of them. 'I have never seen albinos before,' he said.

Around us now, the deep-tanned Italians preen and parade. The women, regardless of age, mostly wear bikinis. The concept of 'beach-body' here seems to be whatever body you take to the beach (although female friends in Bologna have told me of the ritual of *prova costuma*, a designated day in spring where swimsuits are tried on to see what winter misdeeds need to be undone before summer). Most of the Italians rarely swim, we notice – maybe wading up to waists or shoulders but not much more.

When the stirrings of hunger move us, we crunch over the stones to our favourite of the half-dozen beachside restaurants. There, we settle into our late-lunch routine: fried calamari for Peter and the boys, a prawn cocktail for me, wine and soft drinks. We often stay at the beach till sunset, drifting into aperitivo, and then eat on the way home.

Early one evening, we weave our way on foot along the main road to the funicular, intending to take the travelling cable car that soars its way up to the picturesque town of Taormina, high above us. The queue is ridiculous, snaking its way out into the adjacent carpark, so we decide to walk up instead. The path is two kilometres long, a brutal ascent in 34-degree heat. Dripping, we make our way to a restaurant Sicilian Giovanni has recommended. It is set in a garden, the tables placed amongst old orange trees. The food we eat is delicious: seafood sliced raw and drenched with olive oil, grilled swordfish and tiny fried red mullet with artichokes and sweet Sicilian tomatoes. Later, after a wander through an ancient garden dotted with stone grottoes gifted to the town by a former noblewoman, we walk back down the same route we ascended. We pause halfway down to catch our breath and take in the dark sweep of glittering Ionian Sea that we swim in every day.

Every day also, we wake to a breakfast made by Serafina, Giovanni's lively apron-clad mother, who lays out sliced cheese and ham, and squeezes fresh orange juice for us. We eat outside on the tiled terrace. Vincenzo, Giovanni's good-natured dad, stands by as we eat. He is not allowed to do anything in the kitchen, his wife tells us, only to place the coffee in front of us. She mimes this, banging her palm on the table to illustrate her point, and we all laugh.

One morning, when Peter is up early enough to beat the searing heat, he rides his bike up Mount Etna, the volcano that slumbers but is still alive. We travel to the outlet shopping mall two hours away, driving through a desertscape incongruously studded with orchards of lemons and oranges. I remember my book about Sicily and how much of the land was planted by Arab immigrants centuries ago. We head to Realmonte and there, under soaring bleached-white cliffs known as the *Scala dei Turchi*, the Stairway of the Turks, we lounge on beaches covered in sand instead of stones. On our meanderings, we travel via Palermo, the fabled home of the mafia and the Sicilian capital. I recognise the airport, Falcone Borsellino, as being named for the two brave magistrates I have also read about. They were among the thousands of people murdered in the savage mafia wars of the 1990s. We rent an Airbnb where, creepily, the man who owns it comes in at night to do his washing. We swim in a beach at the end of our street described as one of the most beautiful in Sicily; it is strewn with discarded food wrappers and floating plastic bags. (We hardly see litter up north; the piles of rubbish alongside the roads here are horrible. It seems so un-Italian. When I tentatively make this observation to our friends back in Bologna, they look pained. '*Bella Sicilia*', they say. 'Beautiful Sicily.' And then, pragmatically, mysteriously, they add, as northerners often do of down south: 'It is a different country.') It is hard not to speculate that the litter has something to do with the mafia having the rubbish collection contracts. As our friend Andrea said to us in one of our rare conversations about the Cosa Nostra: 'Mafia business is legitimate business now'. The mafia apparently own the cement businesses also, which explains the glut of truly ugly cement apartment buildings often dominating the southern hillsides. And they own the taxi licences, meaning there are only Ubers in Milan and Rome, where the ride-share service is more expensive than cabs. Apparently when they tried to start Uber in Bologna, the cars kept catching on fire.

But litter aside, the 'different country' is rich and raw and spectacular. We visit a twelfth-century palace and marvel at the mosaics in a Byzantine church. Near the town of Agrigento we spend the day exploring Greek ruins, the spectacular remains of temples that once stood in the ancient city of Akragas on a sandstone ridge that overlooks the sea. We eat fried rice balls – the delicious arancini – blood oranges and ricotta-filled cannoli, and buy peaches the size of babies' heads from street vendors.

Driving to catch the overnight ferry back to the mainland, we find a town called Mondello that features a mirage: a butter-yellow art nouveau building that is built out, incredibly, over the sparkling Caribbean-blue sea. Here, we join the 'beach club' for six euros, which gains us deckchairs and admittance to one of the most beautiful places we have ever seen. Golden sands lead to the waters beneath the structure and, wading in, we marvel at the shade, at the ancient wood of the pylons supporting the building above us. When we pop out on the other side into glorious sunlight, we see older Italians above us, fishing over the railings or sitting in chairs lined along the wooden deck, reading newspapers and playing cards. Their belongings are stowed in rows of padlocked closets on the balcony that serve as their summer real estate. Peter swims to the back stairs and climbs up, asking a passing waiter if it is possible to have lunch in the restaurant that splays out over the water. The waiter seems unfazed by the dripping request. Of course, he says. We freestyle back to our belongings, towel off and change, and enter the restaurant through its elegant front entrance. It is glorious. Here we are, above the water, our hair still damp from the sea, but at a table set with linen and glasses of chilled prosecco. Artie and Jannie, who have bought hot dogs from a van on the foreshore, swim in the ocean below us, wrestling and racing, and calling out to us in staccato dolphin-voices.

In Palermo, on an impromptu quest for a souvenir – a pair of the ceramic Sicilian heads that had adorned our balcony in Positano – we stop at an outdoor antique market. There, amongst myriad choices, we find our handsome duo. They are two feet high and ten kilos each: a king and queen, crowned and wreathed in pomegranates and lemons. They are spectacular and, after a successful negotiation with the matriarch running the stall, we go to pay. She looks confused and tells us she only takes cash – of which we have none – so her son climbs into the van with us. He takes the passenger seat next to Peter, directing him through a maze of streets to find the elusive bank that will dispense euros from our Australian credit card. When we return, the stallholder has packed the heads for us in wooden crates. As we leave, she hands Artie a parcel of bubble wrap. It is a gift, she says. Inside is a blue and gold ceramic dish I had admired. I am touched at the gesture. Peter smiles wryly. 'Guess we could have haggled a bit harder,' he says.

Behind us, the stall vendor is standing on the shady street with her son, waving us goodbye. '*Buona fortuna*,' she says, as we drive off. Good luck.

We have already had the best of luck.

We have discovered Sicily.

23

WHAT DO YOU DO ALL DAY?

My many conversations with Hughesy about me leaving our radio show fry his fine mind, and muddle my own. I can't explain to him why it is so important that I give this time to myself, why I would leave a job that gives me such joy. I only know that I need to.

I am continuing to do phone-crosses once a week: sometimes from the roadside; from a balcony in Sicily; standing in the middle of a cherry orchard near a river; from our lounge room. I remain a part of the *Hughesy & Kate* radio show, sharing our family life and adventures abroad but eventually I break it to Hughesy – via the coward's route (again!) of text message – that I will not be returning to the show full-time. My faithful friend is disappointed. Also, he simply cannot fathom how I will fill my time.

'But what are you going to do all day?' he asks repeatedly. The concept of not working is as foreign to my workaholic colleague as the thought of continuing to work is to me.

'You know, go to Italian classes, do yoga,' I reply, vague but determined. Eventually, frustrated by his repeated interrogations (no doubt more dogged because I have previously shown little interest in either of these pastimes), I shut down any further discussion with a short but firm: 'I don't know, Hugh! I will just *live*!'

And as though I have spoken it into existence, I am.

The children are now all back at school, and Peter and I have resumed Italian classes at our own school, the Academya Lingue. We have a plan to spend three weeks learning Italian intensively and then three weeks off to enjoy just *being* in Italy. The charming owner, Andrea, is understanding of our plan and has kindly given us a special rate.

'When I married my first husband and was in California trying to learn English, it was *so difficult*,' our dapper principal says sympathetically in his Italian-American-accented *perfect* English.

So every morning, after I have dinked Jannie or Artie to school on the back of my new secondhand bike (an impractically wide-handled but spectacular turquoise cruiser bought from one of the school mums), we wander through the laneways that lead us to our place of enlightenment.

Our Italian *scuola* is in a building off the picturesque laneway Santo Stefano that leads to a cluster of seven churches (each within the other). The Academya occupies five or six rooms around a central courtyard, with a beautiful upstairs terrace adorned with statues and ferns. There are various teachers: shiny-haired Dora, who is brusque and firm; lovely, laughing Alice, who teaches us songs and conversational Italian. There is bright-eyed Rodolfo, who loves a philosophical discussion; patient Donatella; clever Roberto; and the handsome-but-stern Bob – who loves Peter but rightly takes a dim view of my mental flabbiness. (Although Bob is not so stern when, in one class, he mentions talking to his mother on the phone every day. As he re-enacts a standard conversation with 'Mamma', attempting to illustrate saying farewell, we all start to laugh. Our 28-year-old teacher is talking in a little-boy voice and at first we think he is joking, but we soon realise he is genuinely surprised at our amusement. Later, when we recount the tale to Dora, she shrugs. 'This is how it is with Italian men and their mothers,' she says. She herself is going out with a Spaniard.)

The classes are interesting, and meeting the other students is fascinating, but trying to learn the mechanics of the language is still torture. Just the sight of a sheet of conjugations fills me with despair. My husband, however, is a diligent charge. Most of those studying with us are tourists, here for a week or two. Every afternoon when class is finished, and before our classmates head off on excursions to historical sites in Bologna or nearby towns, we all have lunch together, then Peter heads home and completes his homework lists of verbs and tenses before school pickup. I do not. And at the end of several weeks, Peter (who Andrea has now dubbed 'Super-Pete') is moved up to a more advanced class. When I resume lessons, I am without Peter but with a fresh bunch of newbies: Israelis, Canadians, a Brazilian and an Englishwoman. Always, Americans. They are curious about the fact that we live here whereas they are passing through. It must strike them as peculiar that I am still in a beginner class.

One day when we are doing our get-to-know each other introductions, I say as a joke: 'I am a housewife'. It is really a double joke because I literally say 'I am married to a house'. And also, I am Kate Langbroek. Star of radio and television. Describing myself as a 'housewife' to a group of random Australians would, at least, elicit a light titter. Even out of politeness. It is so self-effacing of me. So modest.

But here, nobody laughs.

I take a beat to digest this. Of course, I could totally be a housewife. Divested of work and out of the context of my home country, that is exactly what I am. It is a strange moment, and it makes me laugh (I am the only one). It is not an awful realisation but it is definitely weird. When I recount the instant to Hughesy (who is still a tad huffy), he grunts and says warningly: 'Be careful what you wish for.'

But my new status is also kind of liberating.

Because my Italian-housewife life, aside from the actual housework, is brilliant. (The only downside to our new apartment is its size. It is enormous. I don't know much about square feet but it is so huge that, one day, after I have swept the lounge room, I am so exhausted I have to lie on the couch to recover. Peter and I have repeated, fruitless exchanges about finding a cleaner. Four children, five bedrooms and seven bathrooms is a lot.)

There is time now to make leisurely breakfasts for us. To have post drop-off coffee at the Brothers cafe with other school parents. To visit Antonella's beautiful house in the hills for a morning tea.

To buy a scarf for the happy and strange celebration that is Denise's Annual Autumn Scarf Swap (like a Kris Kringle but with twenty women of every nationality vying for their favoured scarf). We have a dinner party and invite Italian friends. We head to basket matches and spend weekends at tournaments around the north. There are daytrips to nearby towns and villages, and stunning meals eaten alongside rivers or in piazzas or trattorias perched on hillsides. We drive to Florence many times to go shopping or to have lunch with our Australian friends Angie and Pietro at their incredible historic villa that overlooks the city, and where Machiavelli's cousin once lived. More friends come to visit, and to stay.

One of them is Kat, a sweet, pixie-faced Australian we met earlier in the year at Italian school. She was recovering from a heart broken by another expat Australian, a doctor. Their three-year relationship was scuppered on the rocks of cultural and religious differences and she has returned to Italy in an attempt to further banish her grief. (This country is a self-prescribed cure for heartache: one day I am stopped in the street in Bologna by an older woman who has recognised me from Australia. After confessing that she was hoping she would bump into me, she tells me with that female shorthand – few words encompassing big pain – that she has come to Italy 'to try and love life again'. I look at her: somehow fragile but also beautiful in a new white broderie anglaise summer dress and sandals, and ask if it is working. Her face suddenly breaks into a smile. 'I think so,' she says.)

Kat, our heartbroken fellow traveller, moves into our upstairs spare room and becomes a part of our family. She is smart and accomplished, a dentist who works on a hospital team in England performing craniofacial surgery. But she is so fine-boned and youthful that she looks like she could be my daughter. Watching our various teachers work out that she is not a school student is actually hilarious, so much so it becomes a collective catchcry: 'Not a child; a *dentist*!'

Together, we practise healing Italian-style: we cook and go shopping, where Kat buys a bright autumn coat embroidered with flowers. She hits up Dora for the name of her hairdresser and gets her hair cut and coloured. She flirts with one of our teachers (we are not sure that he notices), has aperitivo in the piazza and watches Italian movies with the other students. The children love her, and she offers to stay with them while Peter and I head to Chianti for three enchanted days with other Australian friends, Thatch and Nidzi. There we lounge poolside and drive down hail-Mary narrow roads, finding picturesque restaurants where we eat unforgettable truffle-topped onion pudding and ravioli, and drink local wine: Chianti, of course. It tastes of sunshine and cherries.

Kat spends two weeks with us then another fortnight at a homestay with an Italian single mother before heading off to do volunteer work on a charity ship in Senegal.

Another school friend, Sophie, the mother of Jannie's adored shock-blond buddy Frankie, puts another piece of my Italian dream-puzzle in place. Soph and her brilliant East-ender husband Mickey have always made us laugh with tales of seemingly permanent hangovers from their rotation of party-hard English visitors. As an antidote, Soph organises a yoga group. Our teacher Claudia, a gentle Bolognese beauty who lived in South America for eight years before returning home, is brilliant. Another school friend, a sunny upstate New Yorker named Trish, volunteers her sweeping terrace for the group class. Once a week, six or seven of us convene there amid the rooftops of Bologna and stretch and breathe. Sometimes we are down-dogging with her new pup, a golden-eyed, fluffy-eared Italian sweetheart called Tartufo (Truffle). It is so perfect that we continue our outdoor routine into winter when our toes turn purple with cold.

The children, like Peter and I, are deepening their roots. The little boys have their coterie of school and sports buddies, and associated birthday parties in parks and restaurants. After one basket match, when Artie has scored his hundredth goal for the season, Peter and I play our part in a team tradition. We arrive with prosecco, soft drinks and dozens of tiny pizzas (Pesce's lovely mum Speranza has come with us to source some extra gluten-free ones) and after the match we all gather in the empty auditorium for an impromptu celebration.

Sunday has found a soulmate, a girlfriend called Bea (short for Beatrice, it is pronounced 'Bear'), and spends occasional weekends at her place with her parents and sister. Our daughter is also going to weekly art classes, which she loves, arriving home with – what looks to Peter and me – minor masterpieces in the medium of the month: oils or watercolour and pastels. She occasionally babysits for fellow Australians Rachel and Dave, spending the ten euros she has earned entertaining their daughter Nellie on mascara from the brilliant Milanese makeup chain, Kiko, or on scented candles for her room. Our teenage girl has also caught the eye of one of the boys at school, an Italian Romeo in Lewis's year. For a few weeks, her 'gentleman caller' is a constant fixture at ours, hanging out with Lewis, but really – always – waiting for Sunday. When she emerges from her room, refusing to meet our gaze, the pair of them head out for walks around town or up to the Giardini Margherita park. He is clearly smitten; it is hard to know what our inscrutable daughter is thinking.

One day, while her paramour is watching soccer with Lewis in the lounge, Sunday refuses to come out of her room, eventually sending the boy a text saying she doesn't want to see him anymore. Lewis, left to comfort his heartbroken classmate, is annoyed. 'He didn't even want to see me,' he says to his sister, after Romeo has left, moist-eyed and sad. 'He only hung out with me because of you!' Sunday is quiet but resolute. 'I don't want it,' she says to me, simply, in the kitchen. I, of course, cannot judge her for breaking up with someone via text. Like mother, like daughter, it would seem.

Our eldest son, meanwhile, has kept the vow he made to us over the summer holidays. Lewis is working harder and more cheerfully at school. And he witnesses the trickle-down miracle of that: he is invited by a teacher to address a Google conference in Florence. He catches the train there and returns elated; next year, he and another student have been selected to represent their school at a school expo in Luxembourg. He is also enjoying his friends. They head to the piazza to hang out or he cooks for them at ours, where they watch various sports and Formula One races. He and Marshall try to indoctrinate the Europeans into Aussie Rules, but our football ('played with-a hands?') is a mystery to them. A group of them have a club, inelegantly called 'Lunch at Guido's Nonna's House', which is Italian-adorable. Every Thursday, five or six of them leave school to have lunch with Guido's grandmother at her house, where she makes them schnitzel, or pasta with ragu (the best he's ever eaten, Lewis says) before heading back to class.

One weekend, Lewis is invited to the mountains by his classmate to go biking and hiking. He is picked up by Guido's glamorous mum Carlotta in her gleaming red Ferrari. They are about to pull away from the kerb when I walk up the street on my way home from Italian *scuola*. At the sight of my eldest son, lanky limbs folded like a pretzel in the front seat of the Italian sports car, I can't resist tapping on the window. He winds the window down, grinning. Reaches his hand out to take mine.

'Are you missing Woolworths now, Luigi?' I ask.

I head to Paris to meet my girlfriend Mac, who has been in Cannes in the south of France for a TV conference. We meet on the street in the 2nd arrondissement on the Boulevard de Bonne Nouvelle, outside the Airbnb we have rented. It is a classic Parisian setup: a fifth floor walk-up apartment, owned by a bachelor. We determine the latter after some standard amateur detective work (no pictures of girls; no female toiletries) and also because the place is slightly grubby. Nonetheless, its position is perfect: on a street bustling with theatres and restaurants and shops but set back in a quiet courtyard.

From our kitchen, we look across and slightly down into a French family's apartment, and it is like a Wes Anderson movie. The lovely twelve-year-old daughter perched at the counter in her school uniform, eating a croissant. The painted tepee that sits in the corner of their stylish lounge room. The father loading the dishwasher; Parisian-elegant, even engrossed in this task, with his crossbody bag and scarf. When we are home, we are either in the kitchen watching our French neighbours' movie-life or sleeping in. When we are out, we could not be anywhere but Paris. We go shopping at the famous Galeries Lafayette department store, where Mac finds me the perfect handbag – a French label that turns out to now be made in Bologna.

We head upstairs to buy hosiery and underwear, and the saleswoman ringing up our purchases compliments my girlfriend's style: 'You look like you are from New York,' she says admiringly, and we are *so thrilled* we preen and chat until the less-impressed Frenchwoman waiting behind us hisses impatiently. Mac finds a French blue faux-fur coat that, against her blonde curls, makes her look like a movie star. I buy a pair of bottle-green patent leather boots that glide on like angels' wings. We eat and walk and get lost and laugh and drink champagne and cups of tea. We end up at a restaurant around the corner that turns into a late-night bar.

Every meal is a memory: breakfast baguettes or towering platters of seafood. We have brunch in a hip restaurant a boy in a boutique recommended where the Japanese girl next to us is eating her way through a burger as big as her head, layered with slices of foie gras as thick as her greasy fingers. By the time we exit the diner, the queue to enter reaches around the block. We have dinner in one of Paris's oldest restaurants, where we drink more champagne and sit in a pink wallpapered room on a rich burgundy banquette and marvel at the brass plaques set in the wood behind us, engraved with names from history. Frank Sinatra. Catherine Deneuve. We are eating where they have eaten. For dessert, our waiter brings us a confection of souffle-light meringue and strawberries that we cannot believe. Our trip could not be any more romantic if it was a honeymoon.

On the way to the airport, I ask our taxi driver to take us down the iconic Champs-Élysées, so we can see the Arc de Triomphe. We stop at a bakery and I pick up croissants and baguettes to take back to Italy, a French treat for my family. And another treat: Mac is returning to Bologna with me. When the children see her back at our apartment, they fall on her. She says: 'I just want to see your life,' and she does. We walk to school. We paint a white t-shirt with thick black stripes for Jannie, who has decided he wants to be a referee for dress-up day. Little Katie, his friend downstairs, makes snickerdoodle biscuits and drops them at our door. Mac's handsome husband Parko, back in Australia, has lost his favourite glasses and can't replace them back home; we find the elusive frames at the optometrist down the laneway from our old apartment. We drive to Florence, where a general strike means the boom gate at the autostrada exit has broken but no one has fixed it so I have to tailgate another driver through the Telepass exit. Mac falls in love with my favourite Italian designer, Twinset; with our beautiful apartment; with our landlord Ferdi, who removes his cap when he meets her; with aperitivo and Manuela's tortelloni; with yoga on Tricia's terrace. Basically, my brilliant friend falls in love with Bologna.

Next year, she says, she will return with Parko. He would love the museums and to see the oldest operating theatre in the world, where statues hold body parts – marble noses and intestines. Maybe we will go to Rome, we think, or further down south to Sardinia or to the Aeolian islands. Who knows what we will do, we say, so laughing and full of joy and anticipation. We decide to discuss it further in a month or so, when we are back in Australia for Christmas. By then, we will have had Yuletide dinners with our Italian friends, knowing that, after a fortnight in our home country, we will be coming back to our new one.

Next year, next year, next year, my heart sings. How brilliant it will be.

PART TWO

24

HOW DID I GET HERE?

I woke up this morning and the fug of my winter cold had momentarily passed, and as I lay there in the dark, I had a moment of intense clarity. It was as though there was a beam of light shining on the terrain that my life has covered so far – illuminating my footsteps as vividly as though I had left them in several inches of snow – and it answered my question (and the question I have been asked by myriad others): How did I get here?

Seriously, how did I get to be sleeping in this ancient Italian palace, with my husband next to me and our four children still abed in their rooms? Why am I not in Australia, in the land that I love, with the life that was, in comparison, so easy and navigable? In the country that my parents chose for me, where I spoke the language and could take advantage of the world I knew; where I knew the pitfalls and the crevasses, the people and the landscape? Where I knew the ropes?

How is it that I am waking up to church bells and the muted light of an early spring morning, to the slippered footsteps of an Italian living in the apartment above us, and the rare sound of birdsong from a feathered friend perched at the brown painted shutter?

I am about to pad down the hallway over marble floors and shifting parquetry to the tiny kitchen I have fitted out from op shops and discount stores, and make porridge from a box I brought back from Australia on our recent Christmas trip. I am about to cut up strawberries from the Market of Herbs two hundred metres from our house. Everything here, even the familiar, is strange.

And yet, when I look back at my snowy trail and survey the footsteps from whence I have come, I can see where I have taken turns that sometimes seemed impossible; where I have pirouetted or come perilously close to toppling over the edge into a ravine of indecision or doubt, or simply made a wrong turn. There are other places, too, where I have summoned up every fibre of will in my body and grappled my way back up to clear air.

And there it all was: the job I had left and people I had abandoned but not forgotten, and the hard slog of one foot in front of the other in what seemed at the time like a blinding blizzard of indecision and doubt – and not always just my own.

But this is what really stood out for me in this early-morning, mirror-lake clarity.

In this life, even when I was not moving, when I felt I was rooted to the spot with fear or anomie or exhaustion, or a sense of being overwhelmed or just not wanting to have to shift, things around me were still changing.

Because that is what the world does. It continues to swing on its invisible axis, to propel itself through time and space, and so, even if you shut your eyes as tightly as you can and hang on for dear life, everything around you is still shifting and evolving. When you open your eyes – sometimes hours, sometimes days or months later – everything around you has changed anyway. People, no matter how much you may love them, become sick. Flowers die. Buildings crumble and are rebuilt. Roads are hewn. Countryside becomes suburbs. Smooth faces become weathered. The cheeks of your baby boy sprout whiskers. Seasons change. Spring buds blossom. Other people may seem to have found their truth, their calling, while you may feel lost and weak and flailing.

So you might as well keep moving.

Because one thing I know: if you don't make decisions, they will be made for you. And you will probably not like them.

Whereas when you gird your loins and pull out your pickaxe (I am short of snow rappelling equipment terms), you at least have some agency, some say, in the circumstances in which you find yourself. And there is immense comfort and strength in knowing that you made the call.

So this is how I came to be living in Italy, in a medieval city made of Roman stone and ancient timbers. This is how I came to forge a new life in a new land, with the same me, who is at once new and foreign and familiar. I have the face I have always had and my attendant fears – some of them fresh and all the more frightening for it – but beneath it all, leading me, is an emboldened heart, beating. It is my heart. *Il cuore.*

Go on, it says. Go on.

(I still don't know how to say that in Italian.)

25

VENICE: A TALE OF TWO CITIES

Who could dream a city rising from the sea?

No cars. No motorbikes. No horses. No roads.

Only canals and bridges: silent save for the lapping of oars in water.

And the crush of several million tourists.

It is interesting, the way (if you are anything like me) you approach with scepticism the much-lauded charms of a place that is known the world over. I will never forget the first time I saw the *Mona Lisa* as an adult, how underwhelming she was in real life – so small and under siege. And yet powerful enough to draw people from around the world. The main impression I was left with from that lovely, modest portrait was of the incredible throng of people clustered around it, the backs of three hundred heads, and the actual physical scrum to try to secure a vantage point not obscured by other desperate tourists, jostling and shoving, phone-wielding arms held aloft, in some cases lifting children overhead and thrusting them over the crowd to the front. I was trapped in an invading force of hot and determined sweating must-see-ers, of which I was one, but nonetheless I felt that illogical, entitled response at being crammed in a tourist logjam; a sulky resentment at all the other tourists.

My expectation of Venice is similar. The first time I visited with my family and mother-in-law Maree, long before our move to Bologna, I had barely imagined it prior to our arrival – due to the logistics of travelling with seven people, including four young children,

I didn't have time. But I have seen so many images in my lifetime, of emerald canals, stripe-shirted gondoliers and watered-silk plastered buildings growing from lapping waters like they are mangrove trees. I have seen photos of friends' round-the-world adventures, drinking beers or spritzes in the main piazza in front of somewhere called The Doge's Palace, and balancing backpacks on water taxis. I have seen the Clooney wedding. So I had braced myself for anticlimax, that this floating city would feel almost like a hollow Disneyland, like a construct. Many tourist-intensive places become so overwhelmed by the power and sheer weight of numbers of their visitors that they can end up being an impersonation of themselves. I am expecting this of Venice.

I am right, and I am also wrong.

Even though my first visit to this jewel of Italy is in the middle of the tourist vac-pack of a steaming hot July, on my first-ever trip to Italy, Venice is extraordinary. Mindful of the absence of parking, the seven of us have left our rented nut-bus (our nine-seater rented van) in Milan in favour of an excellent train, and as we approach over the water and see the boats – so many boats! – it is like nothing I have ever seen before.

I agree with Shakespeare when it comes to entrances and exits: they are everything. So often when we are travelling, we take a taxi or van to our lodgings rather than grinding it out on foot or by public transport. In Venice, there are no roads – at least, none made of bitumen. The only transport here is watercraft, and the public transport is *vaporetti* – water-buses with stops that line either side of the Grand Canal, with timetables and colour-coded routes posted on big signs. Lewis and my mother-in-law Maree have already spent three whirlwind days here on his school trip so they are familiar with the system. This is definitely a bonus.

We alight from the train, making sure we have all the children and that they have their backpacks, and after following instructions from a remarkably upbeat ticket-seller in her booth, and buying some cold bottled water from an adjacent kiosk, we drag our suitcases to the nearest vaporetto stop. The children, pink-cheeked from the searing heat, wait droopily for the boat to pull up. Then we file on and, as we move away from our mooring, with the motion of the boat rendering the air less bakingly still, the city of Venice unfolds around us. Just like imagination, only gloriously real.

Sometimes, in the face of the spectacular, I have the thought: I can't believe what my eyes are seeing, and so it is during my first trip through the waters of Venice. We are slicing through the broad sweep of the green and sparkling Grand Canal, intersected by smaller canals; some glittering turquoise, some shaded and enticing. They are liquid roads; we share them with cruise boats, transport barges, gondoliers and locals tillering their own craft, while on either side of us ancient and breathtaking buildings rise from the lapping waterways. Many of them fly the Venetian or Italian flags, or sport terraces festooned with crimson, pink and yellow flowers. We travel past umbrella-shaded balconies built over the water, past shamelessly fancy hotels and an endless array of museums and banners announcing the annual art biennale, which is in full swing. It is mind boggling. My heart soars, even in the crushing heat.

Then it is back to the reality of an insanely popular tourist destination. Though Venice only has a core population of sixty thousand, it attracts 30 million visitors a year, and it feels as though at least half of them are here right now. We step off the vaporetto into the thick of human soup oozing its way along the hot stone paving, and begin the trudge to our accommodation. We are staying in two rooms in a modest hotel five hundred metres or so down from Piazza San Marco, the main square. 'One day,' I say to Peter, 'we will come back and stay in a hotel on the Grand Canal.' But now is not that time. 'Now' is seven hot and weary travellers trying to make their way to their budget accommodation.

Venice is over a thousand years old. There are ancient bridges vaulting canals everywhere, but practical concessions have been made to accommodate modern tourists. The bridges have metal ramps installed on one side, covering the steps and making it possible to wheel luggage. Every main thoroughfare is lined by street vendors – official stalls selling fans, the famous Venetian masks, multihued Italia caps and lace parasols – and the bridge stairways are flanked by African men selling copies of designer bags. Their position on the stairs gives an excellent vantage point for selling but also for their scouts to see approaching police, in the event of which they give a whistle to their colleagues, who swiftly gather up their wares and scatter into the throng.

Everywhere is a crush of humanity, travellers like us schlepping roll-away cases up ramps and thumping down stone steps in the heat or seeking temporary respite over cold drinks at outside bars. When we arrive at our hotel, set fifty metres back from the main drag, even the small rooms with their panting air-conditioning feel like a sanctuary. With the perfunctory politeness of one who spends his days dealing with a tide of foreigners he will likely never see again, the concierge at the desk directs us to our rooms. We are on the ground floor, where Peter and I will share with Artie and Jannie. My mother-in-law is next door with Lewis and Sunday.

A travelling day is always exhausting I find, even if it is a relatively short trip. We convene to our rooms, where Peter unpacks, and I take advantage of the hotel-bliss of having a plentiful supply of towels and make cold compresses under the tap to wrap around everyone's hot legs. I tell my boyos to pretend they are at a day spa as they watch the Tour de France from the comfort of our firm bed. Later, vaguely refreshed, we venture out to dinner. Even though we are aware of the hard-learned traveller wisdom that the best food is rarely to be found along any main thoroughfare (the better the view, the worse the food), there are too many of us to spontaneously procure a table at any of the small restaurants up the laneways away from the Grand Canal and we, of course, have not made a booking. Anyway, sometimes it is nice to be in the thick of it and accept that you are a tourist. We settle at a large outside restaurant and, in honour of cocktail hour and our sense of elation at having arrived, order aperol spritzes and pizza while we watch the nations of the world flock around us. The heat has subdued us all. After the meal, and a short wander round Piazza San Marco, we return to the hotel where the children climb into their beds and sink into the sleep of the innocent.

The next morning, at the buffet-style restaurant, the children are enjoying the unlimited sweet Italian breakfast croissants and are delighted by the tiny foil packs of Nutella. Aware that we have a big, hot, sightseeing day ahead of us, I try to steer them to ham and cheese and yoghurt while also ordering coffee for Peter and Maree. My mother-in-law has a long black – this is easy for Italians since it is just a taller version of their lifeblood espresso (they call it 'Americano'), but I also request two cafe lattes for myself and Peter. As this is our first trip in Italy, I order using the one tentative sentence I have learned so far in Italian: *'Due latte, per favore,'* and am thrilled when the waitress instantly comprehends, nods, and bustles off.

After a couple of minutes, she returns, with two cups – and two steaming pots of hot milk. No coffee.

It takes me a moment of confusion to register what has happened. Then it dawns on me. *Latte*, of course, is Italian for 'milk'. That is what I have requested, using our shorthand coffee terminology from home, and because it is breakfast, our waitress has assumed we will want the milk hot. This is such a classic Aussie-in-Italy mistake (in fact, few things are more annoying back home than Italophiles who love to say when they hear you order a 'latte': 'You know, latte just means "milk" in Italian!') that we are actually delighted by it. When the waitress passes again, I sheepishly request two espressos – in English this time. When they arrive, I pour them into the hot milk, making our own coffees at the table. I use the rest of the milk to thin the hot chocolate that Sunday has ordered – it is so thick and rich, it is like mud. And of course, there are no frivolous marshmallows on top.

After a day of mild art-gallerying and a delicious lunch on a shaded terrace, we are having a gondola ride tonight. Maree and Lewis have previously enjoyed one on Lewis's school excursion so Peter and I set off with Sunday, Artie and Jannie while the two landlubbers take photos of us from above. As we are pushed out onto the canal by our gondolier, resplendent in his traditional striped shirt and black flat-brimmed hat, us reclining like so many Talented Mr Ripleys on cushions in the beautiful carved wooden boat, Lewis and Maree call out that they will meet us back at the hotel. Jannie and Artie wave excitedly as we sail away.

The tour is just under an hour long. We venture up tiny canals and round corners where, from our position low in the water, we can see into vast living rooms above, chandelier-lit, many with frescoed ceilings. We float past little restaurants, past weary lovers cuddling or posing for photos on bridges, past wanderers eating gelati, fathers carrying spent toddlers on their shoulders, and shops full of glittering masks, jewellery and clothes. The gondolier poles his way round several corners and we are suddenly in dark and tranquil waters, still and narrow, in a silence broken only by his oar cutting through the water. It is magical and secret; ancient and timeless. And then the spell is broken. We are back at the gondola stop. Back among the lights, the heat, the throng that even at ten o'clock at night is heaving.

I still cannot fathom what happened next. I only know this. As the five of us made our way along the promenade, Artie was glued, as he always is, to Peter. Jannie was behind me, dancing with overtired excitement. Sunday and I rose to cross a bridge and, from our momentarily elevated position, I saw the heave of late-night tourists and I reached back for Jannie's hand, but he was not there. He had somehow slipped past me, I thought, to catch up to his brother. We caught up to Peter and I asked if Jannie had run past. He looked confused. 'I thought he was with you,' he said.

At first, it was just a cursory look, with that confident assumption of parents who have looked for many children many times, that we would suddenly see his little cowlicked head darting among the crowds. But that didn't happen. We looked behind us. We waited another minute or two for him to find us, as he always does. Then we climbed over the bridge again and scanned the crowds and doubled back. No Jannie. We called his name, and I ran back again over the bridge we had just crossed and then down the stairs again, and suddenly the surge of people felt foreign and oppressive, and where oh where was our beloved five-year-old monkey?

Artie and Sunday grew fearful then, too, and suddenly we were all calling out 'Jannie! Janneman!' into the throng surging towards us and around us, and then, in a dizzying moment as I looked around and tried to work out what to do next, I saw Venice differently – that it was all water, dark and deep, with shrouded depths everywhere and I realised that a slip of a boy could slip silently away over a steep drop. And then I felt the first gripping surge of fear. We all did.

And then we were all running. The four of us. Darting up laneways and doubling back and calling out, and then Peter – calm, beautiful Peter – said he and Artie would run ahead to the hotel. I was suddenly drenched in a flop-sweat of anxiety and I saw that everyone else, lost in the exhausting magic of Venice, hadn't noticed what was going on – except for the African touts, who were watching us curiously. I ran to the group nearest us at the top of the stairs, and asked if they had seen a little boy on his own, a little boy with brown hair in a red t-shirt. They shook their heads and said they had seen him but only with us earlier. I was nearly sick with dread by then and one of them said, 'You need the police,' but I shook my head. I didn't know where the police were, and Sunday was crying now. The man looked at us and said, 'I will take you'.

So we followed the bag-seller, him loping quickly ahead and always looking around. He made several turns up a dark laneway and then, when I worried there may be something else to fear, he simply pointed ahead to a grey brick wall and disappeared.

There was an electronic bell set in the wall. I pressed the buzzer and pressed and pressed, and then a giant door slid open and we were admitted to a cavernous stone chamber with just a sharply clad police officer standing alone on a platform in the empty room. I approached and babbled at him what was happening. He didn't speak English but motioned for us to wait, and then another giant internal door opened and a detective came out.

He was also immaculately dressed, in a suit, and even in the panic of the moment that had slightly removed me from myself, it was like a scene from a movie: his handsomeness, the breathless mother and her nine-year-old daughter, gibberish with fright. And then he asked us questions, and I couldn't remember the name of our hotel and I didn't have my phone with me, and I felt stupid and sweat-sodden and foolish and frightened.

He was so patient, the detective. He brought us to a main desk, where he offered me a coffee, and we told him where we had been and described Jannie and what he was wearing. Sunday was sobbing, and they brought us water, and I was trying to comfort her but my heart was pounding and I couldn't think. The younger officer asked for the direction of our hotel, and I told him it was five hundred metres away, and he consulted a clipboard in front of him with a list of names of hotels. And I, the idiot who couldn't remember her hotel and didn't have a phone and had somehow lost her little boy, will never forget what the handsome detective said.

'You don't need to worry,' he said calmly. 'In Venice, maybe they steal your handbag, but not your child.'

And then Sunday, my gorgeous girl with her heart of an artist, remembered that there was a giant vertical flag advertising Tissot watches at the turn-off to our hotel and the polizia spoke rapidly to each other in Italian and determined the name of the hotel. The junior officer made a phone call and was put through to the concierge and we could hear their rapid-fire back and forth, and then he handed me the phone, and it was Peter on the line and he said: 'He is here. Jannie is here. It's all right.' And I sagged from relief.

Jannie had run all the way back to the hotel, that little boy. Through the mass of late-night revellers, he had found the hotel I couldn't even remember the name of but he had recognised because Sunday had also mentioned the fluttering landmark flag with the giant watch face to him, and he had privately deemed it a race.

When he'd bounded into the foyer of the hotel, he'd run straight to Nanaree's room, and said: 'I won! I won!'

(And then he leaped into his bed and pulled the covers over himself, all the better to play the family game of 'look how long I've been waiting'.)

His tone was triumphant, his grandmother said, so much so she didn't even begin to wonder at our whereabouts for twenty minutes or so.

Before Sunday and I went back to the hotel, buoyed by air that was suddenly cool and joyous, we turned back to the bridge where the African bag-seller was back at his post.

'We found my son,' I said. 'I cannot thank you enough.'

He nodded and grinned, clearly pleased. His friends looked at us, bemused by the crazy tourist clasping their mate's hands.

In the subsequent years, I have marvelled at what he did for us, this foreigner helping other foreigners. The illegal street vendor, taking us as close to the police as he dared.

And I feel like we met royalty that night in Venice. Some real-life Venetian princes.

Now, after almost a year of living in Italy, we are going back to Venice, my husband and I.

We have booked a babysitter, put in place arrangements for basketball fixtures and school pickups and dropoffs, and now we are free to prepare for a long weekend away. I am so excited, even packing is fun, and I'm reminded of my funny girlfriend Monty, who once remarked: 'The only thing better than having children is leaving them'; a quip that, at the time, reduced us to tears of helpless laughter. And, praise be, that is exactly what we are doing.

It is Peter's vision that we visit Venice, this time just the two of us, and also that our visit will coincide with one of the city's famous Carnevale masked balls. It is doubly significant, this outing, since it will mark the start of the second phase of our Italian adventure: a twelve-month promise to see as much of Europe as possible. Our first year was such an intense period of bedding-in – finding an apartment, organising schools and cars and basketball teams, and attempting to navigate a new language and city – that we have decided 2020, this second year we have painstakingly etched out for ourselves, will be devoted to adventures and travel. We are also looking forward to blowing our hair back, since the year has already been marked by a subdued and painful start.

It is February 2020, and we have been back for three weeks or so from our Christmas visit home to Australia, a stay shrouded with smoke from savage bushfires that ravaged so much of our homeland. Like so many other Australians, our plans for traditional camping and caravan-park end-of-year/new-year celebrations were abandoned. As a nation, it felt like we held our collective breath as we watched much of our country burn, consumed by angry flames. Friends lost homes; too many Australians lost lives. It was truly terrible. Back in Italy, everyone asks about the devastation in Australia with so much fondness and concern, it is moving. At the international school, the parents at the junior school (always the mothers!) have organised a bake stall to raise money for our devastated wildlife. It has been an emotional and taut start to the year and, back in the easing cold of Bologna, Peter and I are looking forward to an uncomplicated and precious few days away.

I say 'uncomplicated' but aside from the arrangements for the children there is still much more planning to be done. In anticipation of our trip, Peter and I have spent the previous week poring over the array of Venetian balls and parties on offer. Carnevale di Venezia is a famous few weeks of festivities involving partying and promenading around the city in fancy dress. The original Carnevale started in the twelfth century and was revived in the 1970s as a celebration of Venice, and an excuse to pay homage – through elaborate historical costuming and masks – to its rich history. It is also apparently an excuse to party (to paraphrase Prince) like it's 1199.

Some of the functions on offer are breathtakingly decadent: boat arrivals at cocktail soirées leading to glorious twelve-course banquets held in palaces alongside the water, and finishing with afterparties that carry on till dawn. They are also incredibly expensive – the most famous at the Doge's Palace is the price of a new car. And you also have to factor in the exorbitant cost of renting the costumes required to attend. A nylon packet Halloween cape will not pass muster at these more extravagant events – attendees are required to dress in full historical regalia. When we tell our friend Riccardo our plans, he informs us how seriously upmarket some of the balls are: 'You will sit next to someone with a mask. And you will not realise it is Barack Obama.'

We have ruled out partying with former presidents and, after much perusal, have purchased tickets to a less opulent but still formal ball in a smaller palace, where we will enjoy a sit-down banquet, live music and entertainment, followed by a late-night disco. Through our school friends, who are vicariously excited at the audacity of our plans, we have been given the heads-up on an atelier in Bologna run by a husband and wife who make costumes for the opera. When we ring the doorbell at the entrance to their low-lying building in the middle of a suburban car park, it is like being admitted to the enchanted workshop of the elves and the shoemaker.

We introduce ourselves, utter the magic word 'Carnevale' and the older couple nod shyly and spring to life. From under piles of feathers and sequins, they produce costumes that take our breath away. For Peter, there is a turquoise blue satin 'officer's uniform' with knicker-bockers and a three-cornered plumed hat. He looks so handsome and transformed we both stand in the fitting room, giggling. Then the wife visually sizes me up and mutters something to me in Italian that I by now understand only too well: for me, there is apparently only one costume in the whole store that will fit. (I am size *grande* in Italy, which limits choices among the fine-boned Italians. Buying a bra that fits here is nearly impossible.) Nonetheless, the outfit she re-emerges with is extraordinary: a giant hooped skirt covered with a rich silk two-piece – a skirt and lace-up bodice in shades of woven apricot and green – topped by a matching veiled hat. It is simply beautiful. And it fits as though it was made for me.

Our wardrobe consultant is thrilled with how thrilled we are, and bustles around finessing us with moulded leather masks that will complete our outfits. Her husband, sewing fringing to a leather waistcoat, looks up and dips his head in silent approval as we parade in front of him. It really feels like we are about to do something special and we head off to school pickup, pleased with our afternoon's work. Not only is the hire of our costumes a tenth of what we would have been charged in Venice, our preparedness also means we have extra time to enjoy ourselves when we finally reach the emerald arms of our Carnevale destination.

And what an arrival it is. Friday-morning Venice is cool and crisp and glittering under a cloudless azure sky. The hotel Peter has chosen is simply perfect – a beautiful four-storey study in cream and yellow. It sits proudly on the Grand Canal, and when Peter tells me that is why he booked it, I am full of love for him and his remembering my dream, uttered out loud those several years ago and now rendered true by him.

The hotel is perfectly situated next to a vaporetto stop near the famous Gallerie dell'Accademia museum and, as we wheel our luggage into the entrance, the manager greets us with a warmth it is impossible not to reciprocate. He is particularly effusive after we fill out our paperwork and he realises we live in Italy. After fielding the requisite questions about what we are doing living in Bologna (when our own country is so famously spectacular), he directs us upstairs to our first-floor room. It is magnificently bedecked in classic Italian style, with a pair of king-sized beds covered with satin lemon-cream quilts, giant gilt mirrors and a pair of silk-sheathed armchairs in front of soaring floor-to-ceiling doors that open to a tiny balcony overlooking the water. We open the windows and drink in the view: boats and birds and sparkling aquamarine, and on the far side of the canal half-a-dozen people in elaborate robes and masks, sweeping along the boardwalk. It is a reminder to hang up our costumes in preparation for tomorrow's festivities before, led by hunger, we venture back downstairs.

In the foyer, the manager announces he has booked lunch for us at a restaurant around the corner. This is typically Italian. We have not asked him to do this or even mentioned our growing appetites but it is by now the sacred and immutable ritual of *lunchtime*, and the national insistence on eating well is one we have learned not to argue with. Also, we, who spend so much of our time organising others, are more than happy to not have to make any decisions so we obediently take up his offer, and head off on the 'No more than ten, no, six minutes walk! You will be happy!' to the restaurant he has forcibly recommended. It is, of course, a complicated twenty-minute expedition across bridges and up laneways. Devoid of crowds in this late winter, Venice is lovelier than I remembered, and it is fascinating to see it, but we get lost a couple of times and we are tired and hungry. Also, Peter and I have a healthy scepticism about what will await us when we finally arrive. Once again, however, Italy is correct.

The restaurant our hotel friend has mandated is set alongside a narrow working canal, well back from the main thoroughfare. The welcome February sun is gleaming off the water and warming enough for us to sit outside at a table at the water's edge. Immediately upon settling, we are greeted with glasses of prosecco and some welcome slices of prosciutto. Then, as though to teach us (again!) to always trust Italy, we are served one of the most delicious meals of our life.

Truly, kings could not eat better. The waitress brings us white fish carpaccio, served translucent-thin on bundles of rocket dressed liberally with olive oil and salt; lamb cutlets with crispy fried potatoes cut into thick ringlets; langoustines so buttery and sweet they make lobster seem coarse; spinach wilted with crescents of garlic and a side dish of crunchy croutons. The feast is enhanced by a rich bottle of Nebbiolo, a wine from the north the restaurant owner has selected for us.

With Neptune our first winter in Bologna.

With our friend Giovanni at his favourite bar, where his mate was always smoking under the No Smoking sign.

Showing my mum and dad, Anne and Jan, around Bologna. We hardly knew anyone who went to church, but there are little shrines everywhere, lovingly maintained (and graffiti-ed).

On the main drag of Bologna with one of the famous Two Towers behind us (they keep shortening the other one because it's at a rakish angle).

Wandering home through the streets of Bologna after the famous annual Giro d'Italia bicyle race, the boys showing off their souvenir caps.

My girl Sunday with her girl Bea. Finding a bestie changed the whole experience for Sunday.

The Italians love kiwifruit because they can make their national flag with it.

International Food Day at the International School of Bologna. Our Aussie friend Rachel (with Sunday and Artie) repped the Australian stall with me. We got lumped in with the UK!

Lewis and his mates Julian, Alessandro and Andrea in our tiny kitchen in Bologna. He went on holidays with them to Puglia – and became their head chef.

Piazza boys.

Meeting her majesty Madonna for a one-on-one interview. We started our conversation literally before my bum hit the seat. She is fascinating. I nearly forgot to get a photo with her. Luckily, Madonna remembered. Also, she is a beauty.

My girl Georgie and me on our way back from a music festival on the France–Switzerland border. We took the train back to Bolo: 300 kph+wine=molto relaxing.

Reuniting in Bologna with Sacha French, our beloved producer of the Hughesy & Kate radio show for eighteen years. Sacha set up a makeshift studio so I could continue broadcasting from Italy.

Sacha oversees my first broadcast. Every day for the next six months I'd get picked up at 5 am so I could join Hughesy on the show from the other side of the world.

Sacha, me, Hughesy and our brilliant anchor Jack Lawrence in our squeezy hotbox of a studio.

My self-made, clever, funny, foul-and-fair-weather friend, David William Hughes, joins me in Bologna.

Me and Hughesy about to go for a drive in a vintage Fiat Bambino. You can tell a lot about a man from the size of his car – he's practical.

When my friends came to town, we made a party: Hughesy, Carrie Bickmore, Tommy Little, me and beautiful Bologna behind; and our Hughesy & Kate Show and Tommy & Carrie Show producers.

Our lovely listeners who won tickets to our 'Spicy Meatball Tour'. They saw the Spice Girls in London, then were flown to meet us in Italy. Commercial radio does some amazing things. Fair to say, nothing looked as pristine as this table after our party.

Me and Sach, with Hughesy and eldest son Lewis before they left on a weekend trip to Cinque Terre. Hughesy enlisted Lewis to convince me to keep doing the radio show from Italy. I resisted.

With friends Georgie D and Carla on Ibiza beach at sunrise. We danced all night.

When you're tired of jumping on fancy hotel beds, you're tired of life.

Positano Beach Club on the glorious Amalfi coast.

Me and the boys: with our comedian friends Lawrence Mooney, Marty Sheargold, Lehmo and Sam Pang before Lawrence and the love of his life, Lou, renewed their vows in spectacular style in Positano.

I love the moment the groom sees his bride for the first time. This is what took Lawrence's breath away: his wife Lou and daughter Maggie. Pure beauty.

Me and the bride the day after. We're not quite so smug. Lou is trying to hide in our lemon grove.

Resplendent in a ten-dollar hat I bought from a street stall, with Peter and Sam Pang at the beach in Positano before drinks on a sunset cruise.

On holiday at our friends Angie and Pietro's villa in Florence.

At a shopping village in Florence. The impeccably groomed men savouring lunch in each other's company in the background is such a common sight that a casual visitor might assume all of Italy is a giant Grindr meet, but this is a cultural trick.

Florence sunset.

Raw prawns are sweet and delicious, who knew? (Sharks, obviously.)

Petie and me in Amsterdam. The only person missing from this happy mess was Snoop Dogg.

Everything is so delicious, it is like we have never tasted food before. And what a gleeful pair we are, toasting each other and our freedom, greedy chins glistening with melted butter, me crunching and sucking at every last crustacean shell like an ecstatic, land-lubbing mermaid.

While we eat, the business of Venice passes alongside us, as if a classical painting came to life but with more pedestrian subject matter: a long boat laden with white bags of hotel bedding headed for a laundry; workmen unloading boxes and wheeling trolleys laden with bottles to nearby stores. A low wooden vessel glides past, reminiscent of an old Viking craft, only instead of a siren-of-the-sea adorning its prow, it proudly sports a new porcelain toilet and cistern, lashed securely and gleaming. As the toilet boat passes, a trio of figures appear on foot through the wintry haze – three women, clad all in white with hooded robes and full-face ivory masks under black veils. They pause at the top of a bridge then drift towards us before wordlessly disappearing down a cobbled laneway. We are in a dreamscape; ancient and modern. We are simply, magically, in Venice.

We punctuate the meal we never want to end with limoncello and caffe, and wander back to our hotel. Even the hit of caffeine cannot stop us climbing onto our vast Italian bed and drifting off into the most glorious, luxuriant, mid-afternoon siesta.

The next morning at the hotel breakfast buffet, we get to enjoy another of my favourite things: eavesdropping on fellow travellers. Firstly, a trio of Americans, so it is not difficult to hear their conversation from our table next to them. (It is a constant source of wonder that the treble of their tone travels more clearly than any other national tongue.)

They are two ladies in their early sixties sitting opposite each other ('Bookclubbers,' I think) and a man of similar age. They are all dressed neatly and practically in the way of worshippers at the Temple of Smart Casual. The man sports a green-checked shirt that is *very firmly* tucked and belted into his beige trousers, as though if given the slightest opportunity it will try to escape. He sits slightly away from the women at an adjacent table, so at first I am not even sure they are together but as their conversation ensues, it appears he is married to one of them. The mood between the married pair is so strange and taut, and such a contrast to the easy chatter between the two women, I am all ears.

They are discussing, among other things, outdoor pool furniture, when the man weighs in with a reminiscence about some of theirs having blown over. His wife looks at him coldly. 'It's never blown over,' she says sharply.

He purses his lips slightly but persists.

'Down the side of the house,' he says, nodding, as though to nudge a corroborating memory from her. 'When (muffled, muffled) had the tornado.'

The wife stares at him as though he is mad.

'We don't live near the tornadoes, sweetie,' she says firmly, and looks away. Her voice is so clipped it is clear she does not find him sweet.

I don't have a dog in the fight, but it is hard not to feel for the man, though his suppressed resentment is palpable. He opens his mouth then clamps it shut again before reaching for a map on the table and studying it intensely. Why does she hate him so, I wonder? The tension between them is so uncomfortable and my instant reading of their situation so dramatic (a past affair? pornography?) that I turn my attention to the table behind them, which hosts a family of French artie types. There is a hipster mother in flared jeans and stripey top. She is on the phone trying to book a water taxi. As she speaks, she flips a wooden high-heeled clog on her foot while the handsome, side-burned father goes outside to smoke. They have two children with them – a tall, teenaged son wearing a designer t-shirt and a classically French, lovely nine-year-old girl, who follows her brother to the buffet and comes back with croissants. All of them order coffee – black for the adults, milky for the children. So French. We are worlds apart, I think;

such products of our respective countries and cultures. All brought together by Venice.

Peter and I spend the morning vaporetto-hopping and exploring the imposing Doge's Palace. There are few other tourists and no queues so we take the luxury of time to enjoy the grand central courtyard, vast ballrooms adorned with richly painted ceilings, as well as the several courtrooms on the top storey. We finish our wandering in the eerie old prison cells on the other side of the canal – bleak and cold stone rooms with barred windows too high to see through. As we leave the dank quarters, we pass over the fabled Bridge of Sighs, a poetic epithet for a cruel reality, named for the sighs of despair prisoners would emit upon their last sighting of Venice on their way to confinement. It is too easy to imagine the misery and the fear of the condemned inhabitants, and it makes me shiver, even though the exertion of climbing the many flights of narrow stone steps should have warmed us.

Downstairs, we are suddenly back in 2020, albeit a heightened, theatrical version. Glittering in the sunlight, costume-clad performers pose for photos under the vaulted archways of the palace, their richly coloured satins and silks a reminder to shake off the more sombre ghosts of Venice past.

For this evening, we go to the ball.

26

CARNEVALE: THE BALL

I do not understand people who do not like to dress up. You know, those naysayers who turn up at a fancy dress or office Christmas party in t-shirt and trousers or a little black dress? Although they are physically present, and may be deeply adored by the assembled, they rarely seem to contribute much to the life of the party. To my mind they are akin to those strange and stubborn souls who refuse to dance. Often they plead shyness, though their refusal to be swayed by either rhythm or fantasy seems to have an unspoken undercurrent of disapproval; that somehow those who are adorned in multi-hued wigs or togas, or pimp suits or naughty nurses' outfits (or have simply draped their normal clothes with strings of tinsel) are foolish or frivolous. Because, if they are shy, why wouldn't they embrace the anonymity afforded by a costume? Let's face it, in a roomful of spangles and colour, you are far more conspicuous in streetwear; just as you are standing, determinedly unmoving, at the edge of a heaving dancefloor.

This is not an issue for the festival of Carnevale in this month when all of Venezia commits to colour and costume. It is much like medieval Halloween, and the prospect of being a part of this is irresistible for me and Peter, who are united in our love of a fancy dress event. It is so transformative and playful. It is fun. Plus, much as my mother says of a wood stack: 'It warms you twice' (with the chopping of the wood and the subsequent fire). You get to enjoy a fancy dress event in many ways prior to the occasion itself. There is the planning, the consultation with friends, the selection of outfits, the glorious anticipation and then, of course, the donning of strange and elaborate garments, all before the joy of the actual party.

So we are in Venice, getting ready for our Carnevale ball, refreshed and steeped in so much luxury. Not just the opulence of our physical surrounds, which are glorious, with the low Venetian sun glowing muted amber through the shutters of our hotel room, but also that we are here without children. No interruptions, no preparing of dinner, no resolving of squabbles or issuing of edicts for the evening ahead. We are two grownups getting ready – for what, we are not exactly sure, but adventure awaits, and we are both here for it.

If there is one regret I have, it is that I don't have a lady-in-waiting laying out my costume. Wriggling into my stockings and giant hooped skirt takes the better part of ten minutes and, although I wanted to surprise Peter by suddenly appearing, transformed, I finally have to enlist his help. He has to lace up my corset, which ties at the back, Scarlett O'Hara style, and (eek!) requires some serious muscle to cinch in my well-fed waist. I need his assistance once more after I have squeezed into the bathroom and wedged my enormous bustle against the wall so I can use the toilet. Propping my hooped skirt up with one hand while reaching over myself in an elaborate pretzel-like twist to grab the toilet paper with the other – without knocking over bottles on the bathroom shelf behind me – is nigh on impossible. Peter, answering my plea for help, comes in and helpfully takes a photo of me, stuck on the loo. I make a mental note to not drink too much tonight to minimise bathroom trips. *Mio dio*, the past was impractical.

But how gloriously impractical. When we are finally ready we stand in the middle of the room, my handsome, turquoise-clad officer and me, now a proper Venetian lady, with hair curled and a shimmering, peachy bosom. We regard each other through our leather masks, and are just delighted. My husband executes a deep bow and offers me his arm. '*Prego, signore*,' I simper sweetly, attempting a return curtsy. Tucking my hand through the crook of his arm, we turn to sweep out of the hotel room but our exultation is short-lived:

we manage only a few steps before getting jammed in the narrow hallway – again, because of the enormous girth of my skirt.

We finally wrestle free of each other enough that Peter can close the hotel door behind us while I tentatively descend the stone steps to the hotel reception. I cannot see my feet on the stairs so I have to shuffle down sideways like a toddler, one step at a time, hands clutching the banister for balance, while my feet blindly feel their way. It is not the kind of elegant entrance I have imagined but nonetheless, as we approach the bottom of the stairs, the hotel night manager is moved enough to look up from his phone. His face registers his surprise and, smiling approvingly, he murmurs the ultimate Italian accolade '*Bellissimi!*'

And he is right; we *are* beautiful.

Stepping out into the laneways of Venice for the fifteen-minute walk to our ball is simply thrilling. Along the way we pass groups of revellers outside bars and Italians enjoying their traditional *passeggiata*, the evening stroll that happens everywhere at dusk. The stories we have been hearing in the news of a strange and deadly virus in China have kept many Asian tourists away so the streets are quieter than they would ordinarily be but there are still many travellers and tourists clustered for the sunset ritual. And tonight, rather than being mere spectators, we are adding to the theatre of it. As we make our way through a wide piazza, men exaggeratedly bow and women murmur compliments. The old people, some of the few permanent Venetian inhabitants, study us from park benches where they are scoping the early evening sights. In more narrow slipways, people step aside so we can navigate the path unimpeded, my heavy skirts sweeping over the cobblestones. Tipsy strangers raise their glasses to us and, when we pass other costume-clad partygoers – harlequins, noblemen and veiled ladies clad in brocade – we acknowledge each other, our respective commitment and the beauty of our costumes, with a slight incline of the head, and a '*Buon carnevale*'.

This promenade alone is nearly worth the effort. When we arrive at the address where the evening's festivities will be held, we are already on a high. Even so, the modern part of us is not sure what to expect. We bought our tickets online so there is always the chance that we have been dudded. It is a relief, then, to be greeted by a quartet of suited men and women at the entrance who check our names off on clipboards and seem to be expecting us. They usher us through two giant arched wooden doors, where we step into our immediate future: the past.

We are in the enclosed courtyard of a grand old palace, filled with ferns and flowering potted plants. On either side of a central fountain, stairs sweep up to a balustraded balcony. A group of cellists and violinists plays classical music in the corner. We are handed glasses of prosecco from behind a long bar and take a moment to relax and, like everyone else, peruse the sparkling array of costumes on display. So much colour. So much opulence. So many assembled lords and ladies. On the twin staircases, performers dance and sway; some clad in fairy costumes with arching gossamer wings, others with horse's heads atop seemingly tiny bodies. My eye is caught by a man clad from head to toe in the most glorious dusky-pink embroidered suit, from under which spills a white silk ruffled shirt with draping cuffs. Under his sweeping iron-grey wig and plumed hat, his face is painted gouache-white, with circles of pink rouge on his cheeks. He looks extraordinary. He catches me studying him and raises his glass to me across the room as a slight woman in a towering white wig appears on the balcony. She throws up her arms in classic circus-ringmaster style, and howls *'Velcome to Carrrrrrrnevaaaaale!'*, which elicits much cheering and clinking of glasses from us below. Then, after promising us a night we will never forget, she invites us upstairs.

There, we are ushered into a long room flickering with silver candelabra, the candlelight reflected in floor-to-ceiling mirrors set amongst draped silken curtains in shades of gelato pink and green. It is magical. There are round tables set for ten, adorned with flowers and sparkling crystal glasses and gleaming silver cutlery. Another band is playing Italian music from a central stage. We manoeuvre through the narrow gaps between tables and find our seats. It is comical to see men heaving their chairs from one side to the other so that giant-bottomed women can wedge into position with enormous bustles tilted to one side.

We settle at our table and soon realise we have struck it lucky with our companions for the evening: a Norwegian couple, impossibly blond-wigged and beautiful, and a lively Greek husband and wife who come annually for Carnevale. On the other side of them is an exquisitely dressed Italian duo and then the only (slightly) jarring notes, a bearded American and his Mexican fiancée. Unlike everyone else at the table, she is unsettlingly quiet – perhaps, I surmise, because she speaks almost no English. That doesn't explain, however, why her companion is equally taciturn. Both of them look faintly horrified when our MC for the evening, a tall and camp bewigged fortune teller with jangling jewellery and a satin turban, bounds up to our table and, theatrically pausing beside Peter, gives him a loud smacking kiss.

The banquet part of the evening passes in a joyous flurry of prosecco and astoundingly good food: prawn cocktails, seafood risotto, fish served with tomatoes and olives and capers, and lots and lots of wine. My resolve to not drink wantonly is forgotten somewhere between magically refilled glasses of vino rosso and bianco. In between courses we dance and chat, and the Norwegians show us pictures of their favourite glacier (could anything be more magnificently *Norwegian*?), cabaret-style performers appear onstage, we mingle with other guests and then, inexplicably, an Elvis impersonator appears at our table and sings 'You Were Always on My Mind'. It is so sweet and strange that we, along with most of the other partygoers, get up and slow dance at our table. The room is crammed with feathers and large skirts swaying and everyone is smiling and clapping and oddly moved and I meet my rose-prince from downstairs (he is Wolfgang Amadeus Mozart, but is also Brian-from-Los-Angeles-originally-from-New-York, and he is in Venice for the weekend to catch up with his Dutch friend Sander who lives in Switzerland).

After dessert (cherries and cream and flaky pastry), we drift to another corner of the palazzo, a beautifully decorated ballroom with painted ceilings, where velvet couches have been pushed back against wallpapered screens, around a huge central Persian rug. Our long-haired compere is in full flight by this stage. He and the other entertainers announce that we are going to learn to minuet, a revolving dance where we point toes, curtsy and swap partners. Everyone is by now well-moisturised so even the most simple moves are a challenge. Our gypsy king, clearly enjoying himself, calls out the steps in Italian and laments our bungling efforts with feigned despair, slapping the side of his head and dramatically yelling 'DIS-ASS-TER!' in heavily Euro-accented English while he lurches around the room with his knees buckling beneath him, mimicking our movements. This, of course, makes the whole room roar with laughter. There are more circle dances – men on the outside and ladies in the middle – where the steps our hosts call out become so mischievously complicated that we end up converging in the middle of the room in a crush of heaving, warm, laughing bodies. It is so joyful. It feels exactly like I imagine it would have hundreds of years ago, if you were fortunate enough to be at a ball in a palace. It is transporting and liberating. It is sorcery.

I can't remember making our way downstairs to the afterparty, a disco with flashing lights and modern music and more newcomers, but suddenly I am dancing with a black-cloaked man with a full-face mask, from which protrudes a dramatic curved beak. He tells me he is a plague doctor, which feels ominous but also perfect. I have a big and hilarious conversation with Amadeus Brian Mozart. He tells me about his life and his company in LA, how he works with lots of Australians and how he is on a plane home first thing in the morning, which is now mere hours away. We try to exchange phone numbers but it all seems extremely difficult. His feet are killing him in his rented buckled shoes, which are not even that high, but I always find it *deeply satisfying* when men attempt high heels and realise the agony of them. We decide to dance through the pain and also arrange to meet in New York later in the year, and then I am ready to leave, so I go find Petie.

He is dancing in a group, with the long-beaked mask of the plague doctor now cradled under one arm. He has angled it so that the disco lights creepily shine through the empty eyeholes like laser beams and he keeps saying in a European accent, 'Haff you met my friend? He iss a doctor!', which is ridiculous but also extremely amusing. Everyone is raucous and back-slapping and we go to leave our newfound friends because we can't bear the enchanted night to end but it is also my life-policy to always bail before they turn the lights on and what is moonlit and shimmering becomes fluorescent-lit and earthbound.

Outside in the quiet cold, as we take a moment to orient ourselves, it becomes abundantly clear that, while I am tipsy, my husband is *absolutely smashed*. He is so drunk, he is hiccupping, and he grabs my arm happily and says, 'This way,' and lurches off through a deserted alleyway. Even though I have a poor sense of direction, it seems opposite to the way we arrived and I say, 'I think it's back that way,' but he is bossy-drunk and confident with the arrogance of one who always knows the way, so I obediently follow him.

At first it is fun walking through the empty streets of Venice under the lightening sky. But we walk and walk, down laneways and across bridges and come to a couple of dead ends and have to double back, and we seem to not be passing anything familiar. My phone runs out of charge and Peter's is low on battery but when I question where we are, he fumbles for it and stares at it glassily and then says things like 'Oh, I seeeee!' or ominously 'Oops!' or 'It's okay, now I know where we are' and by then we have been walking for sooo long that I no longer see the beauty of early morning Venice because my feet are blistered and hurting from trudging kilometres over hard wintry stone. The magic has dissipated and my knees are aching with cold, and then I trip over my skirt and I collapse in a heap of silken brocade on a bridge. Peter tries to help me up but he is still belching and I can't get up because he has his stupid drunken foot on my giant hooped underskirt. When I go to slap his calf away that makes him giggle so hard he collapses on top of me, which makes me also laugh helplessly even though things are not really funny and I need to go to the toilet and I want to be in bed and drunk people are SO ANNOYING.

I realise the only way we are getting home is if I take charge. I look around and see a hotel foyer shining bright so I gather myself up and hobble inside. The dozing night clerk looks slightly startled by my sudden appearance and is helpful but does not know our hotel. I ask where the *Accademia* is and he knows that landmark, of course, and pulls out a map to show me. All I see is the huge curve of the Grand Canal and, with it, the crushing realisation that we are miles away. Literally, we have walked to the other side of Venice. I tell Peter, and he can see how annoyed I am, so he says, 'Don't worry, we'll get a taxi,' and I am all, 'What taxi? Show me a taxi!', motioning despairingly at the deserted waterways. Just then a boat chugs past, and Peter, like a marooned man on an island, waves a frantic SOS and yells at the driver to stop. The driver looks up at us, points behind him and tillers off.

From a side canal, a taxi-boat miraculously appears. Peter hollers at it, jumping up and down in his satin knickerbockers and brandishing his plumed hat, and the boat pulls up to the tiniest sideways jetty in the history of humankind. The driver says it will cost eighty euros to get back to our hotel but it wouldn't matter if it was a thousand dollars – I am so grateful that help is here. We inch our way down perilously slippery wooden steps onto the narrow walkway to the swaying boat. It is lovely and warm inside, with its upholstered cushions and dark walnut panelling, and I sink back, overcome with relief and exhaustion. Peter, by contrast, is really struggling – his drunkenness exacerbated by the motion of the boat – and he is lying on the opposite seat, face down, now alternating his hiccupping with moaning. Yes. He is actually *moaning*. Out loud. It is a solid twenty-minute trip back to our hotel and by the time we arrive and find the secret button to grant us after-hours access and get upstairs, it is nearly two hours since we left the ball. I manage to unlace my costume and crawl under the covers of one of the double beds.

Peter attempts to climb in after me but I am in no mood to share with him. I push him onto the other bed and with my last, tattered shreds of wifely compassion, remove his knickerbockers and shoes.

We pass out, and wake just before lunch.

I am surprisingly refreshed, the adventure and misadventure of the night before – after a great, deep sleep – now making me smile. I am also full of largesse because Peter is suffering doubly; firstly, from his richly deserved, head-thumping hangover and also with a bout of sheepish embarrassment. I go downstairs to the remnants of the buffet breakfast we have missed and come back up with coffee and croissants.

While we have our bed picnic, Peter blearily squints at his phone.

'Fucking hell,' he says, doing a double take that would be comical if he wasn't so clearly perturbed.

'What is it?' I ask. '*What?*'

'They are shutting down Venice,' he says, reading. 'Because of coronavirus. They are cancelling Carnevale. They are closing museums and restaurants. They are shutting the whole city.'

I cannot believe it. The plague we have heard about is here. In Venice. Where we are. Without our children.

DIS-ASS-TER.

The coronavirus outbreak in Italy is in Lombardy – between Bologna and Milan. We are worried there will be a mass exodus out of Venice so I get online and book tickets on tomorrow morning's train back to Bologna. That night, Peter and I venture out for our last meal in Venice. We walk without purpose and end up at a part of Venice that feels open to the ocean. Despite the wide walkway fronting the water, it is utterly deserted.

We wander past a fancy hotel, and the restaurant looks so cosy and warm-lit and inviting we decide to have dinner there. The dining room is nearly empty – there are maybe a dozen diners in a room designed for a couple of hundred. We over-order: seafood and oysters; schnitzel. We drink wine, even though last night's festivities and today's news have rendered us quiet and a bit shabby. Our waitress is wearing silicone gloves. Everything feels weirdly, eerily strange. Bleak. Like end days.

As we eat, some Carnevale-dressed stragglers drift past the window, a small clutch of clowns. A couple of noblemen and women. They are off to the last parties before Venice is shut down; like ghosts, they disappear into the sea mist.

The next morning we are packed and early at breakfast, and end up talking to an Englishman and his New Zealand wife who are there with their tween daughter. They live in Switzerland, where the man is a banker. When he speaks about the virus outbreak in Italy, his tone is amusedly condescending.

In Switzerland, he says, the police would already be in the streets, making sure lockdown is adhered to. Here in Italy, people have gone skiing for a week; treating the extra week off school as though it is a holiday.

Peter and I are guiltily silent. We had spent our morning packing and planning exactly that. Still, there is something I do not like about this man's tone.

He doesn't notice our lack of enthusiasm for his conversational gambit and continues, his mood jolly.

'Ah well,' he says. 'You know the European joke about why Italy is shaped like a boot?'

We shake our heads. We don't know it.

He laughs. 'Because you can't fit that much shit in a shoe!'

He roars with laughter, and though the joke is not without merit, it also hurts me. We love the Italians. We love their shoulder-shrugging attitude to life. We love their hospitality. Their warmth. We love their optimistic pessimism. This outbreak is terrible and frightening but the inference that the Italians are somehow to blame for it doesn't sit well with us. It is strange, this rush of protective instinct.

I want to say to the man: 'Who loves the Swiss?' but I don't.

Instead, we head to the front counter, where the manager who first checked us in is now waiting to bid us farewell.

We say our goodbyes, and thank him for the lovely visit.

'*In bocca al lupo*,' we say. (Good luck. May you travel in the mouth of the wolf.)

The hotelier comes around from behind his desk. He shakes hands with Peter. Clasps my own.

'We will see you next time,' he says, with an incline of his head. Then he straightens, and sweeps an arm towards the window. Outside, Venice shines like treasure.

'Here we will be,' he says. 'Floating on the sea, but not going anywhere.'

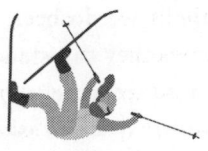

27
WHITE WEEK

Even though coronavirus has now arrived in northern Italy, and our schools (international and language) have been closed, no one is really sure what is happening, or how serious it might be. This is the week Italians call 'White Week', the first holiday after Christmas, in February, when Europeans take advantage of all manner of snow pursuits.

We are in a tiny ski village in the alps about three hours from Bologna near a larger town called Canazei, a popular tourist destination in the Dolomites. It is the second winter we have ventured to the little chalet we have found here. It is a classic, sloped roof *Sound of Music* style building, snuggled up against a base of soaring cliffs cloaked in hay-coloured winter grass and topped by snow. The setting is idyllic – you could imagine a plaited Heidi skipping down the hill to milk her grandfather's goats. It is not fancy. Like so many places we have discovered on our travels, it is not glamorous but it is cosy and clean, and it feels like ours. The lodge provides half-board and while the rooms are small and basically equipped – in the expectation that you will spend little time in them – the food is plentiful: a buffet breakfast with cheese and meats, pickled onions, salad and bread rolls; and a hearty five-course meal of dumplings, soup, pasta and meat for dinner, when the patrons who have been in the snow all day roll in for sustenance. Like I said, it is not fancy but because it is familiar, the owner Stefano is friendly and the kids are excited by it, we have found our way back there again.

Peter and the boys are skiing, kitted out in their own snow gear. Last year we were caught out by our Australian assumption that you could rent ski clothes here as we do back home. In Europe, where many learn to ski as soon as they can stand upright, everybody has their own snow outfits. So last February when Peter turned up to the ski-rental place with the boys in tow and asked about also hiring pants and jackets, the young guy running the place was nonplussed. Hiring skis is one thing but who would want to hire clothing worn by other people? Eventually, sympathetic to the plight of the strange family gaggle in front of him, he produced a box of waterproof ski-gear unsold from previous seasons, and let my husband rifle through those. As a consequence, the men in the family now have their own ski outfits, which makes it much easier for them to head to the ski-lift on our first morning. They have all risen early, while Sunday and I laze about, only leaving our tiny rooms when the cleaners insist on it. We wander down into the little village, past the local horses resting under blankets, hitched to their festive red shiny sleigh, to see which of the dozen or so shops is open. It is a German–Italian town so, as well as the local supermarket, hairdresser and assorted hotel restaurants, there is a wood-carving shop that sells tea towels and slippers, and several butchers. One of them has a portrait of a cheery pig outside, seemingly oblivious that inside, the store sells nothing but vac-packed slabs of speck, the German equivalent of bacon.

We are having a comfort-food lunch – me a giant wiener with sauerkraut and Sunday a lacklustre cheeseburger – when I check my phone and see a notice from the children's school. In accordance with instructions from 'the region', there will be no school next week. In fact, there will be no school until further notice. The teachers are on their week off, working on a plan for home learning. This is a 'gulp' moment for me. For school holidays are fun (and sometimes only bearable) because you know they won't last. The thought that the children will be home all day, every day . . . *mio dio*.

When the boys return from their skiing, I break the news to Peter. It seems almost unbelievable, looking around the crowded dining room, full of groups laughing and drinking and chatting, that a spectre looms.

Later, we are at the little bar at the rear of the chalet. I am wrapped in one of the knitted blankets covered in red and white hearts that is draped over every chair while Peter shares a grappa with the owner Stefano, his big white dog lying at his feet. Stefano tells us they are closing the chalet. For how long, they are uncertain, but after this weekend, the ski fields will be closed.

The next morning, Sunday and I get a taxi for the half-hour trip to the closest town, Canazei, where we will catch the train for the three-hour trip back to Bologna. The boys have decided to spend the last couple of days skiing.

On Sunday, they arrive home fresh faced and wind-burnt, giddy with mountain air and their Dolomites adventures. Jannie proudly shows me a video of him ski-jumping over a snow-covered car. It is hard to imagine that two years ago he was a novice on skis. It is impressive.

On Monday morning we get our new homeschool regimen off to a cracking start. I am fresh and cheerful, and crank out a batch of pancakes with all the fixin's – Gary-the-Butcher bacon brought back from Australia, with strawberries and cream and maple syrup.

The three older kids have to check into Google Classroom with their teachers which, under Peter's supervision, seems to work quite well. They are also supposed to each have their own 'space' to work so they are spread throughout the apartment. Sunday is upstairs in the small spare room that Peter has rejigged as my study; we have tipped the mattress on its side and propped it against the wall to make room for a glass-topped table that now serves as my desk. Lewis is working in his room; Artie is on the computer in the lounge, making good use of his Fortnite headphones that come with an attached microphone. Jannie, the youngest at ten, is simply assigned a list of tasks to complete for the day, which seems so far to consist of roaming around, building Lego and trying to sneak the iPad.

By eleven thirty, they are hungry again. I make a snack, homemade hommus, which is strangely expensive to buy readymade in Italy, though chickpeas are plentiful. This is a staple for us in Australia, where even the supermarket dip is delicious. I fry some flatbreads, the local piadina, and serve it with cucumber and carrots.

Then I go to the shops. Hot dogs for lunch.

At 3.30 pm, when school is 'out', I am frazzled. The children are hungry again. It is day one, and I am already out of ideas, and energy. All I have done today, it seems, is cook and do laundry and clean up after every meal, in time to start prepping for the next.

And I still have to make dinner.

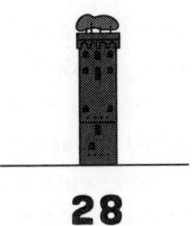

28

WE LIKE-A LUCCA

I am woken by the jabbering of a Russian.

It is early, especially for a Sunday. I lie there for a moment, disoriented, and then the church bells ring. I count them: seven tolls. This is clearly in breach of the Protocol of Sunday Conventions, when anything before 10 am is deemed barbaric and, really, should be prosecuted in some international court in The Hague. And yet, it is not the rich, somehow comforting tone of the church bells that has woken me. At 7 am on what is ostensibly a day of rest, I can hear the Russian woman in the room next door as loudly as if she was in bed next to me. She is actually yelling, first in her native tongue and then in English and seems to be negotiating a divorce. ('We are each paying five or six thousand a month. This is not necessary!') And though I obviously don't know the phantom ex-partner she is bellowing at on the phone, I am firmly on their side.

After our first intensive fortnight of homeschooling, Peter and I both felt the need for a change of scenery and have escaped to Tuscany for the weekend with the two little boys. We are still permitted to travel within our region so we have returned to Lucca – the first Italian town we ever visited together – which is a lovely idea. On the two-hour drive from Bologna, we comment on how unusually empty the roads are. Peter even drives in the fast lane, a feat he usually finds impossibly stressful because of the 160 kilometres per hour required by the tailgating Italians.

Lucca is lovely – a fortified medieval town, which means it is surrounded by a giant wall. Within the confines of the soaring stone escarpment are charming laneways, shops and churches. Usually, the place is full of Italian and foreign visitors, even this early in the year.

But now it is quiet. I mean, not our room, obviously, with our vocal neighbour. But the town itself, normally bustling with tourists and locals, is relatively empty. This is unheard of for Tuscany, which is glorious in every season and attracts visitors by the hundreds of thousands from all over the world. Not at the moment. In fact, I only booked our accommodation as we were walking down the stairs to our car in Bologna, so confident were we that we would find room at the inn.

Our bed and breakfast really is a sweet place. It is called L'Antica Bifore and is inside the old walled town of Lucca in a line of shops that wend up to a stunning oval-shaped piazza. Lucca was the birthplace of Puccini, the composer, and in the Italian manner of celebrating their artists, there are statues of him dotted throughout the town. Our accommodation is owned and run by an Italian/Irish couple (Stefano and Brigid – not hard to tell who comes from where) who greeted us warmly the afternoon before with maps and recommendations for dinner but, in keeping with the new coronavirus caution that surrounds us, no kisses.

The apartment itself is built into an old tower above a pizza restaurant, four bedrooms that open off a central room with a mini-kitchen. When I say 'old', I mean it in a European way: the tower dates from the 1300s, a concept that never fails to fill us Australians with awe. The antiquity is clearly evident in Artie and Jannie's room which is snug, with a double bed sandwiched between exposed internal brick walls. The owners have made it cosier by painting the plastered parts of the wall with frescoes of climbing green vines festooned with pink flowers. They have hung rich crimson curtains, framing the little balcony windows which look out over an internal courtyard shared by other apartments. It is stylish and lovely. Nonetheless, it has a distinctly 'former-prison-tower' vibe.

The boyos are fully onto the slight creepiness of their sleeping quarters. As I tucked them into bed the night before, Jannie pointed to some deep gouges in the terracotta bricks.

'Ith that for where they would chain up the prithoners?' he asks, his lisp accentuated by the slight frisson of fear that clearly motivated the question.

I dismiss his uncertainty with a practised parental heartiness, assuring him that the tower was used for only friendly purposes. 'It was where they used to keep the horses,' I chirrup cheerily. 'In winter, when it was too cold for them outside!' The beauty of the ten-year-old. He accepts my explanation, which is clearly ludicrous, unless horses seven hundred years ago could climb stairs. Still, he is comforted, even more so when I promise to leave both our bedroom doors open so he and Artie can come to us if they are scared in the night.

Peter and I are sharing a room across the common lounge from theirs. It is equally beautiful, with huge arched bottle-bottom green and amber windows which open directly onto the busy strip below. Directly beneath us a sweet and nut stall has laid out its rainbow array of wares. Across the narrow lane, fifteen metres away, if you had really stretchy arms, you could reach out and touch the white marble church opposite.

Between our room and the little boys' is a Danish couple with a baby. We only know this because when we checked in, Stefano, our kindly host, tells us and I note the slightly apologetic tone to his voice. As it transpires, his trepidation turns out to be unnecessary. Once or twice during the night we hear the tiny, lovely squeak of a hungry newborn. I am half-waiting for it to escalate but it doesn't. In the morning, the little family have apparently packed up and left, without us even being aware of their departure.

And this is interesting, in this nose-to-tail breakdown of European cultural characteristics. I mean, it's hardly an exhaustive study, but we are living the bleary proof of it: a considerate Scandinavian couple with a new baby officially make less noise than a solitary self-absorbed Russian woman with a mobile phone.

'We need to come to agreement on this!' she yells in the room next door. 'Are we in agreement?'

No, Svetlana, we are not in agreement.

My husband taps lightly on the plaster wall that separates our room from hers. She ignores it, or maybe she can't hear it over her increasingly impassioned monologue. Either way, she keeps yelling. I roll over and check my phone.

And there it is: the news we have been dreading. In the now daily updates of the coronavirus, as it spreads through northern Italy, it is clear that there is growing cause for concern.

The news this morning is from my school mothers WhatsApp group. Instead of the normally innocuous local knowledge – lunch invitations, dental referrals, school concerts and activities – the group chat is now dedicated to coronavirus updates.

There has so far been a daily escalation of the virus's spread: 120 diagnosed in Lombardy; forty-four dead. Outbreaks in Milano. There are reports of several doctors who have been infected; three of whom have died. Around the world, the coronavirus is spreading but nowhere faster, it seems, than in northern Italy, where we have brought our family to live.

There is a map with entire regions covered in red. These are the 'hotspots' where the viral outbreak is the worst. The graphic is accompanied by an official government press release. I start reading it aloud to Peter then realise it is too important to leave to my faltering Italian. I copy and paste into Google Translate. The news is as bad as we anticipated; not as bad, we suspect, as it's going to be.

I get out of bed and pad out to the communal kitchen to make coffee. The Russian is already out there, still bellowing.

I can barely look at her.

Peter and I get dressed and make our way downstairs. We carry our bags to the car, which is parked on the town outskirts, then walk back to a bike store and hire bikes to ride around the famed walls. The friendly American who runs the shop is coughing but assures us she has not got the virus. She is more concerned, she tells us, about the quietness of the town: the businesses around her going broke, the bike events being cancelled. In ten years as an Italian, she says she has seen nothing like it. We buy the boys some new bike shirts. She tells them to also choose some socks from the shelf behind them and they are delighted, agonising over their gift-with-purchase. Outside, the sun is gleaming as we ride up to the perimeter of the town. While the streets below are quiet, the circuit above is relatively humming. There are walkers and families squeezed into pedal-cars, and couples cuddling in the weak-but-warm sunshine. A young woman runs past us, chasing a puppy that is dragging a branch in its mouth. Children play on the swings and gleefully call to their parents as they soar.

Below, our journey home awaits.

On the drive back to Bologna, we listen to a local Italian radio station. There is an upbeat pop song playing. I can only understand snatches of the lyrics, but in the back seat, Jannie sings along with gusto. His friends sing it at school, he tells us. He knows every word. I am struck by how incongruous everything feels. Outside, the breathtaking scenery whizzes past: fields and fields of neatly pruned vines and well-kept farmhouses with smoke puffing from stone chimneys and fruit trees in early blossom. Nature's bounty awaits.

But spring is not yet upon us. Alongside the roadway, there are still the stark branches of trees that, stripped of their leaves by the winter, reach spidery, thin fingers to the sky.

To an Australian, where the native trees are not deciduous, it is a bleakly beautiful but ominous sight. Among the naked branches, I notice, it is easy to see the nests that birds have built for their summer homes. I wonder where they go in winter, the birds.

We pull into a service station. Peter wants to fill up the tank with petrol, even though it is three-quarters full. 'Just in case,' he says. I don't ask in case of what. The little boys, weary from their sing-along and our morning bike ride, have fallen asleep in the back seat. I go inside and order a couple of coffees from the lady serving food behind the counter. Then, from the small shelf of groceries behind the counter, I select a four-litre tin of olive oil to take home.

Just in case.

On Monday night, the Italian prime minister gives a live press conference. There are to be no more Red Zones, he says. Now there is an Orange Zone. Within the *Zona Arancione* there will be only essential travel: no gyms, no cinema, no restaurants or bars to remain open after 6 pm. There will be no schools receiving pupils. No public gatherings. No weddings or funerals allowed.

And this is the real kicker; the *whole country* has been declared the Orange Zone, from the tip of the boot in the south to the over-the-knee, where it adjoins Austria.

Basically, the entire nation of Italy has been shut down. And we are now shut down within it.

29

SUPERMARKET SWEEPS

Sunday morning. Since the nation-wide shutdown, there has been an increased police presence on the streets and a definite shift in mood outside. Even though we are allowed out of the house to buy essentials, I'm finding it increasingly unappealing to make the small shopping trips necessary to feed everyone. I am nervous I will be stopped by the police. Peter and I debate the exposure-to-virus daily odds: are we better off in small stores, having closer contact with staff, or going to a larger outlet with more space and anonymity?

The former is readily available to us – we have been walking to our local stores every day or so to buy milk, meat, bread and vegetables, but that requires three or four stops. Now we also have to take a ticket from the dispensers installed outside the stores, and wait our turn to be allowed inside. Although there have been no issues with supply of produce here – and none of the vicious/amusing/embarrassing/crazy/panicked brawls over toilet paper that have put Australia on the viral meme map – it is still difficult to buy enough for our family of six on foot.

Today Peter and I decide that we will drive outside the walls to a larger supermarket, where we will not only be able to bulk-buy some essentials, but also be able to load up the van. This is double happiness for me. Because we are not allowed to travel in groups, we will have to leave the children at home. The thought of going beyond the walls is already a huge treat. But without children? In our new reality, this is the equivalent of a honeymoon in Tahiti, so much so that I take an extra ten minutes to do my hair and dress in nicer clothes than I normally would for a day at home. When we are ready, Peter and I practically dance down our front stairs to the car.

At the supermarket, the underground car park – normally a chaotic mechanical ballet of Italian driving and duelling trolleys – is quiet and orderly, so much so that we actually get a park near the escalator that takes us up to the main level. This is unheard of. So far, we are definitely winning the supermarket sweeps. On our way upstairs, a masked security guard greets us. He is surprisingly friendly (most people are pretty dour at the moment) and, in Italian, tells that that upstairs is *'tranquilla'*. It is quiet, he says. We have chosen a good time to come.

When we emerge upstairs, we go to enter the supermarket through the front turnstiles, the way we normally do, but are blocked by more security, who tell us we have to do a one-way loop to join the queue already waiting to enter. At about thirty people, the line is not huge, but since everyone is required to stand a metre apart (not including trolley-length) it stretches back into the mall, past the other shops selling makeup or children's wear or bedding, that are, of course, shut. The line stretches right back to the lovely little bar that we normally stop at for an espresso after shopping, or in the evening, for an aperol spritz and a bowl of complimentary crisps or little sandwiches. It always delights us – to have a drink and an aperitivo snack after shopping. The waiters behind the counter wear crisp navy uniforms that make them look like they work at a five-star hotel, rather than in a shopping mall. But not today, of course. Today, the bar is also closed.

Another security guard approaches. He tells us that we are not allowed to stand together. Nor are we allowed to enter the store together. No matter. We are nearly inside. I am curious to see how many supplies are on the shelves.

Italy, by the way, is not like Australia, where essentially two supermarkets have a stronghold on people's grocery needs. Here, there are a number of companies – Conad, Coop, Pam, Carrefour,

Aldi, Lidl and Meta, among others. As well as the larger stores, most of these also have smaller outlets in the centre, where we live.

We are at our favourite supermarket – part of a chain found only in the north of the country. It is called Esselunga, and it is really beautiful, if such a thing is possible. It is huge – and though it is just a regular supermarket, such is the Italians' love and respect for food that in Australia it would be considered high-end. As well as a breathtaking array of pre-packaged smallgoods and cheeses and pasta, there is also a fresh prosciutto and cheese counter that covers fifteen metres, behind which stand a battalion of white-coated, chef-hatted men and women.

It is such a contrast to back home. Sometimes, in my part-time Coles deli job, we would pre-wrap luncheon meat and chicken loaf into packages of 250 grams (the most common order) and price them, so that we could just hand over the butcher-paper bundles. Here, that would be regarded as sacrilege. In Italy, everywhere you go, your meat is freshly sliced. In restaurants, in delis, in bars and even in supermarkets. It makes it a time-consuming process, for sure – to queue up, select your prosciutto (cured or cooked), from several dozen legs on display, and then watch the counter staff painstakingly slice off the tissue-thin slices, before wrapping them like gifts in foil and paper. But it is also very civilised. And it makes everything taste delicious.

The bakery section is similarly impressive. It sells everything from pasta dura loaves, baguettes and olive-oil focaccia with olives or rosemary or onions or simply salted, as well as custard and chocolate croissants, apple tarts and myriad biscuits, bags of soft pizza dough, and a dozen varieties of the dry, crispy rolls favoured here in the north.

In the fruit and veg department, through which you enter, every piece of produce is artfully laid out in huge piles, and clearly marked – not only with its country of origin, but also its region. There are blood oranges from Sicily; lemons from Sorrento; giant hothouse strawberries or cherries laid out in balsa-wood boxes. There are at least twelve varieties of garlic (Italians, naturally, are militant about which type is most suitable for which dishes – to me, the bulbs are interchangeable). I once counted the varieties of onions: eighteen. Brown and white and pink. Small and large. Yellow and green. Then there are scallions and spring onions and salad onions and Spanish onions and shallots; bunches of parsley as big as a bride's bouquet. Seven varieties of cabbage; one called '*cuore*', which is shaped like its name: in the form of a heart. The other side of the aisle is entirely devoted to tomatoes. These come in every conceivable shape and size and are labelled sweet (*dolce*) for salads or snacking, the more meaty and ripe for passata, green for pickling, and tiny yellow pear-shaped bulbs grown down south in the famous volcanic soil near Mount Etna.

Basically, shopping for food here is fun and fascinating. The variety and array of produce is staggering, but, despite that, some things that we would consider staples are hard to find. There is no cheddar cheese. Barely any coriander. Sour cream is rare (though crème fraîche is a handy substitute). And then there are products that are ludicrously expensive. Peanut butter, for instance, is about twelve dollars a jar. Maple syrup is sixteen dollars for a small bottle. Pistachios are crazy expensive, as are most nuts – except for the locally grown hazelnuts.

The pasta aisle (just the hard pasta) goes forever. The fresh pasta selection is mind-boggling.

And even though there are things that are frustrating (weighing and pricing your fruit and veg yourself; packing your own groceries) I would move to Italy in a heartbeat, just to do my grocery shopping.

Today, though the machinations of shopping are different, the store is comfortingly familiar. The shelves are full. The shoppers, though masked, are calm and engrossed in the business of looking at labels, and surreptitiously squeezing and peering at fruit. There are rules that seem strange; a security guard tells Peter and I we are not permitted to speak to each other, so we mime across the store to each other when we have made selections. When we take our laden trollies to the checkout, the same person has to unload onto the conveyor belt, then race through and pack the groceries at the other end. I nominate Peter for the job, while I make the most of our time in the light, bright surrounds. The plenty is reassuring. Even so, we have bought enough staples for several weeks. Our bill comes to over a thousand dollars.

For the past few weeks, Peter has been leaving the house in the dark, to go for a bike ride up in the hills. It is part of his routine here, and though we have resolved to keep enjoying our limited freedoms until they are removed, he has been increasingly anxious about it.

Today, he leaves earlier than normal. It is about six o'clock in the morning, early enough that I am still asleep when I hear him prise open a shutter for a glimmer of early morning light, then move around in the dim bedroom, putting on his riding shorts, jacket and gloves.

After he has gone, I get up and make breakfast, French toast. The younger boys, who would normally have basketball matches today, are awake; the teenagers of course, still asleep. As the three of us sit down to eat, Peter's place at the table is conspicuously empty. It is well after 9 am but he is still not home. I hope he hasn't had an accident, although with the absence of any traffic on the roads, there really is no safer time to ride. When he is still not back by ten o'clock, however, I start to worry.

An hour or so later, he returns, shaken. He was stopped by the police only a couple of hundred metres from our house. They were initially quite aggressive, he said, but calmed down when they realised he was not being deliberately disrespectful. Still, they detained him for over forty minutes, questioning him about where he has been riding and what he is doing in Italy. Our status as non-Italian-speaking outsiders marks us clearly as 'other' and arouses suspicion. (On the street outside the butcher the other day, a lady heard me and Lewis speaking English to each other and asked if we were tourists. 'What are you doing here?' she asked. We told her we lived in Bologna. That confused her enough to end the conversation, but it was a strange encounter.) The police this morning were equally suspicious about Peter. They have issued him paperwork that we think is a fine. He has been told he will need a lawyer. Luckily, our landlord Ferdinando is a lawyer. The form is in Italian. We try to decipher it: it says the police are suing Peter for breaching the ordinance about being outside.

Until last night, exercise outside was still permitted, so long as you maintained a distance of two metres from anyone else. Now, there have been new restrictions issued, as they seem to be every couple of days.

We will need a permit to go to the supermarket now. Even people with dogs are no longer allowed to take them outside.

We do not know how, or when, this will end. We only know we will find out.

30

THE FIRST DAY OF SPRING

The days are blurry as we make our way through March. Normally we would be engaging in early spring activities: primavera flower shows and day-trips. Instead, we have completed another week of lockdown and our first month of homeschooling. It is Saturday, and so we all sleep in. I don't know why we are so fatigued. Doing nothing, as it transpires, is oddly exhausting.

Only the younger boys are full of pep. Peter has implemented a home workout for them, with a skipping rope, a stationary bike he was given from his Pilates instructor and the imposing front staircase to our apartment. The soaring stairs used to seem decadently elegant, forty-four of them rising to the terrazzo landing outside our front door. Now the stone steps are also a practical solution to the problem of how to stay fit when you are no longer permitted outside.

Peter has Artie and Jannie doing a circuit. Fifty skips. Three flat-out minutes on the bike. Twenty stair runs. Twenty push-ups. He times them, so their natural competitiveness drives them to outdo each other. They come panting into the kitchen where I am making a batch of most unBolognese-style bolognese sauce – no delicate coddling of ingredients – just a smoosh of vegetables and meat I have bunged in a pot together. They are jostling each other, my littlest ones, sweating and laughing. I slice up an apple and give it to them. They receive it like a gourmet platter.

Thank goodness they are so lovely. Thank goodness I am not trying to do this alone, I think.

Around the world, the virus is spreading. Word from friends in Australia is short on detail, rich in imagery. 'People are going crazy here,' seems to be the pithy summation. One moment the federal government decrees there is to be no lockdown, only for the state governments to overrule it, deciding that schools and all non-essential businesses must close. Then the politicians have a joint summit and change that decree. The indecision, even from afar, is confusing and crippling.

It is in some way understandable even though Australia is, at this point, relatively unaffected. Australia is so far away, at the bottom of the currently Eurocentric globe, but my Antipodean countryfolk have seen what is looming and they are full of fear. Quite frankly, they are right to be. Although their behaviour may seem extreme – squabbling over toilet paper and stripping bare supermarket shelves, all the while flocking to the famous Bondi Beach to enjoy a swim and sunbathe on a 36-degree day in the face of looming social isolation measures – I get it.

It is worse, I think, to see the tidal wave coming. Like white mice trapped in a lab maze, there is scurrying and panic, trying to find a way out. Doomsday preppers, once so mocked and maligned, suddenly seem like the smart ones. In Italy, by contrast, there was little warning. We were suddenly thrust amongst it. And while that left little time to prepare, it also left no time to waste on panic.

In our confinement, neighbours and school parents check in with each other regularly, through messages and WhatsApp groups, and the occasional conversation in the shared courtyard. Spirits here are decidedly subdued. Every evening, a government corona-watch website releases the new figures of those affected by the virus. And so far, even though the whole country has been urged to adhere to the 'stay at home' edict, the news is terrible. Newly diagnosed cases are increasing. Six thousand yesterday. On Friday 753 people, mainly elderly – lost their lives. It is well documented that they have died alone; these Italian elders, to whom family is everything. Such is the fear of contagion. Doctors and medical staff, the frontline warriors waging the battle for the rest of us, are also contracting the disease and dying, despite their masks and suits and goggles.

There is alarming footage released from ICU wards at Italian hospitals. It shows patients lined up in cramped wards, encased in plastic bubble-shaped tubes that are helping them breathe. They are wan or gasping for air, even the ventilated oxygen seemingly not helping. In the overwhelmed hospitals, beds are squeezed into hallways and waiting rooms. Government tanks are deployed to carry away the dead. They are scouring the land for room to bury them; the cemeteries in the north are full. Italy has one of the best healthcare systems in the world and it simply cannot cope. What does that mean for the rest of the world?

There are many theories as we wait for a downturn in the number of new infections. There is lots of talk about incubation times and exposure, and how we will see a decrease in cases but not until next week. I hope this is true. Because the feeling of doing all that is within your power (literally nothing), and that still not working is dispiriting, to say the least. To say the most, it is bleak and grim and frightening.

The news from China, believed to be the source of the outbreak, is more heartening. They have had their third day now with no new cases reported. Although that announcement should be cause for cautious celebration, it is also hard to accept that any figures sanctioned by the Chinese government can be believed. There is a growing sense that we don't know the truth about this virus. How it started. How many it has killed. The only thing we do know is that it is difficult to contain, and seemingly impossible to vanquish.

We only leave the house to get groceries at the mini-supermarket a five-minute walk from us or to do a quick drop-off of our organic rubbish to the central bin a hundred metres from our house.

This morning Lewis sloops into the kitchen. He wants to make dumplings, he says.

I am initially reluctant. That is a lot of work, I reason. It means we have to go to the Chinese supermarket about two kilometres from us. It is still in the centre but is down near the station, where my old radio studio was set up. And we have to get pork mince, which means another stop at the little laneway of butchers near the piazza where we used to live. Still, it will be a nice change from pasta, and a meditative exercise to spend the afternoon folding wontons. It is also a chance to stock up on some basics we are running low on – soya sauce, oyster sauce, vermicelli noodles, rice wine. Our Australian palates miss the flavours of Asian food, which has become a part of what we consider our home country's national cuisine. In Italy, it is hard to find.

Peter is not happy about our excursion. Police are patrolling outside, he reminds us, looking for people in breach of the ordinance that requires us to stay *a casa*, in our house. Across Italy, ten thousand people have so far been arrested for breaching the guidelines.

Still, we are permitted to leave the house to get food. I tell Lewis we will ride our bikes: me on my turquoise trundler, him on Peter's precious road bike. It is too far to venture out on foot and it makes sense to cover the most ground with the most speed. Less time equals less exposure to other people; less time out of the house.

Lewis straps on his backpack. I take a grocery bag and check that I have my phone, which has on it a copy of the official form explaining our reasons for being out on the street. I put our passports in my wallet in case we are stopped by the Carabinieri or the polizia, and we head down the stairs.

As we press the button to open the huge wooden doors that access the street from our car park courtyard, an old man enters. He has a mask on so at first I think it is Ferdi, our landlord. It is, in fact, Ferdi's brother-in-law, a twinkly-eyed older man who we sometimes see talking through his window to Edo, his two-year-old great-nephew, in their shared yard. We don't know him well but we are neighbours and it is nice to see someone cheery. We exchange friendly greetings before Lewis and I wheel past him onto the abandoned streets.

THE FIRST DAY OF SPRING

The ride to the other end of town is unexpectedly lovely. It is the first day of spring and the sun has clearly not heard about the coronavirus scare – it is golden and bright and warming. It is so pleasant outside that I am wearing only a light jacket; Lewis needs nothing more than a t-shirt and his treasured Western Bulldogs footy scarf. I have told him to bring this to cover his mouth and nose. He is initially resistant but I remind him of how skittish shopkeepers are when you enter their premises without face cover, although it is not compulsory. And we still don't have the surgical masks we see nearly everyone now wearing. In the absence of any formal face covering, I have taken to improvising with a brightly coloured hair scarf that is sewn onto an elastic strap. I pull it down over my mouth and nose, bushranger style. It is undoubtedly strange. But let's face it, these are strange times.

We follow the back laneways to our destination, along streets empty of all but the occasional pedestrian. Along the way, we pass several patrolling police cars. They slow down as they pass us but, aside from that, don't seem to show much interest. When we arrive at the Chinese store, there are already two customers inside so we wait on the kerb until we are summoned in. I am allowed to enter when the first customer leaves. Lewis joins me inside after the second shopper exits, at which point we have the whole store to ourselves.

Inside, the shelves are still relatively full. Only the fresh produce shelves – normally festooned with Chinese cabbage, daikon radish and starchy sweet potatoes – are bare (no coriander for us) but there is still plenty for us to buy. It is an unexpected treat to browse the shelves and examine the unfamiliar jars and packets. Dried shrimp. Tinned Chinese sausages. Tapioca flour.

Mindful of having to carry our purchases back in my bike basket and in Lewis's backpack, we stock up on noodles and sauces. I am thrilled to find a few Chinese bowls and side dishes sitting dustily on the shelves in the corner of the store. One of my frustrations at home – which I wasn't aware of until I had to produce eighteen meals a day – is our shortage of cups and crockery. I put the treasures in my basket with our other purchases and line up to pay. The Vietnamese lady at the till is now behind an improvised shield, a sheet of Perspex gaffer-taped onto the front edge of the checkout belt. I pay by card; she doesn't want to touch cash.

Laden as we are with our cache of fragile bottles and jars, I don't want to risk riding over the bumpy cobblestone lanes that we took to embark on our mission. And I am emboldened by our ten minutes of freedom – the sun on our faces and the pleasure of being on our bicycles.

We decide to make the journey home along Via Indipendenza, the wide main shopping boulevard that runs the length of the city. I have not been here since before lockdown but it is where all the big retailers have their premises: Zara, H&M and Nike. It is always an impressive sight but today it is extraordinary for a different reason. In all the shopfronts, the windows are still dressed and brightly lit. Store mannequins are adorned in pastels and floral prints, some draped in what was to be new spring wear; others featuring last season's specials. Shopfronts are painted with fluorescent pink and hi-vis yellow brushstrokes announcing sales: 50% *SCONTI*, final discount! This boulevard, normally abuzz with shoppers, strollers, wanderers and tourists venturing out of hotels, immigrants swiftly laying out their copy-designer wares on blankets, nonnas clutching their daughters' arms, sharply dressed men downing espresso at streetside cafes, and humming with taxis and buses and cyclists and joggers, is entirely, utterly deserted. As we pedal up the slight incline towards home, we can see the entire length of the normally crowded strip, our view unimpeded by any other living soul or vehicle, all the way to the Statue of Neptune, who still stands, trident aloft, at the main piazza.

The scene is so apocalyptic, it is hard not to think of Armageddon.

We pass another police car on the way home.

When we arrive back at the apartment, it is strangely quiet.

I peer over our balcony, where I can see Peter downstairs in the neighbours' yard. He has a book on his lap, while Artie and Jannie kick a football around the concrete path. Ferdi is also there, his distinctive cloth cap on his head. I can see from the tilt of his head that he and my husband are deep in conversation.

Later, Peter tells us our landlord was relaying a message from his brother-in-law. He was worried when he saw us leaving the palazzo earlier. Tell them they are not supposed to be riding bikes, he says.

I feel a surge of hot resentment. That's ridiculous, I respond. Firstly, we are allowed out to get groceries. And it is more practical to be on bikes than to walk. Peter, sensing my annoyance, assures me the message was passed on nicely. I'm sure it was, but it still rankles. I don't like feeling that we are being monitored. I mean, I know we are. In a block of apartments shared by Italians? Truly, *Big Brother* contestants would enjoy more privacy. Still, the momentary pleasure of my brief excursion with Lewis is soured.

We make the dumplings. The limitations of the tiny kitchen mean we have to cook them in batches in our one saucepan capable of steaming, and then try to keep them warm in the oven. Even though a few of them are dry, they are delicious. The six of us eat them at our long wooden table in the lounge room. I have made steamed rice and quick-pickled some thin sliced cabbage and carrot. Soya sauce and sweet chilli are set out in our new little side dishes. While we eat, Sunday mentions the September 11 World Trade Centre bombings. It is a somewhat surprising conversational meandering, but clearly not random. Even to her fourteen-year-old mind, the way the world works has raised questions. Everything seems like it may be a conspiracy.

That night in bed, Peter gives me the daily coronavirus update. Once again, it is bad. There has been no decrease in the number of those dying. Similarly, there are still thousands of new coronavirus cases being diagnosed. The virus, it would seem, is thriving, even as the rest of the country shrinks away.

And there is more bad news, a message relayed to me by a mother from school. From tomorrow, the supermarkets in Bologna will be closed on Sundays.

The decree is ostensibly so the staff can have a rest, which makes sense. It must be exhausting and stressful to be stacking shelves or, worse, trapped behind a checkout like a sitting duck while possibly infected strangers file in front of you with their grocery purchases. But for me, whose life has become focused on feeding my family, and whose faith depends on the ready availability of food, it is another restriction in our already constricted life.

We can no longer buy food on a Sunday.

I try to quell the rush of anxiety I feel while mentally I go through the list of food stocks we have. We have enough, I tell myself. And we do. We are definitely okay. It is important that I do not succumb to this debilitating fear. Anxiety, after all, is not only unhelpful, it is often irrational.

Still, as I fall asleep, I am reminded of the naked winter trees we saw driving back from Tuscany those few weeks ago. I feel more and more like the branches that surround us are losing their leaves. Our little nest is exposed, the woven sticks and twigs clearly visible against the stark grey sky, the six of us huddled inside. We have no real protection from predators, I realise. Especially not the invisible ones.

31

WHEN LIFE SERVES US LEMONS, WE MAKE LEMON TART

The mood in our house is subdued. It is our fifth week of homeschooling.

The days seem to be gathering momentum while being long, and though I try not to wish them away, I privately welcome any swiftness with which they pass. There is still no end date to our government-decreed house arrest, and the sense of novelty is long gone as we ploddingly approach the end of our third week of lockdown.

Peter and I are harbouring a secret from the children. Last week, after many protracted late-night discussions and persistent urging from our families, we enquired about flying back to Australia earlier than the end of year booking we already hold. Emirates Airways (which normally flies straight into Bologna) announced it would be making its final flights from Europe on Wednesday. When we tried to book flights last weekend, it was already impossible. No country, it seems, wanted Italian passengers, even in transit. So it is decided. Despite our yearning to be back in Australia, we are staying put.

It is not an easy decision to have foisted upon us but we rationalise it as best we can. My dad back home is susceptible to infection; he has had a lot of skin cancers and his immune system is already fragile from anti-cancer medication, so even if we were there we wouldn't be able to visit him. Or Peter's parents. And here, at least, we are in the routine of homeschooling, with three weeks of lockdown already under our belt. Still, it is hard to be away now. The children would like to be back in our home in St Kilda, with our yard, knowing that friends and family are near. Like us, the strangeness of everything makes them long for the familiar. But that is simply not possible. We downplay the disappointment to each other, but it is a bitter and strangely flavoured pill to swallow: to know that you cannot go home, even if you wish. I'm glad we never presented it to the children as a possibility.

There has been no official word in Italy on when this 'stay at home' period will finish. Though we were initially told it was until 3 April that date, now only a week away, will obviously not hold. Yesterday, the nation's death rate from coronavirus was nearly 700. Every day the numbers seem depressingly similar: too high. New cases are still being diagnosed in the thousands. Spain is now poised to overtake us as the most affected country, with the United States not far behind. It is dispiriting to watch the global numbers grow. Other countries' woes do nothing to alleviate our own, they only cement how inaccessible the whole world is becoming.

I am now relaying reports once or twice a week to various TV and radio shows in Australia. I have become something of a foreign correspondent, I think. Indeed, just like in wartime, the state and federal governments there seem in disarray: flip-flopping on lockdown measures, even as the numbers of deaths and diagnoses rise. Although I am careful to temper any doomsday feelings or predictions in my crosses, the fact is the situation is bleak and whatever I say seems to incense a large number of people, particularly when it is spun into a headline for the daily news sites. These elicit such vicious online attacks (particularly on Twitter, the last bastion of the self-righteous embittered, it seems) that even I, after twenty years of a public profile, am taken aback. I am ugly, they say. I am a fool. I am a 'stupid bitch', a 'pigdog' who is 'desperate to stay relevant'. Given that I abandoned my media career to move to Italy and *not* work, the latter accusation, in particular, is deeply ironic. And ugly I may be – I have barely looked in a mirror for five weeks. When I do, I undoubtedly look a little worn. We are sleeping and eating pretty well but the fact is I'm not being held hostage in a beauty salon with a coterie of staff. I'm a locked-down, love-bound domestic spending my days between a home classroom, laundry and kitchen, looking after the emotional and physical needs of six people. It's hard work.

It is extraordinary though, the odds of my having ended up here in the north of Italy, the European epicentre of this coronavirus outbreak. As my girlfriend Sophie says, it is as though I am a prophet – from only three weeks in the future. It seems inevitable that what we are experiencing in Italy will filter to Australia: the viral spread, the deaths. The head of European soccer was talking on the TV today. For the first time, he said, the whole world is on a level playing field. And for the first time in my life, a sporting official has expressed something that resonates with me. It is true: the coronavirus is a global scourge, scattering in its path jobs and freedoms and homes and lives.

Today we receive a sobering WhatsApp update: a father from school has the virus and is in hospital. His son is in Lewis's class and he is the third person we know who has been admitted to hospital. The first was another dad from school; the second, my lovely and gentle-humoured yoga teacher Claudia. She was (praise be) released by ambulance yesterday after six days on a ward and is at home recovering. Peter and I do some quick calculations; given that we know only 350 or so people here in Bologna, the fact that a trio of them have contracted this virus is alarming. Presumably there are also more people who have not been deemed ill enough to be hospitalised, and others we simply haven't heard about. Though we know the virus mainly claims the elderly as its permanent quarry, none of the three people we know afflicted by it are old. They are in their forties, previously strong and fit. This virus has rendered them weak and fevered and unable to breathe without medical intervention. It is vicious and predatory. It is a brute.

In bad times, as anyone grieving who has received the gift of a home-cooked meal on their doorstep knows, food is a simple salvation. Family meals remain a bright spot in our daily routine and Lewis has recently moved into this terrain with a zeal. His curiosity about what I am planning to cook, and his desire to help, is welcomed, but not without some trepidation. I think he's actually a bit bored with my culinary offerings. I've been schlepping out meals for six people three times a day for a looooooong time now – even before home confinement – so I'm fairly unimaginative in what I produce in the family cafeteria. Porridge or French toast for breakfast; sandwiches or pizza for lunch. For dinner, subject to availability: spaghetti bolognese or chicken schnitzels with salad; tandoori chicken and curries; lasagne or roast lamb with veggies. Lewis Lewis, by contrast, finds more ambitious and elaborate recipes to tackle. Jamaican spiced beef patties requiring pork and (impossible to find) beef lard. Pork and prawn dumplings in hot sauce. A replica of the tiny fried chicken pieces with garlic and chilli we once ate together in Sydney.

He's a natural cook – motivated, no doubt, by self-interest (a force never to be underestimated) – and generally when we end up in the kitchen together, we have a good time. Last night, after hearing Peter express his desire for lemon tart (a wish I determinedly ignored), Lewis announced that he will make one for his father. But here's the thing: my son has never made a lemon tart before. I have. I know it's quite a lot of work. And I know he will require my assistance.

So this afternoon, after the lemon-tart promise, I am prepping for the evening meal. I am looking forward to it – not the actual process of cooking for six in our very limited kitchen, but the meal itself. Lewis and I had an excursion to the butcher yesterday, where I bought a couple of Florence-style T-bone steaks, which are huge. (In the middle of our purchase, while other customers queued outside, the butcher looked at us curiously and asked something in Italian. He wanted to know if Lewis played for Virtus, the Bologna-based basketball team. Lewis, though well over six foot tall, has barely played basketball since we arrived. We told him 'no' and he nodded, but looked confused. It was a strange, but not unpleasant encounter.

Later, we realise it is because we are clearly foreigners. The butcher was obviously wondering why we – two Australians who speak poor Italian – would not have left this town.)

Anyway, the steaks. In the absence of a barbecue, I will cook the big fellas in our frypan with the ridges along the bottom. I have in mind a delicious mushroom and mustard creamy sauce, and will serve the steaks at the table, sliced, with steamed potatoes in garlic butter, green beans and zucchini.

Every time I cook I have to plan ahead. A regret of mine is that, before lockdown, we didn't get a chance to augment our meagre kitchen wares. Tonight, Peter reminds me of six weeks or so ago – in the sweet, simple, olden days – when he and I had idly wandered into the nonna-run op shop around the corner from us and debated whether or not to buy four secondhand IKEA cups for ten euros. I wanted them; he didn't.

'That's nearly twenty Australian dollars,' Peter had said, putting the secondhand blue-and-white china cups back on the shelf. 'That's ridiculous. They wouldn't cost that much in IKEA.'

He recalls that incident now as he is unstacking the dishwasher and marvelling at how precious our three cups and three mugs have become. I smile a little tightly at the reminiscence because I have actually harked back to it many times since, mainly when I go to make a pot of tea, and have to hunt through the house to find one of the half-dozen cups abandoned on desks and at bedsides. (I also recall the moment because at the time I was so irritated at my husband's penny-pinching, I walked out of the shop and left him there.) Now, of course, he would happily pay fifty bucks for that same unremarkable crockery. And in another month or so of home confinement, I reckon the nonnas could jack the price up to 150 dollars and he would still willingly fork over the cash. Nothing increases value like scarcity and in our Italian kitchen, which was meant to be a temporary base, plates and platters and pans are scant.

Because we have the tiniest, second-most-annoying galley kitchen in Italy (the most annoying was in our last apartment), and we are operating with a skeleton assortment of plates, cups and pans, I need to have a clear plan of attack when I cook. Every meal needs to be approached with a Napoleonic battle plan. Today it goes like this: if I peel the potatoes earlier and top and tail the beans, I can cook those first, then leave them on the kitchen table to stay warm while I fry the zucchini in the saucepan I have made the sauce in (once I have poured it into a jug). Then, voilà! – I will have the whole stovetop free for grilling the steaks.

It is a challenge cooking like this. I am constantly burning myself after getting stuck holding a scalding oven tray with nowhere to put it down. Or reaching for a clean plate and realising we have used them all. We are constantly emptying a fruit bowl so it can double as a serving dish, or sharing glasses at the table because we don't have enough clean ones and the designated table setters (Hello Jannie! Hello Artie!) have been too lazy or distracted to wash the dirty ones.

Still, we have been having some simply delicious meals, and because Peter (now in tandem with the younger children or Sunday) does the kitchen clean-up, the thought of cooking is not so arduous. Also, after the initial period of gritty adjustment, lockdown has rendered me infinitely more patient. There is not the surplus energy for frustration, or my previously rich motherlode of maternal rage. That can wait for peacetime, I think.

But now, in the middle of my own meal prep, Lewis is making pastry for the lemon tart, and at every step encounters another limitation in our kitchen arsenal. He is a messy cook, as most people granted the luxury of not having to do their own clean-up are, and has initially tried to make the pastry in a bowl at the kitchen table using the dough hooks on the electric hand beater. As a consequence, there is a snowfall of flour across the whole room. It also appears as though he has separated his eggs directly onto the tablecloth. Naturally, he hasn't bothered to remove it before starting his project and the cloth is now soaked with big slurps of sticky egg white.

Still, since Lewis has always been the most vocal opponent of our life in Italy I am happy he has found something he is excited by, and I bite my lip. It is also surprisingly satisfying, coming up with MacGyver-like solutions to our culinary cul-de-sacs. He goes to roll out his sticky pastry but is momentarily thwarted by the fact that we don't have a rolling pin; he ends up using a tall can of hairspray. When it is time to put the pastry into the pie dish we don't have, we are momentarily stumped. The baking tray I use for lasagne is too deep, as is a saucepan. I debate putting it in a frypan but worry about the plastic handle in the oven. Maybe I can cover it with foil, I suggest. Lewis finds a Phillips head screwdriver. 'I'll remove the handle, Mum,' he says. And he does.

As we move around the kitchen, he starts speaking in a mock Scottish accent. This makes me laugh, and he quickly takes it further; adopting the persona of an impatient and angry chef. In response, I become my own character – Susan, his hapless Irish assistant. Whenever he asks me to pass him something and I don't immediately respond, he puts me in a headlock: 'Yer a fool, Susan! A good-fer-nuthin fool!' In response, I hand him a utensil then pretend he has punched me in the stomach for my tardiness, doubling over with imaginary pain while still mumbling a humble 'Yes, chef. Sorry, chef'.

Scottish Lewis dishes out the abuse. Susan takes it with stoic and flat-footed doggedness. Between his sledges at how useless I am, we melt butter and squeeze lemons. I mutter passive-aggressive digs at his failed fictional restaurant and his lack of knowledge about 'blind-baking'. It is a fun game, if a little wild, and Peter, who is not given to accent-speaking or role-playing, watches us with a cross between a frown and a smile as he cleans up after us. Although he initially urges caution as Lewis drags me around the kitchen by my head, and I swat at him with a wooden spoon, it is undoubtedly amusing, and he is soon laughing.

'You two could have a cooking show,' Peter says.

It is such a funny idea, Lewis and I are delighted. And the Angry Chef and Sous-Chef Susan are such full-fledged, archetypal characters, it would actually make compelling watching.

A cooking show would be fun, I say to Lewis. What would we call it?

My eldest son looks around the kitchen we have been trapped in for weeks; at our bench crammed with saucepans and steaks and lemon rinds. He looks at the bags of rubbish – plastic and paper, waiting to be taken to the rubbish bins outside; at the table covered with pots of steaming potatoes and remnants of flour and pastry, illuminated by the last beams of afternoon sunshine filtering in through the shuttered windows.

'Shitaly,' he says.

'Let's call it "Cooking in SHITALY".'

It is such a perfect, unexpected summation of the situation we find ourselves in. The three of us laugh until we are gasping for breath.

That evening, after dinner, Peter and I are on the couch with the little boys. We are watching the movie *Groundhog Day*.

Lewis comes in carrying the big silver tray our landlord has left for us in the kitchen.

On it are four saucers with four slices of warm lemon tart.

It is so unbelievably delicious. Stunningly, gorgeously, decadently delicious.

I am glad we made it.

32

HAPPY ANNIVERSARY

I don't want to come across as some kind of perma-tanned, gypsy-clad Instagrammer posting platitudes in a hackneyed drifty font, but *there are unexpected blessings to being in lockdown* (ED: print in drifty font, please). Time itself is the main one. No rushing around is another. There is no need to hurry when you have nowhere to be. Like most blessings at this time, however, what makes the gift ultimately beneficial is also what makes it difficult.

So, when you have conflict with one of the five people with whom you are confined to quarters there is nowhere to hide. There is no 'giving each other space', distracting yourself with an outing, shopping or any social activity. There is no going to yoga to blow off some steam, no basketball or bike ride or walk on the beach. There is no mother to have a cuppa with to seek counsel, no delicious restaurant meal to lift your spirits. No cinema to transport you momentarily. No hairdresser to refresh your locks. No apology gift or flowers to buy. No wild night at a gig to remind you of who you are. No parties. No babysitters. No girlfriend to walk–talk a park circuit with. There is no job, no work, no office, no car. There is only you and them. There is no outlet. There is no diversion. There is no fresh air. So you have to sort things out. Like I said: a tough blessing.

This is the case as Peter and I approach our seventeenth wedding anniversary. Seventeen years ago, this coming Sunday, Peter Lewis and I were married on the top of a mountain in Victoria's high country. It was a most brilliant lost weekend. In an old alpine chalet, with eighty of our friends and family, and a brilliant ragtag band, we promised to love and honour each other. In sickness and in health. For better and for worse. My parents, even though I was five months pregnant with our first child (and they are devout Christians), were beaming with happiness.

My vivacious mum Anne mingled with our fancy-dressed friends and held court. My father Jan, so tall and handsome in his dress suit, walked me down the long steps onto the lawn where our guests awaited, righting me when my heel caught in the grass.

My beloved mother-in-law Maree read us the Irish blessing that still makes my eyes prickle with tears:

May the sun always be at your back.
May the road rise to meet you.

My niece Chloe, the eldest daughter of my brother John-Paul and wife Stacey, was a flower girl along with her lovely sister Bronte. Chloe got stung by a bee in the middle of the vows and stood silently, tears streaming down her cheeks. Everyone thought she was just deeply sentimental.

My funny brother gave a speech in which he referred to our nuptials as me marrying my 'stalker'. (The sledging was a highlight for Hughesy.)

Our photographer, attempting to take a group shot with all of us assembled on the steps of the chalet, kept yelling at my father-in-law Bryan to move and frustratedly complained that he was ignoring her. We thought it was because Bryan wasn't wearing his hearing aid but it turned out she was actually shouting at Bryan's identical twin brother, Uncle Kevin. How was she to know?

Our dessert was also our cake: eighty choux-pastry swans filled with raspberry cream, made by the brusque Frenchwoman we had befriended in the country bakery that the locals stubbornly avoided, but who magicked buttery baked goods like the lady in the novel *Chocolat*.

The next day we had a recovery barbecue by a lake and lazed around; everyone was shabby-shanks and gritty-eyed and so happy.

My goddaughter Loqui later saw one of the horses in the stable licking the fat off the cold barbecue plate.

Her dad, Paatschy, sang a rendition of a Human League song that slayed.

Then we joined my parents-in-law at their caravan for the rest of our honeymoon week. It was simple and glorious and humble and heavenly.

In normal times (before the coronavirus) our anniversary was a low-key milestone, marked by just the two of us with a lunch or dinner squeezed in amongst various family and sport and work commitments. This week, however, in the reflective mood of our various conversations back home with grandparents and friends, the subject has come up quite a bit. And it is amazing how much children enjoy hearing stories from their parents' wedding.

So it is especially lovely when Lewis announces he will cook us a celebratory meal to mark our special day: Vietnamese bao buns and crumbed calamari. The other children will act as waiters, he has decided, and Peter and I will eat by candlelight in our neighbours' borrowed garden. It is a grand plan, a week in devising. But, while the days outside become noticeably warmer as we move deeply into spring, there is now a distinct chill in our apartment.

The reason is this: two days ago, we got an email from the school deputy principal, asking us if everything was all right with Lewis. He has made no contact with his French teacher, it said. Will not reply to her, or the school. And then, the sucker punch: Lewis hasn't attended his French class for three weeks.

I am shocked. I go straight to Peter, who is working at his computer in the kitchen. From his grim demeanour it is clear that he has also received the news. He is, in fact, furious. Lewis has always openly disliked French: it's a school subject that he decided he wasn't 'into' about two years ago. To be honest, our eldest son is one of those people who doesn't normally work overly hard at even those lessons he enjoys and his unwillingness (we don't believe it's inability) to push himself has been a long-standing thorn in his father's side.

Although Peter often comments on what a poor student he himself was, this really isn't the case. He is the most diligent person I know. By contrast, I have been less inclined to worry about Lewis's lack of academic rigour. I was always an erratic student, getting by with last-minute swotting and sometimes impressive improvisation. I was also a terrible procrastinator, never starting an assignment until the day it was actually due. I hardly feel inclined to judge Lewis for his lack of interest in academia. Besides, he is bright and charming and quick off the cuff. In life, I reason, he will be fine. But wagging class is something else, and to refuse to answer emails from a teacher or vice-principal is not only rude and disrespectful, it is embarrassing.

When we talk to him, Lewis, though fiery-cheeked, is unswayed. He hates French, he says, and he will not do it anymore. The argument consumes us for a couple of days, and bleeds into our normally enjoyable mealtimes.

As is the case with deadlocked parental–child conflicts, we tag team before Peter, defeated, asks me to deal with the situation. Given that he is often the enforcer when it comes to overseeing routine and schoolwork, I accept that this is my challenge to sort. I speak to Lewis again. He is particularly angry with Peter: a combination, I think, of old moose and young moose locking of horns, shame, and his and his father's shared, bone-deep, righteous inability to budge. Lewis and I often resolve our differences with humour and gentle ribbing of each other; but not this time. I am uncharacteristically firm. I tell him he needs to write to his teacher and apologise. And, I remind him, whether he enjoys it or not, French is on his curriculum, and the fact he has used homeschooling as an excuse to skive off has left us deeply disappointed. Besides, it is a very unattractive trait, to believe that you have to enjoy a subject in order to work at it. It hardly sets someone up for life, that attitude. Lord help them if they ever find themselves under real pressure – under house arrest, for instance, in the middle of a global pandemic.

Lewis waves me out. He is in the middle of English class, he says. He will talk to me later.

The manner in which it plays out later is unfortunate. I am in the kitchen (surprise, surprise) when Lewis, unannounced, drifts in to ask if I need help with dinner. I am in the final throes of the meal – making gravy, taking vegetables out of the steamer – so I ask him to set the table and, when he has done that, to unstack the dishwasher. Lewis is not one to normally front-foot it with mundane chores. He likes to help cook and do the shopping. He keeps his room relatively tidy (with daily reminders) and has become our unofficial tech troubleshooter, but rarely seeks out domestic grunt-work, so his offer to help is appreciated. I believe it is his way of building a bridge and, to my mind, will be the start of our French conciliation.

Over dinner though, the mood is again strained. Lewis, primed for the intervention he knows is brewing, is sullen. He is still, however, imbued with his natural sense of smartarsery (courtesy of his mother, apparently) and when Peter fleetingly alludes to the French debacle, he arcs up at him. Things become increasingly taut. They clash as often as they bond, these two, something I believe is not unusual for fathers and firstborn sons, but given the stifling restrictions under which we are living, the tension escalates more quickly than it usually would.

After dinner, the little boys are clearing the table. Lewis has been instructed to oversee clean-up, but in his eldest-overlord manner, ends up teasing his brothers instead, flicking them with a tea towel and wrestling around the kitchen. We can hear them from the lounge room, where Peter is watching the news, waiting for the updates on the coronavirus figures. It's always a pretty anxious time of day, and the sounds echoing from the kitchen don't help. Lewis is playing rough. Things are noisy. There is a loud yelp and Artie runs in, crying, with Lewis in hot pursuit. Peter, who is already on edge, hits the roof.

'*Lewis!* I told you to clean up the f-ing kitchen!' he yells. 'Just f-ing do something to help for once!'

It is so loud, and so angry, that Lewis is shocked into obedience. It is also slightly unfair. Peter's words (sans the swearing) would normally not be unreasonable, but tonight are misplaced. Lewis has helped me earlier. He knows this, and so do I. Still, he retreats to the kitchen, where he actually does a remarkably thorough job. After an hour or so, I enter to find the stovetop and sink are sparkling and completely clear of dishes. I go to compliment him, but he roughly brushes past me and stalks off to his room.

Jannie asks how long we are going to be angry at Lewis.

'It gives me a sore tummy when you fight,' he says.

I understand his consternation. I, too, feel flat and despondent over this seemingly unresolvable stalemate. Also, I know that there will be no special dinner for our anniversary. It is ridiculous, but in these days of so few pleasures, I feel slightly crushed by it.

Before bed, I stop by Lewis's bedroom. He is lying on his bed, playing a game on his computer. His face is still a flushed and angry mask. I put my hand on his knee. He swats it away.

'I hate him, Mum,' he says. 'And I don't like you, either.'

I understand. But so must he, I reason. We all have responsibilities we undertake that we don't like. It is such a tedious and cliched parental refrain, I almost feel a kinship with those musical artists who have to sing the same song, their greatest hit, night after night. I nearly lack the will to explain it myself. Still, like Celine Dion in a Las Vegas residency, tackling her umpteenth version of 'My Heart Will Go On' (but with fewer sequins) I take a deep breath and explain the way we all do the things we must. I get up every morning and make breakfast and do the washing. I go food shopping and make meals, even when I don't feel like it. Peter pays the bills, does an endless grind of paperwork, cleans the kitchen and supervises homework. We can't just pick and choose what we want to do, and when. That is life.

'But what does it achieve, to yell at a kid like that?' he asks.

I pause. Decide to play my natural game.

'I dunno,' I say. 'It got the kitchen cleaned.'

Despite himself, he laughs.

The next morning, we all sleep in before I get up and make croissants for breakfast. The food stores are closed now on Sundays so the pastries are actually from the French supermarket that only sells frozen goods. They are really good, fresh from the oven. We all crowd into the kitchen to eat because the lounge room table is strewn with the pieces from a 1000-piece jigsaw Artie and I have started the evening before, post-storm.

Later, Lewis comes into our room, where I am changing the sheets on the bed.

'I might go to the shops after this,' he tells me. 'To get stuff for dinner. Wanna come?'

It should be an olive branch, this offer, but instead only highlights his ignorance of our daily lives.

'You can't,' I remind him. 'There are no food shops open on Sunday anymore. Remember?'

He is quiet. So. No anniversary dinner, then.

That afternoon, Peter presents me with an anniversary present, a pink and purple yoga mat he has ordered and had delivered before online deliveries were limited to only 'essentials'. He is so thoughtful and well-organised. I hate being empty-handed. I have nothing for him, I tell him, except the love that Tom Hanks had for that basketball in the movie when they are shipwrecked on an island together.

Later, we head downstairs to our neighbours' garden, to sit in the last of the sun and have a moment with just the two of us. We are carrying glasses of pastis, an alchemist's drink that goes cloudy when you pour it over ice and water. We bought the bottle of Pernod – the liquor that makes the magic – on our family road trip to France last summer, a bottle that has so far sat untouched in our Italian kitchen. Downstairs, we speak to our Chilean neighbour, Claudia, who is on her outside patio. She is cheerful and brusque. We talk about Sweden, where she and her husband and son previously lived, and speculate about whether their lack of lockdown – in the hope of raising 'herd immunity' – will work in ultimately reducing the severity of the corona crisis. Then she tells us of a good takeaway place that delivers.

That night, we have fried chicken and chips delivered to the house. Lewis has ordered it, after much frustration, on his phone.

I am lying on our bed reading when the food is delivered. I am not overly interested in joining my family for dinner but when, slightly anxiously, Artie comes in for the second time to tell me it's mealtime, I relent. I go out to the table that has been set with six places. On it are cardboard containers of imitation KFC with the generic phrase 'Fried Chicken' written on the boxes. Despite the slightly creepy packaging, the food is surprisingly hot and fresh. The kids are thrilled, both with the novelty of getting food delivered and in particular with the curly fries Lewis has chosen. I am picking at a crispy drumstick when Lewis tells us he has sent an apology email to his French teacher. And he will be in class tomorrow.

Jannie has a sip of contraband Coke and, emboldened by sugar, asks Peter if the two of us did 'smoochy-smooch' on our anniversary. Sunday mimes dry-retching and gets the rare pleasure of making her brothers roar with laughter. And just like that, without fanfare, without digging deep or agonising over who is wrong and why, the air has cleared. Our family feels normal again.

Artie is so happy, he leaps up from his seat and starts dancing.

Peter is laughing. I am laughing.

We are a little bit bruised, but we are all okay.

It is, I realise, the way the jigsaw of a family fits together.

Seventeen years ago, with love and optimism in our hearts, and a lanky teenager in my belly, we faced each other on a mountaintop on the other side of the world. We said for better. We said for worse. 'For better' is infinitely preferable, obviously, but just like our entire adventure in Italy, we haven't quit just because things get tough.

Because if you do that, you won't be there when they get better.

And things will get better. Like the song says, our hearts do go on.

I just really, really hope we're not on the *Titanic*.

33

GOOD BAD FRIDAY

Day drinking is a bad idea.

It is Good Friday, which, surprisingly, is not a public holiday here in Italy.

I am reminded of how we were caught out by this last year. We had only been in Bologna a few months and we had friends arriving from Australia, who had booked a big house for us all in Tuscany. In anticipation of a traditional Easter long, long weekend, we went to pick up the kids from school on the Thursday afternoon to get an early start to our road trip. We had traipsed up the stairs at the international school, excitedly relaying our plans to the lovely school administrator, Olivia, who inexplicably looked confused. She informed us the children were actually expected in class the next day. Even though Italy is one of the most Catholic countries in the world, Easter Friday, it turns out, is not a holiday. The Monday is. What we call 'Good Friday' in Australia, the first of the traditional four- or five-day Easter break, is just another working day.

We were both amazed and I recall seeing Peter – always a stickler for keeping commitments – waver; he was considering delaying the Tuscany weekend. I guess, similarly, he could read the expression on my face. After four exhausting months of getting up at 4 am in the middle of winter to do my radio show, and setting up a new home in a new country, I desperately needed a break. We all did. My wood-chopping expression clearly conveyed this more eloquently than words. So, with apologies for the school day to be missed, we had our brood summoned from class and headed to the hire car place down near the station.

Our willowy friend Jojo, her wolf-sideburned husband Noddy, and their three-year-old prince Ambrose met us there. What joy to see their familiar faces. After a brief reunion, sympathising with their travel woes – booked-out trains! the last hire-car in Rome! – we piled into our own leased VW van for the drive to Tuscany. (All of us, that is, except Lewis, who had set off on his boys' own adventure to the Balkans with his school mate Marshall.)

The pleasant two-hour drive to the Tuscan hills we had anticipated was more of a descent into one of the circles of hell. We already knew that no one likes to get out of town more than Italians but, even so, we weren't prepared for the density and volume of the Easter traffic. It was simply horrendous, worse than anything we had ever encountered in Australia. After a couple of hours of idling in the numbing congestion, we had travelled no more than twenty-five kilometres. The children, crushed in the rear seats of the van, were hungry and restless but pulling over into one of the equally congested roadside petrol stops was out of the question so JoJo and I did the time-honoured road trip mother-backseat-twist. The pair of us fossicked through the groceries we had bagged up, assembled mortadella and cheese rolls on our laps, and passed back iPads, pillows, our battery-drained phones and the mobile picnic. It bought us another hour of peace on what seemed like the ultimate road to nowhere.

Our enforced car-confinement at least meant we could catch up on various friends' lives back in Australia: new jobs and houses and babies and Noddy's latest pub venture. Meanwhile we were pressed for the headlines on our own grand adventure. That part of the conversation centred on what we had learned to date: the shining brilliance of the food and Italian people; the mystifying frustration of their bureaucracy and disorganisation. As if to illustrate our point, our van suddenly came to a complete halt, butted up against a massive line of cars waiting to exit one part of the paid freeway, only to join a bigger queue to re-enter the next section. Surely, Peter lamented, there was a better system than this waiting-for-ticket, scrabbling-for-change debacle.

Even going through the many tunnels on the autostrada – normally a thrill of engineering innovation when you pop out of a kilometres-long arched tunnel that has been drilled through the base of a mountain into the glorious circle of light at the other end – was a trial. We were jammed amongst hundreds, probably thousands, of cars, bumper to bumper. Some of the drivers actually turned their engines off, anticipating a considerable wait. It was brutal. And though the Italians around us seemed to be taking it with their philosophical acceptance, there was a palpable sense of weary exasperation all around. *Piano, piano*, seemed to be the silent mantra. Slowly, slowly.

I don't know why this is, but there seems to be a firmly held international convention that roadworks must be scheduled for the busiest times of year: let's paint the new lines on the bitumen at Christmas lunchtime! Let's block two lanes of a major freeway right before a holiday weekend! Italy, it seems, was no exception to this thinking.

As we nosed our way into yet another tunnel, we heard a sort of commotion; a distinct beeping of horns and distant yelling. How strange, we thought. An accident? It seemed unlikely, given our five-kilometre-per-hour crawl. And yet there was clearly some sort of tension ahead. Then we saw, fifty metres or so in front of us, a team of three men. Alongside a barrage of flashing lights illuminating the gridlock, one of the men was trying to block off the left lane of the three-lane tunnel. He was physically weaving between stalled cars, and laying out witches hats, which was an obvious exercise in futility, because there was simply nowhere for anyone to move. We were trapped nose-to-tail in a tunnel – jammed up against each other like corralled metal-clad cattle – and he, driven to frustration by the drivers' refusal to vacate the lane, and no doubt overcome by the hot and fume-filled tunnel, had simply had enough.

Fascinated by this unexpected drive-by entertainment, we watched his fury escalate as we drove closer. Signor Roadcrew had abandoned his witches hats now, and had started actually lunging at cars. He was banging on the bonnets, gesticulating wildly, and yelling at those behind the wheel of the offending vehicles. Noddy craned his head out the window to see more, then suddenly said: 'Is that . . . FIRE?'

As impossible as it seemed, the workman was brandishing a flaming flare. In a jam-packed, fume-filled tunnel, old mate thought the solution to his problems was to light an open flame. And continue to scream. As we drew alongside him, we could decipher his bellowing: 'Get off the road! *Move!*' Still, no one heeded his shrieking commands – no one could – and our guy finally went totally ape. He snatched up the two other blazing flares he had placed on the road, waved them above his head and, cursing wildly, hurled them against the wall of the tunnel.

It was madness. It should have been alarming, and it was, but it was actually so INSANE, so *pazzo* as the Italians say, it made us laugh. The children, astounded, watched him, bug-eyed. As we moved past Crazykins, still swearing and flailing, we could see other drivers shaking their heads in bemusement. One of them, perilously close to the flight path of the burning missiles, was smoking a cigarette. He looked over at us and shrugged. Ah, we said to our friends. Flares. Fire. Temper. Patience. Welcome to Italy.

Six hours after our two-hour trip began, and a shameful McDonald's stop later, we finally rumbled to a stop outside our rented stone house.

That weekend was perfection. If ever a place deserves its reputation for beauty, tranquillity and old-master painted vistas, it is Tuscany. At night, we slept on hard Italian mattresses under piles of woollen blankets in creaky-floored rooms rendered tranquil by shutters and age. We ate pancakes for breakfast and in the afternoons wandered out for gelato and aperitivo in the local square. We ventured to nearby villages where we ordered steaks as big as besser blocks and drank wines Noddy selected from the vineyards around us. At a market wending through a tiny town made of stone and steps, I bought a chopping board made of olive wood from the old man who had carved it. Little Ambrose cemented himself as an honorary Italian by eating nothing but Parmesan straight from the bowl at every meal and, enamoured of his honorary siblings, clung to Sunday and wrestled with the boys. The trees and fresh air seemed like a miracle after months surrounded by cobbles and marble. The children ran on the grass and played ping-pong in the open garage and we all swung on the swing. Mostly, we marvelled at the beauty that surrounded us, drinking in hazy hills and rows of vines ascending to the castle on the hill opposite us, and waving to the farmers tinkering with their tractor in the paddock next door. Noddy made a fire in the giant hearth, and our hearts and bodies were warmed. Sunday morning, like magic, the Easter Bunny found us. He (or she) brought Australian Easter eggs and, most gorgeously of all, t-shirts for each of us. They were black and emblazoned with yellow stars that read: Boogie Tuscany, in honour of the music festival Peter and I attend every Easter in Australia, the festival where we all first met.

This year, of course, Tuscany, or any destination other than the lounge room, is but a distant dream. All of us have given up everything – not just for Lent, but beyond. The stay-at-home orders are still strictly in place; not just here in Italy, but now around the world. There will be no trips away. No friends from Down Under, more of whom were due to arrive last week. No Boogie Festival.

So the suggestion of a Zoom party seems like a beautiful idea.

Petie and I received notice of it a few days ago. It was planned by the group of friends who normally organise Boogie, and others, like us, who are enthusiastic participants. Given that the companionship of friends and the joy of live music are two facets of our regular lives that we are missing hard this strange and uncharted April, the timing couldn't be better.

Boogie the Festival, by the way, is a gorgeous three-day fiesta on a dry country property about an hour up the northern highway from Melbourne. About three thousand people gather to dance in the dust and set up decorated tent-towns around eskies and folding tables laden with cocktails and dips. There is a late-night disco in a dusty dirt amphitheatre. There are Box Wars, where people make armour out of cardboard and battle it out till only one gladiator stands. There is always some strange cabaret, and peacocks and sheep in the nearby paddocks. The festival has its own currency – big coloured, shiny Boogie Bucks – and outdoor wooden shower blocks our capable friends have built, and it is untamed and friendly and just perfect. Though there are lots of children there, Peter and I normally drop ours off with his mum, Maree, in their version of heaven (the country caravan park where she's been spending holidays for over fifty years) and head off for a couple of days of our own grown-up festivities. We camp and dance and eat tacos from the taco truck, and take afternoon tea and cakes at the Clubhouse, a wooden structure inhabited by the old gay couple who owned the dustbowl of a farm that hosts the shindig.

The farm was sold last year and Bruzzie, one half of the duo to whom it once belonged, has died, so things were always going to be different. But this is beyond different: for the first time in thirteen years there will be no gathering at all, aside from what we are about to enjoy via technology. It is significant, and our fellow revellers – committed party people – are primed. For us, this social meet is a rarity. When we click on the computer, it is morning in Italy: 8 am. On the other side of the world, it is cocktail hour and our friends are making the most of lockdown – they are variously drinking, smoking herbs, prepping snacks and dinner. Many of them have dressed for a party.

Isolation means something different back home, at least in these early months. I have noticed this on my social media feed, which is now chock-a-block with people baking and sunbaking, often picture-bragging about their opulent surrounds while simultaneously posting platitudes about 'gratitude' and what they have learned in lockdown. They are a couple of weeks behind us in their stay-at-home measures and, hopefully, will never be subject to what we are here. The coronavirus numbers in Australia are positive. Or, should I say, nowhere near as 'positive' as here. Italy has 100,000 coronavirus cases; Australia has 3000. So the social distancing edict seems almost a game for many, a welcome interruption from normally hectic lives. And no wonder. They are allowed to visit each other's homes (so long as no more than two at a time). They are permitted to exercise outside, also in pairs. They can go to the beach. Florists are open. Seriously, in Australia, they can still buy *flowers*.

It's not a competition (and if it is, it's one we are clearly losing) but for us there is no going outside. No shops. No jogging. No parks. No bikes. No friends. No visits. No deliveries. No beaches. No sun. No fresh air. We are essentially in solitary confinement but with six of us.

The Zoom party, then, is an unexpected starburst of energy. Inspired by our friends' glittering faces and party vibes, I go to the wardrobe and pull out a couple of fur hats. Mine is blue and fluffy; Peter's is white. We are like a pair of glamorous Russians, and suddenly look festive, though we are both still in bed in our pyjamas. Peter, buoyed by the mood, pads off to the kitchen and returns with a beer, and then, for me, a bottle of Lambrusco, our fizzy blood-red local wine. I have made the children a pot of porridge, but for the first time we leave them to start homeschool by themselves. It is so nice to see some familiar adult faces; to talk good times and shoot the shit. To feel naughty. To be at a party. As people drop in and out, others join. We are all around the world, this eccentric, sweet fraternity. Sydney, Melbourne, Brisbane and Tasmania are represented in Australia; we, of course, are in Italy, while other friends are on-screen in America and Germany. The tech-savvy change the backgrounds of their Zoom surrounds; the Northern Lights, palm-fringed islands, prison bars. There is much laughter and talking over each other, and no one seems in a hurry to leave.

It is such fun. We move into the kitchen, where Peter angles the computer so our friends can see me do the day's cooking. I make a pizza for morning tea for our school pupils. Then a couple of lasagnes. I have prepared the ragu the day before but it is still an elaborate assembly line: the bechamel sauce, the meat, the pasta sheets, layered with eggplant and zucchini I have fried in olive oil and will secrete between the other layers. At our party, a girlfriend plays the guitar and sings a song. Another friend keeps reminding us there is always a silver lining on a dark cloud, even on the bleak cumulus that is the virus. For instance, she says, this will be the first Easter in thirteen years she has been home with her dog. She repeats this revelation with tipsy monotony until I point out that, unless the dog has a messiah complex, it has no idea it is Easter. Onscreen, everyone has suddenly started drawing freckles on their faces with coloured markers, or lipstick, or whatever they have to hand. A friend disappears from his virtual *Brady Bunch* box, then pops up in another. He has left his home to drive to another mate's house to pick up a delicious-looking homemade icy margarita.

The Zoom gathering continues throughout the morning until the American platform provider sends a message: we are being cut off. Four hours, it seems, is the limit for this particular party.

The lasagne is now ready for lunch but we have missed the official school break. The children are back in class, unfed. I don't care. Peter takes them bowls of pasta to eat at their desks.

I lay down on the bed.

Like I said, day drinking is a bad idea.

And then Peter reminds me we actually have to go out. Aside from the essential bread and milk, we need to find Easter eggs for the children. For Sunday.

The thought of this is almost too much. Though going to the shops – our only sanctioned outing – has normally been a bright spot, it has been getting harder and harder. Our last big trip to the supermarket saw a two-hour line of people waiting to enter the store. Still, Peter is right, in our efforts to keep things as normal as possible, we need something for the Easter bunny to deliver.

We decide to walk to the small shops on the other side of the main piazza. I love to see Piazza Maggiore, even though it is empty now aside from army trucks and police.

On the deserted street, a cop car cruises past.

I don't realise at first what has happened. I am taking a photo of the statue of Neptune; its water jets turned off for the first time since we have lived here, with the mermaids, suddenly dry-breasted, clustered thirstily at the water king's feet. I understand turning off water in a drought. But why now? I ponder. It's not as though there's a crowd of tourists clustered around, breaching social distancing measures. The arid fountain seems symbolic – as though we are being reminded that, in Covid-time, there is to be no joy. Not even fleetingly passing a beautiful fountain.

Behind me, the cops have done a U-turn and are now pulled up beside Peter on the kerb. They are questioning him about why he is out. Because he has already had a run-in with them for riding his bike, he is chastened and apologetic. But I have been subconsciously preparing for this. Coupled with my skin-full of Lambrusco, I am ready to go.

I come over. The police ask why we are together. Only one family member at a time may be outside, they tell us, even to go shopping.

But we have four children, I say. One person cannot possibly carry groceries for six people. That is too much food. Even in my broken Italian, my tone is terse. Almost aggressive. It is, in fact, very old-school Italian mamma. I start to walk off, to continue our mission. The police call me back, and ask my address. We live about three hundred metres from where we are standing. I can see they are a little taken aback by my certainty, and they don't issue a ticket. They do, however, nod curtly when Peter volunteers to go back home. And then they simply drive away.

I am left to get whatever chocolate I can muster, on my own.

Normally, the Italians are madly into Easter and make the hugest, most ornately decorated eggs. They wrap them like a bouquet of flowers, with a big bow tied around a soaring plumage of coloured foil. These eggs would ordinarily be in every shop window at this time of year, along with general *Pasqua* decorations: giant sugar rabbits pulling carriages of eggs, or farm scenes crafted entirely from chocolate.

Of course, there is none of this for Easter 2020. I end up at the local convenience store, the only one without a queue outside. Their last Lindt egg is broken. I find two Transformer eggs for the boys. A pink-wrapped one for Sunday. I look for some mint chocolates for Lewis, but there are none. I buy him a multipack of Snickers and head home.

While I was out, the Italian prime minister has given another update on our isolation measures.

They will now continue till 3 May. Another twenty-three days. More than three weeks.

Fark. How dispiriting.

As Peter points out, they are just kicking it down the road. Eking out what could, and probably will, go on for months.

I hide the stash of Easter eggs on our front landing behind some bags of plastic recycling, then go back inside and lay out some leftovers on the kitchen bench. Heat up some sticky ribs from the day before, toast a flatbread, and put some salad on a plate. Bung it all on a tray and take it to our bedroom.

Peter looks surprised. We're going to eat in bed, I inform him, and the kids can help themselves from the food I've left out for them.

My husband, recognising my fuel tank is unusually low, joins me momentarily on the bed. Then he gestures to the big round table against the wall on my side of the room. It has become a repository for the detritus of our life – past and present. My hair tong (rarely used); a tin of jewellery; a fine cloak of ancient dust.

I can move the table under the window, Peter says. And we can eat like we're in a hotel.

It seems like too much bother – everything does – but I reluctantly get up and wipe down the table. He returns with a couple of chairs, and two glasses of gin and tonic.

The idea is actually brilliant. There we are, eating in a new place. Just the two of us, face to face over a set table, looking out over a blossom-strewn garden and dusty-pink apartment blocks, as the Mediterranean sun beams its late-afternoon best.

Across the way from us, in a neighbouring building, an Italian man, hanging out his window and smoking, raises one arm in a greeting. I wave back, and raise my glass to him.

The G and T is perfect.

I realise the secret to day drinking.

You just need to keep it going into the evening.

34

STOCKHOLM SYNDROME

There is an old Buddhist saying (they are all old, the good sayings, aren't they? I mean, there are newish fleeting ones, like 'OK, boomer', 'OMG, literally *obsessed*' or 'Sorry, not sorry' but they somehow don't seem to carry the gravitas or sense of the poetic that is called for in these challenging times).

Anyhow, the mantra I am thinking of that seems so appropriate for now, is simply this:

Before enlightenment: chop wood, carry water.
After enlightenment: chop wood, carry water.

You see, I have had a weird epiphany.

I am starting to enjoy isolation.

I mean, *really* enjoy it.

At some point, over the last few weeks of our two-month-long confinement, something has changed. Or I have changed. I know this is the point of life – that we constantly re-evaluate and grow – but I have spent so long internally railing against the lockdown (and stoutly resisting any added burden of discipline or self-improvement during this time) that this latest realisation is astounding. I am so happy, it makes me smile.

In the scheme of things it sounds like nothing. Eight weeks is only fifty-six days, after all. It's not time enough (for me) to become fluent in a language or learn to sew (ditto). It is long enough that bread would get impossibly stale and hard, cheese would grow mould, and a newborn baby would learn to lift their head, and chuckle. For me, it is 1008 individual meals cooked and served ($3 \times 6 \times 7 \times 8$);

56 loads of washing, hung out and dried, folded and put away; 112 dishwasher-loads of dishes, stacked and unpacked. It is at once the blink of an eye and an eternity. It is a long time to be shut in your house and not allowed outside.

I am also reminded of the story (possibly apocryphal) of someone once asking Einstein to explain his theory of relativity. He replied: 'If you put your hand on a burning hot plate, ten seconds feels like an hour. If you find yourself in conversation with a pretty girl at a party, an hour feels like ten seconds. That's relativity.'

I don't know how much of that anecdote actually happened. For starters, it sounds more like the wit of Oscar Wilde than that of a world-changing physicist. Also, I am not motivated by speaking to pretty girls at parties. Or physics, for that matter. But it pops into my head now because the sense of it has never felt more true.

See, at the start of our lockdown, I was gripped, as so many were, with fear and disbelief and uncertainty. Everything had changed; the whole world seemed tipped on its axis. I was tired and puffy-eyed, anxious about whether we would be able to get food, trying to make everything okay for the children, to stay level, to keep things feeling smooth and almost humdrum, in keeping with the nature of a vigorous family life. But inside, I had knots in my stomach. I felt exhausted and overwhelmed.

The housework was too much. The thought of Google Classroom. The washing. The cooking. The preparing of lunch for homeschool and afternoon and morning tea. The shopping for groceries. The folding of clothes. The changing of sheets. The forbidden outdoors. I felt heavy and leaden – 'draggy', as Lewis once said, when he was so ill. When our cleaner Valentina announced she was not allowed to travel and could no longer come for her weekly stints, I was gripped by desolation, even though it was awkward with her having to work around rooms filled with all of us at our desks, also working. But the significance of her not being able to come, and the looming lack of external help, seemed like a further step on our descent into some unfathomable darkness.

Then, as we moved into our new life, things began to shift.

About six weeks ago, Peter, my ever-practical and forward-thinking beloved, designated Sunday as our family cleaning day and allocated chores accordingly. Lewis was on vacuuming duty; Artie and Jannie (always a team) were to clean toilets and bathrooms; Sunday was to help fold clothes and mop the acreage of marble and timber floors. I changed sheets and cleaned out the fridge, while Peter swept and emptied rubbish bins and hung rugs over our window-sills for a good Italian-style beating, and was general cleaning-crew overseer.

The children and I were initially resistant – them complaining and squabbling, me silently resentful of this interruption to our normally tranquil, relatively lazy Sundays. And then, after three weeks, something amazing happened. The notion that our previous day of rest was now the day for chores became an accepted part of our routine. Peter and I would make sure to flag it over dinner the night before – 'Tomorrow is cleaning day!' – in order to get any mandatory grumbling out of the way early. (If there is one thing I have learned about parenting, it is to always issue reminders before the fact, to help everyone set themselves internally for what is to come.)

And now, six weeks in, we are living what seems like a minor miracle. The cleaning regimen happens seamlessly; cheerfully, even. Last week, Lewis woke up before anyone else and started vacuuming, and had half the job done before we had made the first morning coffee. Likewise, Artie and Jannie now compete to complete their bathroom duties, singing and jostling. Our daughter, more of a night owl than a morning bird, is sleepy and silent as she undertakes her tasks, but is still placidly compliant. In an hour and a half, the jobs, shared by many, are done, and when we sit down to have lunch together, the day still yawns before us. It must be true that hard work is its own reward because we are all elated with the sense of satisfaction at what we have achieved. And there is no doubt that a clean and orderly house lifts everyone's spirits. It vibrates at a different frequency. Throughout the subsequent weekdays I notice the children are more conscious of avoiding spilt crumbs and dropped socks when they know they will have to play their part in later cleaning them up.

How basic these life lessons are, and how much of my own life has been predicated on trying to circumvent them. I have always been a reluctant housekeeper and, aside from cooking, find other household chores overwhelming at best; draining and dispiriting at worst. Learning to keep my bedroom tidy has taken me my entire life to this point. But my babyish no-do-because-I-no-like is in defiance of the very laws of nature.

If you (or the blessed bakers) don't get up and punch the dough before dawn, there will be no bread at breakfast. If you do everything for your children, or simply outsource your domestic work, because you can; if you don't push through the difficult parts, embrace the metaphorical (or literal) chop of wood and carry of water, you also miss the end rewards. It is simple to say; difficult to accept. On days I have flubbed through this lockdown (and there are many of those), not exercising or writing, or going unshowered until evening, still in my pyjamas at sundown, I feel sluggish and heavy, like I am wading through treacle. At the start of the day, everything feels like a stolen pleasure; by the end, I am grumpy and impatient and heavy-headed. I try to comfort myself with endless snacks, or seek the solace of a rumpled bed. By contrast, when I push through and make myself do even relatively little: a set of stair runs or twenty minutes of online yoga, speak with relatives back home and wash my hair and get changed, I find I am energised by the very thing I have dreaded doing.

Similarly, with a schedule – even this barely onerous one – comes the most unexpected gift of time. Peter and I will often watch a movie in the evenings, together, or with the children. We have started a perverse movie theme night called 'The Crying Game', which involves selecting sad movies and seeing who in the family cries first. (It is always me and my sentimental Artie.) And on a side note, it gives me an odd surge of pride how many of these movies star our own Russell Crowe: *A Beautiful Mind*, *Les Misérables*, *Gladiator* (which reduces us all to sobs, even Jannie, who normally delights in the nickname 'Captain Stoneheart'). Also, I have read more books than I have in years; so many, in fact, that I have exhausted our meagre library (*Pachinko*, *The Dutch House*, *Under The Tuscan Sun*, *Boy Swallows Universe*) and am being left novels (*The Expatriates*, *The Husband's Secret*) in our shared liftwell by our cute and cheery American neighbour Denise.

The children have also ceased resisting what needs to be done; they automatically clear the plates from the table after meals now and take them to the kitchen. My husband has started cooking: delicious Indian curries, homemade naan bread, his mother's fruit cake – for which I slice the rind off lemons and oranges, and steep them in a sugar syrup on the stove to make candied peel for the cake. Everything, it seems, has taken on a newfound ease. My daughter is blooming. My sons are energised and playful. At dinner the other night, when Peter and I commended the children on the beautiful way they have grown into their tasks, they lowered their heads in silent pleasure, drinking in the praise. In what was – and still is, in many ways – a bleak and frightening time, everyone is inexplicably joyful. It is not the way we ever would have envisaged living but there is a simplicity to it that we have happily surrendered to. Peter says one night, as we all sit down to the evening meal: 'We are like farmers; we go to bed early, we get up early, and we see the same people every day.'

Every afternoon now, as spring extends its hold, the sun shines with a looming summer warmth directly into our bedroom. While Peter sweats it out on his fixed bike in the lounge room, I have taken to opening the shutters wide and, stripping down to bra and knickers, sunbathing on our bed. In the privacy of our room, I can lightly toast the parts of my body (pizza-dough belly; winter-white thighs) that on a public beach or by a pool would feel too exposed. Often, fatigued by my righteous exertions and lulled by the warmth of our solar friend, I actually fall asleep and wake, sun-kissed and refreshed. Truly, an afternoon nap and a sunbathe? What impossible riches.

It seems as though I am going to leave lockdown more rested, and with the best tan I have had in years.

When we are finally released from our house arrest, I may well be the prettiest girl at the party.

As we used to say in Australia: good one, Einstein.

35

SUNDAY'S BIRTHDAY

Girl, I always say, is born a woman.

Sunday Lil, my complex, lovely, sloe-eyed beauty of a daughter, is turning fifteen in isolation. She is often a mystery to us, our second-born: an artistic, introspective girl, unexpectedly funny and calm but fiery when she kicks off. 'The Jamaican girl' my mum and dad call her and, indeed, her colouring and her strong-minded creative streak seem very much a through line from my maternal grandmother, herself a Jamaican living in New York, my grandma Kate (after whom I am named). It is from her, and maybe a little from her mother, that Sunday has her stubborn temperament; her keen eye. Her eccentricity. Her tread-her-own-path sense of herself. It will stand her in good stead in life, we think, but it has also been a challenge for Peter and me, particularly from August last year when a sullenness descended upon her, as though a soul-poltergeist had rearranged the crockery of her psyche and flicked a switch marked: 'Parents Bad. No Talk'.

Today is Sunday's birthday and we are grateful for the thawing over the last couple of months of the icy demeanour she has previously presented to us. It is an unexpected upside to our enforced intimacy (thanks, coronavirus). At times now, she even fronts up, unbidden, to bestow upon us an amusing snippet of gossip from school or to escape the relentless coughing from the apartment above her room. (The coughing from the person upstairs, by the way, is indeed horrendous; deep and persistent and hacking. We don't think it is a Covid cough, but Sunday firmly believes it is. One night, she records it, and all six of us huddle around her phone, analysing the bark of our anonymous neighbour, and assuring Sunday she couldn't be infected through half-metre-thick 500-year-old walls. We are not sure of this, by the way, but it seems to comfort her.)

Anyway, the girl, our only girl, has requested cinnamon rolls, fried chicken and waffles for her birthday dinner. We rarely eat any of these foods – or at least, not in that combination – so we figure they must be ideas she has discovered on TikTok, her most faithful digital companion.

In the lead-up to her big day, when it becomes apparent that we will still be very much in lockdown, and deliveries are still for 'essentials' only, we start planning the housebound festivities, which will revolve around the birthday meals. Lewis volunteers to fry the chicken. I find a recipe online for cinnamon scrolls.

In preparation, yesterday I set out to go to the French frozen supermarket to buy boxes of waffles. As I am prepping to depart – wallet! mask! permission-to-leave-the-house document! passport! – Jannie, who is bouncing a ball in the lounge, unexpectedly asks if he can come with me. Throughout the entire lockdown, he has not once railed against our home confinement, has not asked to leave the house, has never once complained. So his request takes me by surprise. I hesitate. Technically, he is not allowed to accompany me, though on previous trips to the supermarket I have seen an occasional child with their parent. Solo parents, I guess, or with one parent deployed at work. You can't leave a child at home alone, after all. And we are all buoyed by the news that, from next Monday, we will be allowed to go outside – the government has stated that parks and gardens will finally be reopening. I look at Peter, and even though he raises his eyebrows – silently disapproving of our premature foray into the outside world – he doesn't argue the point. I nod at Jannie. He gives a whoop of excitement and runs off to find his shoes. I follow him, instructing him about the necessity of wearing a mask outside, and that he will need to keep a metre away from other people. He, of course, has not experienced any of our Covid-avoidance measures.

It will be unfamiliar to him but outside is a new world he has to get used to.

We still don't have medical face masks so I rig him up with Peter's ski muffler. It is thick, too warm and too large for him. Ever the joker, Jannie sticks his whole face through it, like a car-accident insurance fraudster wearing a foam head brace. It makes me smile but I impress upon him that strangers will not find mask antics amusing. He nods gravely, then runs down the stairs.

I follow him to the inner courtyard where my bike, neglected for the last couple of months, is looped to a railing against the wall. Jannie has eagerly scrambled onto his familiar place on the back before I have even unlocked it. It is over three months since I last dinked him to school and though he has clearly grown and does not perch as lightly as he once did on the rear flat tray, the trip is exhilarating. It is a ten-year-old boy's first glimpse of life outside his apartment in more than nine weeks and he keeps a running commentary of the empty streets, amazed that the neighbourhood he knows so well now looks so different. As we bump over the cobblestones on the long lane that leads away from our apartment (lined on both sides with shuttered bars and restaurants), he opens his mouth and croons a single long wolf-howl; pleased at the vibrato provided from our corrugated ride and how it ricochets around the deserted alleyway.

At the French supermarket, Jannie peruses the rows of freezers as though they are the promised land and gives a squeal of pleasure when I tell him he can choose whatever he wants. As well as the waffles and some frozen croissants, he selects a raspberry tart and a box of chocolate-filled churros. And a tub of vanilla ice-cream. It's Artie's favourite, he informs me cunningly, thereby securing quinella credits; the thoughtfulness of choosing something for his brother and the ice-cream itself. As I wait to pay, Jannie shows off how quickly he can pack our purchases. Behind her mask, the checkout lady's eyes crinkle in a smile as she watches him. It is nice to see a child, she says. He is so happy.

As we are leaving, laden with our goods, we see the cleaning products store next door is open; miraculously, with no queue outside. We enter, seizing the opportunity to stock up on plague essentials: bleach and detergent, and then, unbelievably, we find a display of cosmetics. Jannie picks out four tiny bottles of nail polish; green, purple, mauve and turquoise. There is also a rack with lace-trimmed pairs of socks. A stand of blushers and tinted moisturisers. Things a girl would like.

Later, after we have returned home with our booty, Peter ventures out to the old man whose tiny pen-and-paper shop has reopened around the corner (yay!) to buy some wrapping paper. Normally the old fellow is there with his wife; she sits on a chair, squeezed in the corner, chatting to the infrequent customers as they make their purchases, or berating her husband when he gets prices wrong. In the afternoons, after the store has reopened after the three-hour midday break, they often move their chairs outside, this husband and wife, where they socialise with passers-by, only venturing inside if someone stops to buy a pen or notebook. This is a standard Italian phenomenon, the fusion of socialising and work. Today, however, there is no wife; only the elderly man, masked and alone behind the counter.

As he is paying for the sheets of gift paper, Peter spies a dusty assortment of boxes and old gifts on the shelf above him. It is a strange jumble of goods from the past: an old Barbie doll and other clutter that looks as though it has been there since the 1970s, untouched. He points to a mug with a picture of a dog on it and a vintage-looking tin with a hinged lid. The old man seems a bit uncertain but when my husband explains he is looking for a *regalo*, a present, for our daughter, the old man brings over a ladder, worryingly shuffles up the steps to retrieve the treasures and proceeds to wrap them, slowly and ornately, with ribbon and patterned paper.

Breakfast the next morning is light-hearted and fun. The cinnamon rolls are impossibly sweet but impressive to behold and teeth-achingly delicious. Sunday is thrilled by them, and even more so by the first of her simple gifts. She marvels at the socks and is so pleased with the makeup ('How did you get this?' she repeatedly asks). She holds the bottles of nail polish up to the light, admiring their audacious colouring. I am reminded of the Dutch saying: a child's hand is easily filled.

My beloved girlfriend Alice, Sunday's godmother, has sent videos featuring her, her boys and a new baby we have not yet met: a long-haired black puppy called Saski. Nanaree and grandpa FaceTime from Australia. There are messages of love from my parents and other friends. Sunday, unused to being the focus of so much attention, is flushed with pleasure. As I watch her, I am reminded of a feeling when I was about her age that still makes me shrink slightly inside. I felt so unlovable, I remember, so weird and emotionally misshapen, it was almost unbelievable that not everybody felt the same way about me. And here is my daughter, sitting across a dining table from me, decades later, almost giddy with joy. Beaming, she giggles with her brothers as she opens the card we have written for her. She peruses it in silence for a moment, then looks at her brothers and squeals: 'Guys! I'm being sent to boarding school!'

It is funny, all the more so because a few months ago, when she was so dour and angry and despondent, that seemed like a real possibility. We all laugh.

That afternoon, Lewis and I prepare the chicken, which we have marinated in homemade buttermilk, along with some herbs and spices. We dredge it in egg wash, then flour and a new recipe Lewis has found for seasoned batter.

True to his word, my son does the frying while I crisp up the waffles in the oven and steam some green beans.

The little boys have set the table, and next to her plate have put the two remaining wrapped gifts. Sunday goes to take her seat and hesitates, confused.

'Those presents,' she says to her dad quietly, 'who are they for?'

Her innocence is beautiful.

She opens the mug and then the beautifully wrapped tin. It is such a humble offering but she studies it carefully, running a finger over its painted patterns of snowmen with carrot noses, her face alight.

'I really love tins,' she says.

The dinner is delicious. Strange, for sure, with the combination of maple syrup and fried chicken. Later, after we have had chocolate cake and sung rounds of birthday songs in Italian and English, I am clearing up the table.

The birthday tin is still on the table. I see, stuck to the winter-wonderland enamel, as though it was camouflage, a white paper sticker with feathery writing on it. It is an old person's scrawl. In Italian, it says 'Stamps and Pens'.

It was the old man's tin.

He actually used it in his shop.

I go to peel the paper sticker off, but then decide to leave it.

One day, I think, Sunday will be an old lady herself. The world probably won't know what pens and stamps are by then. Perhaps, too, this plague will have passed from most memory.

Sunday, I am pretty certain, will always remember.

36

MAY THE FOURTH BE WITH US . . .

The first thing I notice when I wake and head to the kitchen is that workmen are downstairs. They have not been here for weeks, and yet there they are, uncharacteristically early for Italy. The church bells have just chimed seven yet Franco, the burly resident handyman and his friendly mournful-faced offsider, are unloading bags of concrete in the central courtyard. I poke my head out the window and see them leaning against the wrought-iron gates in their overalls. They are laughing and have pulled their masks down, all the better to chat and smoke. This somehow makes it official; Italy is resuming normal programming.

This long-awaited date, 4 May, finally marks the first easing of our lockdown. Today we are permitted to pick up takeaway food from restaurants, to exercise outside. The parks and gardens, firmly gated for the last nine weeks, will be opened. The thought of this is almost overwhelming. What to do? Where to go? Peter has already announced he will take Artie and Jannie to shoot hoops at the local basketball stadium before homeschool.

I bring him a coffee as he rouses the boys. Still sleepy and unaccustomed to what once was their twice-weekly routine, the three of them wheel their bikes downstairs.

In less than an hour, they have returned.

The police. Again. They arrived at the end of their skills session as the boys were handballing a footy to each other. They were friendly enough, Peter said, but nonetheless sent them home. Yes, you are allowed outside, they said, and yes, you may now ride your bikes, but ball sports are still forbidden. ('No squad,' as the polizia put it.) Jannie, always prone to the dramatic, is clearly frustrated. 'I hate the government,' he says, banging his fist on the couch. Artie is more philosophical. 'At least we can ride our bikes now.' Still, they are both subdued. They were so looking forward to shooting hoops again. And they're no Ned Kellys, my boys; only outlaws enjoy a run-in with the cops.

Later, Peter goes for his own ride, solo, up to the hills. He sees a lot of other cyclists there, many of them wearing masks, as though riding eighty kilometres up hill and down dale is not difficult enough already.

In what is a bright spot (a relative concept), Peter and I have now got proper facemasks. There are still none of the surgical type available – they seem to instantly sell out – but one day we are walking back from the supermarket and see the local tailor (closed as a non-essential business) has a makeshift sign out the front saying Mascherine. Underneath is a hand-drawn arrow directing us up a laneway to the rear of the store. There, in what feels like a most clandestine black-market exchange, we buy two fabric masks for the rather exorbitant price of 20 euros each. At least, I say to Peter, we know they are beautifully stitched. But apparently not. Two days later, the ear-elastic snaps off Peter's couture mask, rendering it useless. He is annoyed. My guess is that the tailor hasn't much expertise in mask-making, but it looks like that may soon change. By the end of the pandemic, he will be a master-masker.

When he comes home, I put on makeup and get changed. It takes me a while to find my handbag. After an exhaustive hunt, I find it upstairs where it has slouched next to my desk, unused, for the last few months. Just a small thing, yet there is not another time in my adult life when I have not used a handbag for more than a couple of days; normally, my life is inside it. (Now my life is actually inside.) It is a beautiful bag, a memento of a precious five days spent in Paris last year with my girlfriend Mac but, as gorgeous as it is, I decide I can't be bothered with it anymore and just take my wallet.

We drive to Giovanni's restaurant to pick up the much-anticipated takeaway. It is golden hour. The roads are full. People stream past on the footpaths and on the central bike path between the divided lanes, with dogs and on bikes. Quite a few are on rollerblades, as though in their downtime they have fossicked through their unused sporting equipment and vowed to resurrect it the second they are permitted. The trees are green from the recent rain. The sky is bright blue, deepening into the royal indigo of summer evenings. Outside the restaurant, in its little garden setting, the jasmine is in bloom. Honeysuckle perfumes the air. Lights are on in the apartment blocks nearby. People are on their balconies, bringing in washing from a gravity-defying system of racks and lines strung over railings, watering potted flowers in every cheerful hue, or simply smoking and enjoying the street view over an evening aperitivo. Everything once again feels so open and alive; so full of tentative possibility. It is intoxicating.

At his Ristorante Lambrusco, Giovanni has set up a table across the wooden front doors with a large printed menu and an EFTPOS machine. His offsiders are expecting us and, as we wait for our order (pasta with sausage, sliced meats, fried bread, soft cheese, tomato and onion relish, parmigiana), Giovanni comes out in his chef's apron, perspiring lightly from the heat of the kitchen. Above his mask, I can see his brown eyes sparkling. We are so pleased to see each other, I want to hug him. Instead, he elbow-bumps Peter and, preening, shows off the tan he got today on his own bike ride. It is already a deep brown in a classic cyclist's configuration: mahogany from the wrist to halfway up his shoulder, where the Lycra covering ends and the flesh suddenly returns to pale. One hundred and forty kilometres, he says, and we marvel. Even under his covered face and long apron, you can see how thin Giovanni is, how fit. He is pleased, he tells us. He has lost twelve kilos in lockdown. No pasta. No bread. No wine.

Of course, tonight, with his restaurant finally open again, he will enjoy all of those Italian pleasures. 'Why not?' he says. 'Our life is coming back.'

We all do prayer hands. Long may this freedom last, we say. May the Fourth be with us; with all of Italy, and around the world.

37

THE FIRST SUPPER

We are going to a restaurant tonight.

This, of course, is a French word. In Italy, they call it a 'ristorante' but apparently the principle is the same. It is a place that sits you down at a table and they BRING YOU FOOD. And WINE. You're not related to the owners of this establishment; in fact, often you don't know them at all, but they insist on doing this for you. Incredible, no?

And at this *restaurant*, they have set the table with a CRISP WHITE CLOTH so you don't have to allocate that job to children (or attempt to explain to them the pre-isolation concepts of 'crisp' and 'white'), or listen while they bicker over who will do what and wrestle around in the kitchen trying to squirt each other with water from their mouths – *mio dio*, from their actual mouths, the filthy urchins – and then intervene when it gets too wild and a glass shatters on the floor and their father comes in bellowing 'STAND STILL! DON'T MOVE!' while he huffs and puffs and sweeps up the shards around their bare feet.

At a *restaurant*, they deliver the meal right in front of you on beautiful china that all matches, with plates that are not chipped from anyone using them in a secret and oddly violent coin-tossing game when they are supposed to be in their homeschool English class. Also, the glasses are glorious, sparkling and crystal-clear and distinctly lacking in smears and smudges. And they have separate vessels in every size and shape: for white wine! For red! For liqueurs! For water! Restaurant water itself, like a magic elixir, comes in two varieties: sparkling and natural (not the two I have become accustomed to: 'tap' and 'spilt').

The only responsibility they entrust unto you in a *restaurant* is to decide what delicious concoction to select from a LIST OF DISHES that they present on a thing called A MENU and then (and I believe this all to be gospel true), they will make it for you. SERIOUSLY. They do ALL THE COOKING. And the PREPARATION. You don't have to go to the supermarket or the butcher or even the greengrocer and stand in a queue to buy any of the ingredients, or feel a late-afternoon, back-aching sense of despair when you realise you don't have any lemons or have run out of olive oil and must run back to the shops. You don't have to burn your hands wrestling a hot casserole dish out of the oven or curse as you set yet another tea towel on fire while trying to lift a scalding lid off a saucepan to see if your pasta is cooked. You don't have to peel or grate or boil or broil (whatever that is), or slice or toss or soak or chop or knead or sauté or grill or mash or blend or steam or sear or scrape. They DO IT ALL.

This already sounds more than enough. But that's not the extent of it.

If, when you take your place at the table at said restaurant, they have, for example, forgotten to put out the salt, all you have to do is ASK and someone called a *waiter* will bring it to you. They will be calm and unflustered. They won't burst into tears, accusing you of being angry at them, claiming that it was somebody else's job to put the salt on the table, and that everyone else is your favourite and that you hate them and they always get asked to do everything. Nor will they then break into a scuffle with their sibling over who gets to jump on the scooter that is leaning against the couch in the corner and zoom off, banging into the door jamb, only to utter a giant 'Oops!' upon their return, when it transpires they have been holding the salt shaker upside down and have left a Hansel-and-Gretel-like trail of gritty grains on the floor all the way from the kitchen. (If, perchance, that DID happen at a restaurant, they would never look helplessly at you, waiting for you to drag yourself from your chair to sweep up the spilled salt. No. They would simply magic the mess away with such little fuss and commotion that you would barely even notice it had happened. Your only job, apparently, is to stay seated AT ALL TIMES while food and drink are brought to you – as much food and drink as you choose.)

And at this mythical place called 'restaurant', they also CLEAN UP AFTER YOU. Uh-huh. You don't have to gather up the plates and platters and condiments and balance them in a leaning-tower-of-catastrophe back to the kitchen. Nor are you required to rinse off plates before you stack the dishwasher, or yell at kids to stop bickering over who will dry and who will wash, or mop up drips and splotches and grains of sticky rice from on and under the table and chairs, or put stained placemats and tablecloths and sodden tea towels in the washing machine or work out how to jam leftovers in the fridge, or sweep away piles of cooking debris and onion peels from the floor around the sink, or attempt to scrub singed foodstuffs that defy carbon-dating from the bottom of a charred pot. At a restaurant, you are actually NOT ALLOWED TO ENTER THE KITCHEN. Seriously, they won't let you in there, even if you beg them. (I know! I KNOW!)

I realise this all sounds unbelievably perfect, but, much as every paradise harbours a serpent, and every pot of ointment a fly, restaurants also come with a downside.

Apparently you have to put clothes on to go there.

You can't just sloop to the table, barefoot, in the nightie you've had on all day or wearing the same grimy t-shirt and trackie daks that've become your uniform for the past twelve weeks of lockdown. It also seems the people who work in *il ristorante* appreciate it if you wash your hair and put on knickers and a support garment called a 'bra' (you may wish to Google this) before enjoying their hospitality. Convention dictates it is not the done thing, at a *restaurant*, to turn up smelling slightly of perspiration with lank and matted tresses tumbleweeded atop your head, while your breasts, like two puppies in a pillowcase, threaten to burst forth from under a threadbare and pilling singlet.

This, of course, is a price I am happily prepared to pay to enjoy our first restaurant meal in more than three months. (As well as the actual cost, which could be ten times what it normally is and still seem like a gift.) In our period of home confinement, I work out that I have made more than 1200 meals. I am ready to be waited on.

Aware of our much-heralded anticipation of our night out, Lewis offers to cook the other children dinner, his first risotto. By the time we leave, the meal smells so good, and he is so proud of it, that we are tempted to stay and enjoy it ourselves. We resist that temptation. By then, also, I am showered and perfumed and have put on a festive yellow top with a flowered skirt; it feels like the first time I have dressed for something other than housework in weeks.

Peter and I set off to walk across town, through the piazza, curious to see how many places are open and how the Italians will marry the new concept of social distancing with their ancient social traditions of kissing in public and dining out. We are heading to a restaurant that nestles under the porticoes for which Bologna is famous. We have eaten there before – pre-Covid – and have taken several visiting groups of friends there. The owner, Giancarlo, as well as making delicious food, is renowned for getting smashed and flirty and singing opera as he moves from table to table. In previous visits he has often recounted stories of his relatives who moved to Australia in the 1980s and had a banana crop decimated by some weird banana-disease before moving to a seaside town and opening a cafe where they now serve lasagne. This latter move on their part enrages him. They are, apparently, from the wrong part of Italy to make the dish. 'What they fucking know from *lasagne*?' he often laments. 'I say, I come to Australia and show you fucking *lasagne*!' We love his indignant fury and it makes us laugh, but Giancarlo is not joking. He is, it seems, the only sanctioned lasagne-cook in the family. Anyone else is a pretender.

On the walk to the restaurant, the sky is markedly heavy and dark. There is a loud crack of thunder. Italians, who hate to be caught in the rain, huddle in doorways and under the porticoes for shelter, social distancing suddenly forgotten in the face of the drops descending from the heavens. They are, in their attitude to precipitation (and so many others ways), totally the opposite of the Dutch, who – through necessity, I guess, because of their damp and rainy climate – are undaunted by moisture. The stoic Netherlanders actually have a saying: 'You're not made of sugar'. You won't melt. I utter this maxim repeatedly whenever we are caught in inclement weather, so much so that it annoys the children. (This is much like the way my mother, in her rich American accent, would always intone: 'I'm afraid you're gonna live', whenever my brother or I injured ourselves. VERY ANNOYING. Because 'mother'.) Anyway, the Dutch in me has clearly come to the fore again tonight; it is so nice to be outside in the warm and humid evening air that we continue our walk in the rain, undeterred. I don't even mind that the moisture is flattening my hair that I have spent half an hour 'doing'.

Peter and I have our masks with us and as we turn down the familiar laneways into the student quarter, we notice several groups – five or ten young people, beers in hand, laughing and jostling each other as they perch on seats or balance on the edge of street planter boxes. Bologna being a university town, normally these bars and backstreets would be surging. Tonight, the groups are sparse: they are obviously the students who were left behind in the great Covid exodus when everyone returned to their home regions. Nonetheless, it is nice to see a hint of former life returning to the streets. There is a sense of conviviality and the fragrance of smoke – pot and tobacco – wafts through the heavy air. None of the students, we notice, are wearing masks.

In the three months we have been sequestered at home, we have lost our fledgling sense of the geography of our adopted town. Peter and I have to stop a couple of times to make sure we are heading in the right direction. That, coupled with me stopping in front of newly lit storefronts to longingly gaze at homewares and summer dresses, like a kelpie at a butcher shop window, means that when we finally arrive at the restaurant we are half an hour late or, as the Italians call it, 'early'. Giovanni is surprisingly already waiting, unperturbed, and slightly slurry. He had been going to drop in at his favourite bar around the corner first, he tells us, but that of course is still shut. Instead, he came straight to the restaurant, where he is now sitting at a table outside its front doors, nursing a glass of sparkling white wine. What a vision it is. The lighting is fabled Italian gold; every table has a candle flickering. Vines are tendrilled through the arches that frame the street. It is like a mirage.

We take our places as our waitress welcomes us. She is sporting a mask and gloves, and in response to our queries, tells us they are hot and uncomfortable to wear but she is extremely happy to be back at work. We are barefaced, all the better to enjoy the complimentary glasses of prosecco she pours for us, along with welcome slices of fatty and salty mortadella. We toast and drink, then settle on a bottle of Sangiovese, the red wine of the region, while we choose our meals from the blackboard menu and from a list the waitress recites in rapid Italian.

Pasta first, of course. Peter orders a traditional dish – tagliatelle with ragu, the classic Bolognese sauce – while I select a pasta I have not encountered before: long almond-shaped folds that the owner's friend makes somewhere in the south of Italy. Giancarlo, who suddenly appears at our table when he hears me order, says, 'This one is from the wheat flour and the flower of the wheat; no one else can make this one.' It is served with *salsiccia*, the local coarse and seasoned sausage, removed from its casing and stirred through the dish.

The wheat-flour-flower pasta is so good. Every mouthful is a joy, but it is also dense and extremely filling. I can barely imagine eating my *secondi*, yet it feels poor form to not enjoy the customary two or three courses at this precious establishment's Lazarus-like resurrection. The boys have ordered steaks, thick and cooked rare, which arrive with roast potatoes and vegetables; I have requested roast beef. And it is just that: a plate covered with wafer-thin slices of quickly seared beef, still pink inside, and liberally sprinkled with chunks of salt and olive oil. The meat is so delicate and the condiments so flavoursome, we all end up sharing it. (If Giovanni has coronavirus, we all do now.) At the end, we rip little pieces of bread from our rolls and make the tiny boot, and wipe our plates clean.

In the background, incidentally, the soundtrack to our gorgeous meal has been less than idyllic. While we eat, a team of workmen are busy setting up shallow, flat platforms over the cobbles on the street. This improvised outside area will be how the restaurant seats customers over the coming summer since the close quarters of their indoor area is pretty well off-limits. The configuration makes perfect sense; the timing less so. The workmen are making a helluva racket as they back up their smoking lorry, drop three-metre-long pallets onto the road, then drag and bang and drill the railings which frame them into place.

This is so Italian, it makes us laugh. Three months they have had to plan and set up the outside arrangements for the long-anticipated reopening of this restaurant. Instead, they have waited until tonight – the first night they are allowed to welcome customers – to boom and crash and weld things into place. At times the noise is so loud that we have to yell over the cacophony as we try to converse over our meals. Giancarlo, seemingly oblivious to the racket (and, I suspect, actually proud of his enterprise), bustles over to sit with us. He has a bottle under his arm and pours us more wine. He sings a little. We enquire as to how he fared during lockdown. He gives us the customary Italian shrug. He renovated his cellar, he says, and drank many bottles while doing so. He laughs at his own humour then rubs his tummy appreciatively, and we all toast again.

Dessert arrives: crazy big bowls of creamy mascarpone sweetened with sugar and whipped into a soup-like consistency, topped with peels of grated dark chocolate. It is accompanied by a bottle of marsala, which is simply placed on the table. I love this Italian tradition where it is left to the diner to help themselves. If you wish to have a glass or a whole bottle, that is up to you. The fortified wine is sweet and musky, and with it comes another food-history lesson. Giovanni tells us about the wine as we drink. How other wines were once blocked from being transported through disputed trade routes to England so the English taught the Sicilians how to make marsala. The drink is named for the southern town where it is made, and Peter and I realise we have actually been to Marsala last year on our driving trip around Sicily. It warms me, like the golden liquid itself, to know the physical place where this nectar is bottled. I feel a little bit more connected; a bit less like a foreigner. Obviously, I am giddy with wine and food and the scent of looming summer and the sensual headiness of it all. Maybe I am just tipsy.

As we go to leave, Giancarlo brings a gift to the table, a bottle of red wine. We cannot drink any more, we explain; he tells us to take it home. Then, sliding his face mask off, he takes my hand and, after a long and flowery exposition in rapid Italian (I only catch a few words, 'beautiful Australian woman' being enough) he presents me with the red rose from the vase on the table. He lingeringly kisses my hand as Giovanni and Peter chant at him '*Un metro! Un metro!*' (Where is the one metre distance?)

As we recite our litany of goodbyes, our thank yous, our good lucks and our see you soons, Giovanni and Peter elbow-tap our host farewell. Behind him, the real reason for the workmen's seemingly odd timing is revealed; the three of them are now sitting down to dinner. There they are, seated expectantly at a linen-clothed table, still in their work gear, about to enjoy a magnificent meal in (aside from their high-spirited conversation) now blissful silence. Of course. What seemed strange earlier now makes perfect sense. The contractors scheduled their job so that they could enjoy a meal together afterwards. Italians, naturally, have missed the pleasure of a restaurant experience more than anyone.

I watch for a moment as the workmen *salute* each other, then I turn to Giancarlo to say my own goodnight. I proffer my elbow, and he hesitates for a moment, then suddenly pulls me in for a giant bear hug. It is a ridiculously demonstrative embrace – and would have seemed excessive, even in pre-Covid times. I slightly protest, but there is no point, really. I am pinned tight. As he releases me, he delivers a giant kiss on both of my cheeks.

Old habits die hard, it seems, and the new ones have not yet taken hold, particularly with people relaxed by wine. Giovanni, who has been watching our farewell grapple, smiles and shakes his head.

'Things get lost in the bottle,' he says, poetically. 'I think this may happen also to social distancing.'

He offers us a lift home, but Peter and I decide to walk. When we stood from the table, I realised how full I felt, how unaccustomed to the quantity and richness of restaurant food.

Besides, it is a sweet walk home. Back through the piazza, still damp with rain. Over the glistening cobblestones, under the hanging moon.

I am reminded of an elderly lady I saw the other night on the news in the middle of lockdown. She was standing forlornly outside her neighbourhood strip of shops, which were shuttered and dark.

'Italy without restaurants is not Italy,' she said, and wiped tears from her eyes. Actual tears.

I hope she has been able to go out tonight.

Going out is good.

38

STEPPING OUT

Last night, in another step towards normal, we went to a bar around the corner from our apartment. It is owned by an Australian girl, Grace, and her Italian boyfriend Eddie, who we had just met before we were all slammed shut. Now, over serious cocktails beautifully made by Eddie, we commiserated with them on our respective unfortunate timing.

They opened their bar in November last year, just before winter, but thoughtfully, in time for us to celebrate Peter's birthday there, with a group of students from our Italian school. We'd had such a great and festive night there, and our custom and group of fun friends was appreciated by Eddie and Grace, for whom building a new business was naturally a little slow. Between Italian bureaucracy and their own limited workforce of two, it had taken a year to refurbish the space. Their 'Elektrobau' is just around the corner from us, so not in the bar district, and with the Bolognese being so habitual, they knew it would take a while to lure locals from their regular haunts.

Their cocktails are stunning – a far cry from the standard aperol spritz (which, of course, they also serve). Eddie, originally a lawyer (like seemingly everyone in Italy), actually worked in bars in Australia for five years, where he met Grace, who was serving drinks at a lovely rooftop bar in Melbourne called Madame Brussels. And now they've made their own bar and it is beautiful. It's a large room at street level, painted matte black inside, with a giant wrought-iron lamppost in the middle, and dark and intimate tables and booths. Along the back wall are mirrored shelves with glistening bottles ready to be used in Eddie's concoctions. It's unusually spacious and has an Australian bar-vibe, with theme nights for every festive occasion advertised with Grace's clever drawings plastered in the glossy black windows. Things were just starting to happen for them when Covid struck.

They are cheerful and positive, even though Grace has let her trademark cherry-red hair fade in lockdown, they have a litany of people they owe money to, a landlord who is sympathetic but still needs his rent, and are staring down the barrel of a summer with few tourists.

They have also been in lockdown for three months with Eddie's parents at their apartment a minute's walk up the street, so have been on a bit of an incidental detox. When they reopened a week or so ago, they realised they had lost their ability to drink. On their opening weekend, they had a huge night with some locals, who also appeared to have forgotten how to hold their liquor. There were twenty people – half of them friends and the others strangers – and, because it's Italy, there was also a dog. They kicked on until 5 am, when two of the men got into a spirited altercation. When Eddie told one of the men he had to leave, he was indignant.

'Why me?' he asked. 'Why am I the one sent away?'

'Because this other guy is my friend,' Eddie explained. At which point, the punchy Italian started to cry.

Yes. He cried.

A cop car cruised by slowly, and Grace, who was slightly nervous because of lockdown restrictions and social distancing rules being breached, realised she was bone-tired and that the sun was rising, and she had no reserves left to comfort a weeping Italian. She had had enough. She kicked everyone out. Even the dog.

We are sitting at the bar now, hearing of their exploits, happily interrupted by the return of normal Italian life – neighbours walking past and saying good evening and stopping for a quick chat; a random Eastern European lady stopping by, dancing solo in the middle of the room, while asking for cigarettes.

A trio of well-dressed men come in. They are new to the place but pick up on the fact that we are speaking English, and ask where we are from. When we tell them we are Australian, they are overjoyed. It turns out two of them lived in Australia ten years ago; working first to meet visa requirements at a tulip farm in Victoria, and then in hospitality at The Prince Hotel, just down the road from our home in St Kilda.

They are so cheerful and fun. They can't believe we live here. 'Australia is the greatest country in the world!' they say. Then they tell us, as Italians always do, which regions we must visit while we are here. Where to go to drink the best white wine (Campania). Where to go to eat the best ham (Parma, of course). They insist on buying us another round of drinks.

In return, Peter shouts a round of toasties with cheese, and a house specialty with mortadella and Vegemite that Grace makes on a tiny kitchen bench screened off from the main room.

We have made a date with our new Italian friends, Daniele and his Napolitano sidekicks. We will meet them next Friday night at the bar. Then, the following morning, we will walk up to the hills with them, to the villa in the park that has a view over Bologna.

Little do I know that next week, instead, I will be attempting to fly back to Australia to see my adored father, who is desperately ill.

39

STRAWBERRY THICKSHAKES

Lewis and I are racing.

It is a baking day in June and we are at the station in Bologna, the first time we have been here since everything was locked down in February. Although Peter dropped us off twenty minutes early we are now about to miss our train. We are panic-dragging suitcases down and up stairs and I have two that weigh over fifty-five kilos together, one of them *the worst suitcase in the world* – it's huge and unbalanced with a munted handle and wheels seemingly designed by the Antichrist himself.

Lewis is helping me as much as he can, but he also has his own large backpack, and together we are overwhelmed and desperate. The station's normal throughfares are blocked off because of social distancing (we think, but it may also be a touch of 'Italy'), and we are now a pair of hot and frantic rats in an *Amazing Race* maze, trying to get to our platform to get our train to get to Milan to get a plane to get to Australia.

We are attempting to fly home. Back to Australia. Back to Melbourne.

And we are mired in Covid-complicated caca.

The international airport in Bologna has not yet reopened so we have to make our way to Milan on the train. From Milan Centrale we will get a cab to Malpensa, the international airport, then a plane to Dubai, and from there, another on to Melbourne. Peter and I have spent the last week in contact with Australian authorities in Italy, and, while we are permitted to travel on compassionate grounds, when we reach Australia (which has so far done an impressive job of containing the virus), we have to complete mandatory quarantine in a hotel room for two weeks. That leaves us a week or so with Mum and Dad, friends and family, before we (godspeed), make our way back to Italy. Since Lewis is so close to my dad, and has finished his end-of-year exams, it is decided he will accompany me to Australia. Peter will remain in Italy with Sunday, Jannie and Artie, who are still finishing their school year. Phew.

The compassionate grounds are these: my beloved dad Jan has been sick, and as often tends to happen with someone who has accumulated an impressive collection of years on earth, things have recently lurched from bad to worse.

The cruel irony is that he was supposed to be in Bologna now, with Mum, visiting us, as they did for three weeks last year. Instead, he is in hospital after a seemingly minor skin cancer removal led to a blood infection. Over the last six weeks, he has been in and out of hospital and he is now on such strong antibiotics that they render him constantly nauseous. He has not eaten for three weeks.

This is twofold worrying. Obviously, for my lovely *pappetje* who has become terribly, ominously frail, but also for my devoted mum who is trying to manage things. Mum and Dad have a staunch group of helpful and loving friends (many from their church – how glorious is the fellowship of a church when it offers what it should?), but the confluence of Covid restrictions and the general exhaustion of hospital is clearly getting Mum down. Also, some weird stuff has happened: last week, when she had to call an ambulance to pick Dad up from home, the crew arrived in full science-fiction hazmat suits, demanding to be led to 'the patient with the virus'.

Mum assured them neither she nor Dad had coronavirus, but the paramedics were adamant. They had been told, apparently. So they bound Dad up in sterile plague-coverings, like one of those cling-wrapped suitcases you see bound for Bali, and they took him away. At the hospital, they admitted him to the Covid ward. Who puts an immunocompromised, elderly man in a Covid ward if he doesn't have Covid? It was like they were trying to kill him.

Dad, always so positive, did his best to keep his spirits up, and on the phone assured me that both his Covid tests had come back negative. When I expressed disbelief that he was still in the coronavirus ward, he said to me in his adorable Dutch accent: 'Don't vorry about me, darling. Nobody in de vard has de virus.'

The hospital has always looked after Dad beautifully, and he has been going there so long, a lot of the staff know him and are fond of him. But I can't bear to think of him suffering and weak, and not being there to put my hand on his beautiful bald head, especially in these times when people are spending their final days alone and fearful, denied the comfort of their families.

The journey back to Australia is fascinating, in an eerie 'new-normal' way.

Mid-June is the traditional kick-off for summer tourists in Europe but when we finally reach our platform and make our way onto the train, we discover we are the only two on our carriage. The fast train to Milan from Bologna is empty. Once we have found our seats and clutched sweating hands in a panting high-five, the food cart trundles past. This is standard on Italian trains, which are generally magnificent. As well as travelling at 280 kilometres per hour, there is a restaurant carriage serving hot food and wine, and a food cart pushed by a white-gloved attendant who offers fresh coffee and food. Today the trolley is tended by a masked woman wearing plastic gloves. She hands us a paper bag containing water, extra face masks and gloves. Then she asks if we would like sweet or savoury snacks (always savoury!) and hands over a bag of crispy, salted bread twists. As she moves off, Lewis takes his mask off to tuck in, and she wheels her trolley back and, in curt Italian, instructs him to leave his mask on. Ah. Okay . . .

For the rest of the journey, as the train speeds past green, green countryside and through tunnels, Lewis makes me laugh by pretending to eat his hard round pretzels through his cotton mask.

In Le Marche before a beautiful birthday seafood dinner at our friend Giovanni's mate's restaurant, Torpedine, in Porto d'Ascoli on the Adriatic coast.

At Agrigento in Sicily with Artie and Jannie at the ancient Greek ruins of Akragas. A refreshing 40 degrees! After this we had the greatest lemon granita of our lives.

A palace in Palermo, the Sicilian capital and fabled home of the mafia.

So many beach meals. This was at Giardini Naxos in Sicily, overlooking the sea. The waiters crossed the road to bring our food.

Seafood platter, Sicilian style.

Sicilian Arturo. Everyone offered the children wine.

The Breasts. (I'm not sure what they're called in Italian, but it's got to be something to do with boobs.) And the fabled cannoli.

With Sicilian-Giovanni's parents Serafina and Vincenzo in the kitchen of their bed and breakfast in Taormina. I am wearing a crocheted flower necklace Serafina made for me.

Five take Puglia.

Preparing for the ball at Carnevale in Venice. My only regret was not having a lady in waiting. I was hoping to surprise Peter with my transformation but I had to enlist his help to get into my giant hooped dress and Scarlett O'Hara-style corset.

Lady Kate and Lord Peter of Bologna. Most excellent fun.

Mozart and companions. Smart casual.

Who are these mysterious and beautiful ball-goers? This officer and lady.

Embracing what the Italians call 'White Week' when schools have a week off and everyone heads to the snow. In Italy many people can ski before they can walk. We discovered the perfect *Sound of Music* chalet in a tiny village about three hours from Bologna where Peter and the boys enjoyed skiing – and the odd blood nose – while Sunday and I lazed around and admired the scenery.

In our final weeks in Bologna, I would cry every time I saw Ferdi, the landlord of our beautiful palazzo apartment. (A portrait of his dad, also a lawyer, hung in our entranceway.)

Ferdi's massive ongoing renovation of his historic building was often impeded by discovery of ancient frescos on the ceiling. The renovation of our apartment was a story of its own. The same two tradies every day but they got the job done.

The day before her 14th birthday, Sunday and I went to Florence to see Jannie play in his first basketball tournament where he was billeted with an Italian family. He was so happy to see us.

My daughter Sunday and me in Florence. Pardon our smugness.

Jannie strewn with confetti from a street fiesta in Bologna.

Italian humour.

Every park in Italy has a bar or little restaurant. Even in Covid times, and in the middle of winter, they are welcoming and well frequented.

Covid reared its head but in October 2020 we were still allowed out in Bologna. Also, I am carrying a Gucci bag so double happiness. Our old apartment is behind us, with scarlet blinds open.

My yoga friends Francesca, Johanna and Simona in my courtyard in Bologna. Our teacher Claudia has the bike.

On the streets of Bologna, walking to Sunday lunch.

Bistecca + vino. And a mouth-watering sample of the magnificent Michelin-starred food we enjoyed for our farewell dinner in Bologna.

At our unforgettable farewell dinner hosted by our friend Riccardo at the renowned Ristorante Il Portico, once the domain of a pope.

When we arrive in Milan Centrale an hour or so later, it, too, is a shadow of its normally bustling self. There is a snaking line of taxis outside, waiting for non-existent passengers. On the half-hour trip to the airport, unimpeded by any other traffic, the driver tells us it is his first airport run in months.

When we arrive at the main Departures entrance, the doors to the terminal are locked. We follow the few other people we see to the other end of the concourse, where a single door is open. Inside, after a temperature check, we pass security who wave us into the empty terminal. There is a lone coffee shop open, with a smattering of travellers queued. Everything else is shut. At midday on a weekday in tourist season, in one of Europe's great cities, the empty, echoing airport is an unbelievable sight. We make our way to the check-in desk. It, too, is closed.

We pass the waiting hour on seats directly next to the counter, with a view to the other end of the vast and empty terminal. In that time we see no more than fifty other people, many of them cleaners.

Every stage of this journey feels like a minor victory. The six-hour flight to Dubai is relatively normal, except we are forbidden to carry onboard any cabin luggage, the flight attendants are wearing disposable surgical scrubs over their uniforms, and passengers and crew are required to leave their masks on 'at all times'. (The latter means when you are speaking to someone, they can't hear you over the compressed cabin noise, and obviously can't lipread, so they need to incline their head toward yours to work out what you are actually saying. This would seem to negate the purpose of the social distancing measures.)

When it's time to fill out the two-page health check the cabin crew have distributed, required to transit in Dubai, the flight attendant tells me he is not permitted to lend me a pen. We share a moment of confusion as I digest this small but peculiar restriction. I mean, it is going to be very difficult to fill out a form without a pen. And I have no bag. The flight attendant looks stricken. This is one of the airline's first flights back, and I guess this dilemma has taken him by surprise. He glances around conspiratorially, then produces his own pen and covertly places it on my tray table. I place it back on the armrest when I am finished filling out the forms. Later, when I return from the toilet, I see the pen has disappeared.

Dubai airport is normally a heaving mini-city with terminals linked by trains, and lengthy queues of transiting passengers staring sandy-eyed at huge screens displaying hundreds of flights. Tonight it is so quiet we hear our own footsteps reverberate through the cavernous hangar. Ground crew have checked our temperature as we disembarked the plane. A security guard checks again as I go to enter a duty-free store, which the salesgirl tells me has only reopened that day. I am the sole customer, and I briefly wonder how their business will fare. I have to put plastic bags on my hands to enter, as well as my mask, and every product tester has been removed from the shelves; even for perfumes. Who, I wonder, will buy a new fragrance without smelling it first? I lose interest in the joyless store, and check the departures board, where a single screen displays all onward flights. There are eight of them.

When our aircraft touches down in Melbourne fourteen hours later, we sit onboard for nearly an hour, waiting for health officials. There are not many passengers, maybe 120, and when we are permitted to disembark we file down the empty corridors past the 'Last Chance' duty-free store, which is closed. Instead, there are multiple trestle-tables set up outside the collared doors, where government workers are allocating quarantine hotels.

Lewis and I are given a slew of paperwork. We agree to our detention and state that we are free of any virus symptoms. There are more sheets with details on Covid-19.

Everything else is standard, but slow. We get our suitcases from the single operating conveyor belt. Declare the food (some gifts of aged balsamic vinegar and packets of hard pasta) we have brought from Bologna, and then, after being checked by biosecurity and clearing immigration, we are shepherded the back way out of the airport, along linoleum corridors and through 'staff only' doors, to a cluster of waiting SkyBuses.

There is some confusion as we attempt to load our suitcases onto the waiting coaches. Because of cross-contamination fears, the drivers have been told not to handle luggage, but a lady in front of us, juggling an infant, a stroller and a couple of suitcases, is physically overwhelmed. She simply cannot lift her suitcases with her baby on her hip; we know, because we watch her several failed attempts. Normally, Lewis would step forward to help, but we have been firmly instructed to keep our distance. Eventually, another waiting bus driver, frustrated at the holdup (and, I suspect, the lack of practical chivalry), steps in and resolutely hoists her bags onto the bus. Then, under her instruction, he collapses her stroller for her. He is swift and practical and assured, and when he is finished he says, 'There you go, love,' which is so comforting and old-school Australian, it makes me love him.

Three hours after touchdown, we are finally delivered to our laneway hotel in the city centre, where we are directed to stand on taped markers – a metre apart – as we wait to be checked in. We are flanked by security guards and a contingent of Department of Health staff, and there is a slight kerfuffle as a passenger on the bus tries to have a cigarette, heading back out to the street twenty metres behind us. He is told that he cannot 'under any circumstances' walk backwards along the corridor. He pleads that it will be his last cigarette in two weeks. The official is staunch. Another colleague quietly intercedes on behalf of the smoker, but to no avail. Lewis and I exchange looks over our masks. It seems extreme, but we are prepared for the reality of entering a 'rules are rules' realm. When it is our turn to shuffle our way, weary and bleary, to the check-in desk, the suited, masked man behind the counter takes us by surprise with his warmth. He is positively beaming – you can see his eyes crinkling above his mask.

'Welcome to The Pullman!' he says. 'Is this your first stay with us?'

He is so friendly, so upbeat and cheerful, behaving like we are normal travellers who have just arrived for a normal stay at his hotel. It is so incongruous to our 'now' – lined up with masks and gloves under armed guard – that it makes me laugh. Unexpectedly, I also get a lump in my throat, and a prickling of stupid tears. I am more tired than I realised.

The manager (lovely James) offers us a choice; because I am travelling with my teenage son, there is a standard room with twin beds, or another – a 'suite' with one bedroom and an adjoining lounge. The latter is not large, he informs us, and has only one bed, but has a long couch we can make up for Lewis to sleep in. Then we will at least have a door we can close between us, he says; two weeks is a long time. I am so dazed, I can barely make a decision, but on his recommendation, we take the suite option, and head upstairs, accompanied by security guards, who travel in the lift with us.

Our two-week quarantine is a blur of jet lag, which proves surprisingly difficult to shake without the sun to reset our body clocks. Lewis and I are both strangely unmotivated; some days it is all I can do to have a shower and make our beds. We punctuate our erratic sleeping with binge-watching *The Office* (American) together, and listening to the occasional cage wrestle of drug addicts from the pedestrian mall outside. Still, the hotel is clean and well-run, and unexpectedly welcoming. My girlfriend Jane sends a huge bunch of flowers, which is so crazily kind, and somehow makes our room seem opulent. Our beloved Sacha puts together a care package for us; we are apparently allowed one a week. She is not permitted to drop it off. Instead, it is picked up from her house via taxi and delivered to the hotel. She has packed snacks for Lewis – chips and boxes of the Aussie lifeblood Barbecue Shapes; coffee pods and cheese for me, plus a yoga mat and several books. The latter two, it turns out, are laughably ambitious. I seem incapable of anything other than sleeping and staring at my phone, doom-scrolling Covid numbers around the world.

There are thrice-daily door knocks to deliver our meals, which are left at our door in brown paper bags. The food is wholesome and fresh, and in surprisingly generous quantities. For breakfast, muesli and yoghurt; sometimes croissants or hash browns. Lunch is a salad or wrap; quinoa with chicken. Dinners are curries or slabs of fish or chicken with vegetables. One day, a week or so in, a Domino's menu is slipped under the door for an upcoming 'Pizza Night'. This is very exciting. I have also told Lewis we can now order an Uber Eats every second day. He chooses Vietnamese, Japanese or Chinese; dumplings and crispy Szechuan chicken, and sushi – delicious foods we have missed in Bologna. These arrive the same way as our normal meals: via an anonymous knock on the door. We leave a minute for the delivery person to scamper away, so they don't have to come in contact with our plague-selves. When we open the door, there is often a security guard sitting outside, watching our floor. They must be such long, dull days. The guards are mainly on their phones; sometimes sleeping, the opening of our door jolting them awake.

Every day we receive calls from Department of Health employees; checking us for symptoms of the virus, and asking about our mental well-being. In between, I am on the phone myself: to Mum, back to Italy, or to the hospital where Dad is being looked after. He sounds so weak that, one day, after we have tried to speak to him, and he is lapsing in and out of consciousness, Lewis and I both sit on the edge of my bed and cry. We are willing him to hold on, to find some reserve of strength in his increasingly empty arsenal; to wait for us to get out, to rally. I speak to a health official about applying for an exemption to get out of quarantine early. She has obviously fielded a few of these difficult queries, and carefully explains that exemptions are basically only approved for 'end of life'. Mercifully, my father is not in palliative care. Fark. Such a sobering, heavy thought. Such a weird and painful limbo we are in.

In the meantime, I speak with Dad's haematologist, Simon, a truly lovely man and gifted doctor, who has pulled off medical miracles in the past ten years he has been treating my father. One night I message him as he is making a roast dinner for himself and his husband. He texts me back, assuring me that he has been constantly astounded by Dad's strength of will. It is a heartening reminder to remain strong myself.

Three days before our release, several nurses appear at our doorway with a trolley and we are offered Covid tests. These are strangely not yet compulsory for quarantinees, but we want to make sure we are clear before we are released; after all, we are heading straight to the rehab hospital Dad has now been moved to. The next day, we get the results. We are negative; a huge positive.

Tuesday morning. We receive a call that we will be released any time after 1 pm. It is surprisingly difficult to pack; Lewis and I have had hardly any fresh air – two fifteen-minute breaks in fourteen days, and we are both sluggish and slow. My eyes are perpetually itchy. Also, we seem to have accumulated a lot of extra junk in quarantine. When the departure knock comes at the door, we can scarcely believe it.

We are signed out and put into a waiting taxi. Outside, it is winter-grey, but the world looks bright and amazing. We head straight home, where we are met by Sacha and her son Milo, and hug them till they beg for mercy. Then we jump in my car – which starts like a charm, thanks to Sacha's regular running of the engine, and leave to pick up Mum, who is waiting.

We are here. We are home. And we are going to see my father.

'The power of love' sounds like a platitude, a hokey song lyric, but I have lived it, and never more so than when we first see Dad.

On the way to the hospital, we have stopped at the McDonald's drive-through to pick up a strawberry thickshake – my father's favourite. Mum is impatient at the detour. 'He won't be able to drink it,' she says. 'He can't keep anything down.' Still, Lewis and I are insistent. It is important that, in the face of our helplessness, we bring him this tiny treat that we know he loves.

Ten minutes later, when we have signed into the visitors' book downstairs, and we finally enter Dad's shared hospital room, I am shocked. He is gaunt and breathless, and although his eyes light up when he sees us, he can barely speak. Lewis and I perch on the bed on either side of him, stroking him, cuddling him. We remove his knitted beanie so we can kiss his bald head, patchwork-quilted by his various skin cancer removals. We arrange pillows and extra blankets, and tuck his feet in at the end of the hospital bed. Lewis falls into the gentle teasing manner he has always had with my dad (he calls him *Slow-pa*, a play on his Dutch grandpa-title *Opa*), and though my father tries to smile, it seems to take more energy than he can muster. We offer the strawberry thickshake, but he shakes his head.

Over the top of Dad's hospital bed, I check out my mother. Mum is normally a robust, hearty-laughing, life-of-the-party person, but the past months have stripped her of her usual vitality. As we know only too well in our family, hospital confinements are exhausting – especially when it seems you are 'losing'. Mum, clearly overwhelmed by all the travelling to the hospital and doctors' meetings, and running the household and general anxiety, spends a lot of time with her hand clasped over her mouth, in that seemingly universal manner of mothers digesting bad news. She has done such a good job, holding things together, but is undoubtedly depleted. When visiting time is over, and we leave to drive her home, Dad, who has been resting quietly, manages to warn me not to speed.

'You are not in Italy, now, sweetheart,' he says, which makes us all laugh. And indeed, a flash of his normal nagging self is the most positive sign we could have.

Then, when we are tidying up the room, and go to bin the untouched thickshake, Dad says to Mum, 'Put it on the table next to me, Anne. Maybe I vill hef a little zip.'

And he does. Just a sip. But his eyes gleam, and he says, 'Delicious.'

The next morning, a miracle. Dad is sitting up in bed, and wants to go for a walk up the hallway. His progress continues throughout the week; little things that mean the world. Walking to the bathroom. Sitting on the edge of the bed and raising himself to his feet. Every day, when we visit, we walk the hallways. By the third day, Dad is calling out comments to the nurses as we pass; introducing us to them, and telling us their backstories. It has become a victory lap. The nurses are beyond beautiful; that perfect mix of compassion and firmness; patience and humour. The head of the ward takes me aside to tell me how much they love looking after Dad. 'He's such a gentleman,' she says, a phrase I have heard often in my life. And it is true. Even at his lowest ebb, Jan Langbroek is gracious and impeccably mannered. And watching him – my tall, proud, stooped father, leaning on my tall, loyal, straight-backed son, as they slowly make their way down the carpeted hall together – makes my heart swell so much it hurts.

Every day, now, on the way to the hospital, we stop and pick up a strawberry thickshake. By the end of the week, Dad is reaching for it greedily. We have also started bringing in chicken nuggets, which are also happily received (with his standard routine: 'Should I hef von? Maybe just a little bite.') Dad is now walking and talking. When we arrive in his room he is often holding court with his roommate, a sweet faded-rose beauty called Charlie Allen, whose daughter visits faithfully. When Dad sees us, he demands to know why we are late. He reminds Mum to pay some bills. Asks for his phone charger so we can call him. Together, we FaceTime my brother John-Paul in Queensland, and Peter and the other children in Italy, and Dad talks quietly with them. Not a lot, and he is weary afterwards, but my beautiful Dutch dad is back. We can see him. His inner light, so dim when we first arrived, has been switched back on.

In between hospital visits, which are getting more complicated as Covid cases rise again in Victoria, we squeeze in some normal Melbourne life. I get up at dawn to go to early-morning yoga – impossible in late-rising Bologna, where the earliest class is normally at 8 or 9 am. I have breakfast with Hughesy. I go into the studio with him and see Jack and Ed Kavalee (who has brilliantly replaced me on the radio), and the three of us do a couple of shows that are so fun and funny. Lewis has a night with his old school friends. We drive out to Peter's parents' house for dinner, and are welcomed with my mother-in-law's magnificent roast lamb. Some girlfriends surprise me with Friday night drinks. We are limited to five visitors because of coronavirus restrictions, which suits me fine. We drink and eat celebratory prawn cocktails and end up dancing in the lounge room. I am so tired, but so happy.

On Monday, Sacha sets the whole day aside to help me book our flights back to Italy. Now we just need to find a plane that will take us. There is a flight departing on Wednesday; it is cancelled the next day. Then we are rebooked for Friday, on a flight back to Milan.

At the airport, our check-in takes a couple of hours, as we answer reams of questions posed by the woman at the airline counter. We are surrounded by other travellers – individuals and families – pleading their case, variously crying or shouting. Some are turned away; the lucky ones are sent to another queue, to present their documents to the ominously named Border Force (who have already checked ours). It is a very confronting scene. Lewis and I sit quietly, waiting.

I pull out my phone and dial home, expecting Mum to answer. Instead, it is my dad on the other end of the line. He explains he was released from hospital that morning. After ten long weeks, he is finally home.

It is so amazing. It is a blessing; a gift; a miracle.

It is, truly, a testament to the power of love.

(And strawberry thickshakes.)

The week after we leave, our home state of Victoria is plunged into a lockdown that will last for 112 days; the longest in the world.

40

THE BEE IN BEE-ACH

We are back in Italy, and it is almost the country we knew before – still a little bruised and tentative from the lockdowns, but also optimistic. The mood of the whole country seems summer-ready and bright. Now that some of the restrictions have eased and we are allowed to travel out of our region, we have happily seized on the chance of an overnight trip to the beach with our friends Monica and Riccardo, and their beautiful smiling son Robbie, who is fast friends with Jannie. The younger boys are in the same class at school, and also play for the same Italian basketball team, but because the basket season has come to an abrupt Covid end, they are starved for the bouncing of a ball. So today Peter, Artie, Jannie and I are going to a beach club an hour or so from Bologna where we will meet Robbie and his parents.

Coming from a country where the beaches are free, and free of private enterprise, the European beaches are always a surprise. The miles of oceanfront are often privately owned or leased, either by the hotels behind them on the shore, or by clubs that set up for the summer season. The infrastructure is extraordinary – with wooden boardwalks, colour-coded umbrellas and recliner chairs for rent, stretching as far as the eye can see. If you are staying at a corresponding hotel, you cross the road, and are given a towel and an allocated spot. The clubs, though primarily for members, are also open to the public, for a daily rental of the day beds, which are lined up in uniform rows for one or two hundred metres, all the way to the edge of the water. They often offer sports facilities – basketball or mini-gyms and sometimes even tennis courts – and all of them, of course, have restaurants. A day at the beach is such a popular escape in Italy that when you look from one end of the beach to the other, all you see are thousands and thousands of fluttering umbrellas.

We are heading to a beach club called Umberto, a place so well-frequented in our hometown Riccardo jokes that all we will see will be Bolognese sunning themselves. It is in a town named for the pine trees that line the main street, and it was once *the* destination for well-heeled Milanese. Now it is a family place, with dozens and dozens of hotels, most of which are still empty, or creakily coming back to life after the lockdown. Because of this, we have decided not to bother booking accommodation beforehand; we will take our chances and hopefully snare a bargain once we arrive.

When we cruise through the town, we drive past a hotel that is so white and splendid, it dominates the street. The watered lawns are green and lush and freshly mowed; the surrounding wrought-iron fence a perfect frame for the weight of blooming jasmine that cascades down to the footpath. To top it off, there is a red Ferrari parked at the entrance. The latter seals it for the boys – 'Can we stay there?' they request in unison. My thoughts exactly. And though it seems decadent to even enquire about a family room at a five-star hotel, Peter parks, and we go in.

There is another couple at the check-in desk as we enter. They are stylish-rich Italian: impeccably coiffed hair; decked from head to toe in Dolce & Gabbana resort wear. By contrast, Jannie and Artie are in their Aussie uniform of nylon basketball shorts and thongs. Still, the impeccable lady at the desk is smiling and welcoming. She gives us a decent rate on a family room up in the rafters. It includes breakfast, down by the huge blue pool surrounded by more lush green grass and festive flowers tumbling from pots.

After a lunch of the most insanely over-dressed tuna carpaccio (edible flowers and pickles and sauces and croutons), we head to our deck chairs at the beach. It is still too cold for grown-up Italians to swim, but Peter and I take the first plunge of summer with the children. Afterwards, the boys head to the basketball court to dry off and bounce. Jannie comes running back twenty minutes later and says Artie has been stung by a bee. Riccardo is sleeping on the recliner. Artie, who is quiet and dazed, goes white and red and blotchy. He starts to throw up. Can't eat an icy pole. We wake up Riccardo. He snaps awake, instantly grabs his keys, and hustles Peter and Artie to his car. They drive to the nearest hospital. It is closed. Riccardo – ever the hospitality professional – is furious at the hotel front desk for not knowing, in a pandemic, which hospital is open. He heads to another hospital. Drives 160 kilometres an hour; Petie, in the back seat, holding Artie, is petrified.

They whisk Art into emergency. Three doctors attend to him; the senior doctor is well into his seventies. They are swift and kind and efficient, they give him a cortisone drip and hydration and, after three hours, Artie is released.

He leaves with medication for the next six days.

We go out to dinner that night. Artie has had a long bath, which Jannie insisted on joining him in, and the combination of little-brother adoration, medication and relaxation has seen him much revived. At the restaurant, the boyos are positively giddy. They are shown by a waiter to their own table across the room, where we can see them ordering illicit soft drinks while Robbie – already brimful of food knowledge, instructs them on what to order. We all eat fried seafood – calamari and sweet white fish without bones. We drink wine and toast Riccardo for his kindness and for driving like an F1 champion. He laughs and says he drove like an Italian.

That night, we sleep like logs.

41

PLEASURE. PAIN. PUGLIA.

I am watching a man kill an octopus.

He is a family man – Italian, of course – for in this reprieve from lockdowns and restrictions, we have headed down south, to Puglia, the high-heel of the boot of Italy, and though it is remarkably free and sun-drenched here, there are few foreign tourists.

The man is with his mother and father and wife and teenage daughter, and they have, like us, clambered down the steep rocks to get to the water. Unlike us, after a few minutes of swimming he emerged from the deep blue with a soft pink mollusc. He called out excitedly to the others before swimming back to the rocks with his briney prize captured in his diving goggles, held aloft like a platter. Now he is slapping the octopus against the rocks, then hands it to his daughter, who rinses it in the sea water before passing it back to her dad for another intense slapping. Finally, the man – this hunter – flips the creature inside out, nestles it in the goggles, covers it with seawater, and resumes his swimming. The family group are pleased; I hear their plans to eat the octopus, now tender and dead, for lunch.

We are staying in a two-bedroom apartment we have rented across the road, Sunday in a room of her own while Artie and Jannie share a fold-out bed in the loungeroom. Lewis is with us and yet not with us; he is in Spongano, a quiet town five minutes inland with a group of his friends from school – Julian, Alessandro, Paolo, Lucy and Andrea. They are staying – unsupervised – at the stunningly fitted-out old tobacco warehouse Andrea's father and mother bought some years ago and have renovated. The five of us remaining have followed our eldest son south, fleeing baking Bologna and overnighting on the way at a beach town with salt pans and flamingos. Ostensibly, we were to pick Lewis up after his weeklong idyll with his mates but when he sees our cramped quarters he opts to stay at the villa, where the crew is living large. It is three storeys of opulence, overlooking a resort-style swimming pool framed by ten-metre-long fluttering curtains. Like I said, stunning. There, Lewis cooks for his friends every night, and a local woman from the village, Rachele, comes and indulgently cleans for them every afternoon. It is obviously too good to leave, the dream holiday set-up. The independence. So now we are in the strange situation where we sometimes bump into our son and the others at the Castro town harbour, where they have lined up to jump off the sea-wall or are borrowing a boat to explore the coastline. Once, we (intentionally) meet them all for dinner at the giant seafood restaurant up on the hill above the town before the gang heads off to a nightclub on the beach.

Puglia, by the way, is the present holiday hotspot of Italy, and has been gaining in popularity over the past few years. It is easy to see why. It is spectacular and the coastline majestic but compared to the glamour of Capri or Sorrento, it is rustic and raw. The food is glorious; seafood is plentiful, and the bread is outstanding (this is especially noticeable after Bologna, where the bread is more like a male model: good-looking, but dense and disappointing). Also, Puglia is cheap. A buttery breakfast pastry with coffee costs less than two euros.

Much of the coastline here is rocky. We have to painstakingly make our way over jagged volcanic shards to get to the water, and have learned to lie on them to sunbathe. We make day-trips looking for sandy crescent beaches or head inland, past seemingly endless kilometres of the olive groves divided by stone walls for which Puglia is famous. The walls are so ancient (Puglia is well over two thousand years old) that the stones are bleached and porous like old bones. Though the scenery is stunning, dry and flat and bright, there is a blight here. There is a bacteria, introduced from imported trees, that is killing many of Puglia's olive trees. This is, simply, a catastrophe. The region produces more than a tenth of the world's olive oil from more than 60 million trees; now a third of them are dying. When you see them, in their tens of thousands with bare and twisted limbs reaching denuded to the cloudless sky, it looks as though they are in a tree cemetery. It is, of course, impossible to not also think of the pandemic that is sweeping the globe.

Italians do not speak freely of such a blight – or maybe just not to foreigners. I initially heard of the dying olive trees from the photographer who took pictures of us for an Australian magazine spread about our new life. Paul, a most delightful and cheerful Englishman (who, despite his modesty, turned out to be a photographer of international acclaim), was telling me and Peter over post-shoot drinks about his own place in Puglia, a property he shared with a Venetian friend of his for over twenty years.

'It is terrible,' I remember him saying in the noisy laneway bar where we were squeezed on benches alongside a throng of students. 'I love the trees so much. It is like watching friends die.'

Anyway, I am thinking of our photographer friend now and wishing I was better at keeping in contact with people. As it is, I can't find his email and neither Peter nor I can remember his surname, or where exactly in Puglia he had his summer base. Everything was so foreign then. But the trees make us think of him as we drive highways intersecting tiny towns and see whole groves bulldozed. We think of him, too, as we see where optimistic farmers have turned fields and planted them with fresh trees, lovingly watered and tended in the belief that they, one day, will also get to be ancient.

Anyway, the olive saga forms a sobering backstory to what is a glorious, sun-drenched southern-Italian summer. After several days in our pretty apartment in Castro, we move to our own villa. Although small, it is beautifully set in its own olive grove, with a shaded stone terrace wrapped around it and a timber-decked swimming pool up a pathway next to our own trullo house. (The little stone conical huts known as trulli date back to the fifteenth century or earlier. You see them dotting the landscape throughout the Itria Valley in Puglia. Many of them are restored and can be rented as hotel rooms so it is incredible that ours is used as a storage shed.) Lewis joins us and the six of us spend our days by the pool or cooking on the outside barbecue the owner drops off wood for. Inside the villa is another tiny, ridiculous Italian kitchen (seriously, in a country that prizes food so highly, the kitchens are often laughably inept. This is the topic of much discussion. Maybe, we think, it is because much of the work – pasta making, for instance – is done outside the kitchen?) Anyway, this cucina is literally the size of a closet, and impossible for two people to stand in. In a way, though, its limitations provide me with holiday freedom; the mandate to eat out.

We take day trips to markets in nearby towns, where we buy bags of stone fruit and dusky grapes and feast on pizza and local burrata, oozing-soft and milky – and always, when it is offered, fried calamari. Once, we find ourselves at a rustic restaurant in the square of a small town, opposite a church that is holding a night service on the cobblestones outside. The trattoria is run by a hard-working but friendly mother and son, and when the octopus we have ordered is placed on the table, to the accompaniment of the hymn being sung in the background, it turns out to have been fried completely intact. Its beaky head is full of sea-gore. Even Peter and I can't face it, but – not wanting to hurt the feelings of the lovely madre cooking, who is so pleased with her international guests – we undertake a covert family operation. We pass the fishy offal into napkins under the table, which we then leave discreetly around the corner for the circling street cats.

Back at our villa, we seem to have acquired our own cat. At first, he seemed like a trick of the light – this skinny, white feline slipping among the olive trees like a four-pawed ghost. When Jannie first enticed him to the living-room door with a sliver of prosciutto, I was not convinced. He was skittish, ribby and scarred, and had one eye. Jannie, however, was instantly smitten, and named him Oliver. 'Because of the olive trees,' he said adoringly; a lisp-challenging explanation, for sure. Jannie was outside for hours the first day talking to his new furry friend. I grudgingly accept Jannie's love of the stray but have sternly warned my littlest son not to feed him. Of course, by the end of the week we are buying Oliver tins of tuna. We have bathed his eye, and it is miraculously opened and healing. After five or six days, our olive-cat is looking sleek and plump. One morning, Jannie calls him and he actually comes running. Jannie is elated.

This, of course, is the universal power of being loved. But there is more Italian magic at hand.

One day, we take the twenty minute drive down the coast road to a charming town called Tricase that has become a favourite haunt of ours. We surmise that it was named for the original three houses that must have grandly lined the shore – one of which, a stunning deep-pink villa, is still there, abutting a rare treasure: a tiny block of sandy beach. We have taken to heading there after a late breakfast – the Italians are so habitual, they vacate the packed beach at around 11.30 or 12 to head home for lunch, leaving it relatively free for us. This late morning, we have settled on the sand with our towels and sheltering beach umbrella. The three boys have raced around to jump off the rocks in the boat harbour, and Sunday is sunning herself on the shore, so Peter and I wade out for a swim. I start freestyling ahead of him, am momentarily confused when he doesn't overtake me in his customary show of physical superiority. I flip onto my back and scan the waters behind me. I can't see my husband through the paddling crowds, but I can hear his voice. He is speaking to someone in English, and laughing. Then I spy him, talking to a man in the chest-deep water. He beckons me over, so I swim my way to him. And what I see is unbelievable. Peter is with our photographer friend from last year. Paul, who we have spoken of so often here. And who we had no way to contact. He is here with his wife, Jasmine, and their children. His surname is Stuart (of course!) His villa is a mere half-hour drive away, ten minutes from where we are staying. He is also astounded that we would have found each other here, in the water in this tiny town in this densely packed country. And he had been wondering what had become of us; if we were still in Bologna, or in Italy at all.

Two nights later, we join him and Jas for family dinner at their villa, a modern low-slung white building set among the parched and brown tree-friends he told us about over a year ago. The boys all play ping-pong outside while Sunday bonds with their daughter, Xu, who is her age, the girls drifting off to a treehouse at the back of the property. The following week, after roaming the white-stone baroque laneways of Lecce, and visiting a beach called Gallipoli (how could we not?), the six of us moved to a three-storey beachside apartment in the town quaintly called Santa Maria al Bagno (literally, the bathroom of Saint Maria). Our English friends make the hour-long drive to visit us there. We swim in water so clear you can see where an underground spring pumps sweet water into the salty, making syrupy eddies. We jump off rocks and swim with a morning club of elderly ladies, who all wear shower-caps and clutch pool noodles. We wander the streets, and nod to the Italians sitting outside on their plastic chairs, all the better to catch the evening air and to gossip and neighbourhood watch.

There is a festival that night, and fireworks plume over the glittering sea, and we all drink wine from plastic bottles we have bought from a roadside stall, which we are expecting to be terrible, but which is surprisingly good. We barbecue meats and dress salad with olive oil we have bought from the same roadside man, and the teenage girls wander, giggling, down to the market opposite our apartment and return with secrets and trinkets.

And Italy is beautiful. It is not without viruses, of course. But it is never, it seems, without beauty.

42

SICILY: MOLTO, MOLTO GIOVANNIS

It is early October and the autumn days are, as they should be, cooler and noticeably shorter. So predictable is the change between seasons in fact that on 21 September, the night of the autumn solstice, the temperature dropped and we slept under more than a sheet for the first time in months. I find it comforting that the natural world is working as it should (at least in this regard) and have taken to making proclamations like: 'Well, the seasons are like clockwork. Someone better tell Greta'. This amuses me doubly, mainly because the reference to activist Greta Thunberg annoys my climate-marching daughter (the same daughter who sleeps with a hoodie *and* the aircon on, by the way). Also, I am feeling pretty cocky because, as it transpires, we are not yet done chasing the sun. Peter and I are heading back to Sicily.

As is often the case in our family, this impending trip has its genesis in cycling. As well as keeping my husband fit and making him deeply happy (he often returns home from a ride with a satisfied salt-crust of exertion on his face), Petie's pedalling has contributed much to our discovery of Italy. Whenever we head away, his road bike is loaded in the back of our Volkswagen van so he can take it for an airing every second day or so. Frequently on his expeditions, he will pass a restaurant or castle or lake which is so spectacular we all revisit it later. Peter has ridden since well before I met him and, through him, I have learned to also enjoy the sport – at least from a spectator's vantage. (In retrospect, I think the years spending so many late nights watching so many Tours de France played a part in our decision to move to Europe. The beauty of the multicoloured peloton snaking along country roads. The majestic scenery. The inevitable commentary about *food*. It is as though I have absorbed it by osmosis.)

This year the Covid-postponed Giro d'Italia (the Tour of Italy, which forms the cycling holy trinity with the Tours of France and Spain, and last year conveniently started outside our window in Piazza Maggiore) will commence in Sicily. It seems a perfect excuse to return to that stunning part of this country, the island ball being kicked by the Italian boot, where last enchanted summer we had such a glorious time with Artie and Jannie.

We have planned this trip for several months and now that it is upon us the timing couldn't be better. A week ago, after much discussion, Peter and I gave notice to our landlord, Ferdi. Our original return flights to Australia are still scheduled for December, and it seems the time is right to head home. It has not been an easy decision; Peter and I are both feeling intense sadness at the thought of leaving Italy, and apprehension about returning to our home country. We are grateful, then – almost desperate – to have the opportunity of this last hurrah; a final taste of Italian sunshine and freedom, before winter and the grind of packing up our household closes in on us.

It is Saturday and we have already had an emotional whirligig of a morning. In Australia the boys' beloved AFL Bulldogs team were playing against St Kilda for a berth in the finals. Peter returned from the little boys' basket training with their coach, Tall Giovanni, in time to see the end of the ultimately heartbreaking match. The Doggies had miraculously clawed their way back from a 26-point deficit, only to miss a goal in the crucial last moments of the game, resulting in a meagre-but-major three-point defeat.

We were all clustered in the lounge room, passionately barracking and cheering and willing victory – only to be left with that wounding last-minute loss. It hurt, watching my boyos watch their adored team's campaign come to such a bitter end, but sport,

I have come to grudgingly learn, is one of life's great teachers. So much of it is about redemption, about preparation and sacrifice, and valiantly pitting yourself against others who want what you want but may simply be better prepared or more talented or genetically blessed. And, reduced to its essence, life itself is just love and loss, isn't it?

Still, this is an academic analysis of what was simply a brutal, dying-embers defeat. Peter and Lewis shouldered the pain in stoic silence. Even Artie, I noticed, was able to digest it with a quiet reddening of the eyes and a brief head-ducking exit from the room – a sign of how he has matured this past year. Jannie, however, still bursting with the passionate, blindly loyal faith of a child, was so devastated he ran into the hallway and kicked the marble floor in fury until he hurt his toes. Then he flung himself on his bottom bunk and, pulling the doona over his head, railed at 'unfair umpireth' and 'cheatth' and howled and howled and howled.

I tried to comfort him with the platitudes of one who doesn't know that much about ball games: 'There is no shame in that loss' etc., but swiftly realised I would be better off making a batch of consolation pancakes. So I did, and we all gathered around the table and ate them with cups of tea, and eventually, soothed by lemon and sugar, maple syrup and bacon – and the comfort of family – peace and hope for the future was restored.

So we have resumed packing for our trip to Sicily. The expedition has been organised by our mate Giovanni for a group of his cycling buddies, and though we cannot do the entire ten days they have planned, we have nonetheless carved out a pleasing five-day escape, where we will lap up some lingering southern sun and seafood. The schedule is simple but pleasing: Petie and his fellow *cicliste* will ride the Giro course every second day while I will wander down from our bed and breakfast (the one run by Giovanni's Sicilian friend, Also Giovanni) to a beachfront day bed at the perfectly named Isola Bella (Beautiful Island), where I will drink almond granitas and read. In the evening, Also Giovanni's mother will cook us dinner.

Back in Bologna, we have booked our student-babysitter Veronica to hold the fort. She has coordinated her uni classes so that she can stay at ours for the week, dropping the boys at their relentless (and often conflicting) basketball training, supervising homework and seeing the children back-and-forth to school. Because she can't drive into the town centre, Peter has nutted out the details for her; he has drawn maps and cross-referenced bus timetables and colour-coded movement schedules in his thorough and patient manner, while I have spent the last few days cooking so that there will be ragu and meatballs; quick meals for the time we are gone.

Although we are not flying to Sicily until tomorrow afternoon, we are to drop our bags off today – along with Peter's prized bike – at Giovanni's restaurant Lambrusco, where (in a classic Italian complicated-but-ultimately-practical arrangement) another friend will drive all the bikes fourteen hours south in a bus borrowed from Giovanni's landlord, Older Giovanni. This will save on Ryanair's baggage fees and leave the rest of us with nothing but their satisfyingly low airfares – sixty euros a head for the hour-and-a-half flight. If all goes to plan, the plan is genius. En route to the restaurant, we will also deposit Jannie at a friend's paintball birthday party in a park twenty minutes away. Phew.

It is now 3 pm and we are in that pre-trip, mid-organisation zone: weary from our endeavours, but buoyed by the prospect of looming adventure. Petie and I are lying on our bed with Jannie, having a cuddle and mentally checking off final arrangements before we leave for the park and restaurant. Nothing, I think to myself, is more satisfying than when a plan comes together.

As though I have conjured it with my thoughts, a message pings on Peter's phone.

It is from Veronica.

She has some bad news. Her study partner from uni has just tested positive for Covid.

Of course this means Veronica may also have the virus. She is waiting for her own test results. In the meantime, she is in quarantine.

She had asked another friend if they could replace her as our babysitter but realised this friend has recently also spent time with her so she may also be infected.

Fock fock fock fockitty fock fock fock.

FUCK.

I have a childlike flare of my own frustration at the news, not unlike Jannie's earlier floor-kicking tantrum. I am sick, too – sick of Covid. Sick and tired of the disruption to every plan; sick of every heartbreak that, although seemingly minor in the face of a life-robbing pandemic, is nonetheless heartbreaking. The months of isolation; the homeschooling; the friends who could not come visit; birthdays spent alone; anniversaries unmarked; the cancelled plans of those we know and don't know around the world; the grief and tales of brutal lockdown in our home state in Australia where cases have risen; so many struggling in isolation and my father's illness and pregnant women being arrested for challenging government decrees and wearing masks and ruined businesses and having to be cheerful and constant hand-washing and EVERYTHING – rational and irrational – is brought to a head by this eleventh hour kick in the guts. In America, even President Trump has been struck down by the virus. It is an impossibly insidious foe. There is no point in fighting it.

We will go anyway, I say rashly, jumping off the bed and zipping up my overnight bag. Veronica will not have Covid. She does not have it. It will be fine. Peter, flattened by his own disappointment, stares at me as though I am mad. In fact, he actually says, 'Are you mad?'

No, I say. I am not. (Knowing that I am.)

He tells me not to be ridiculous. Veronica cannot come. She is in quarantine until she gets the results of her test. Even assuming she is negative, this will take days. And we have no one else. Plus, he says, he has spent hours putting in place arrangements that only she is capable of executing. And the boys cannot miss basketball training.

It is his insistence on the latter that really trips my anger, and we have a furious face-off. Lewis can look after the children for five days, I say desperately. He is seventeen, practically an adult. And *you* are always saying he needs more responsibility. Plus, there are other grown-ups in our apartment block who can check in on him if he needs. Also, I continue, why is the basketball training of an eleven-year-old and a thirteen-year-old the only sacrifice that cannot be torched on the altar of coronavirus? Why must we give up everything and not them? I am sick of having to care about basketball.

It is rare that we fight, and the flames of this clash burn fast and bright, but because we do not (ever, really) allow ourselves the luxury of walking out, we continue to hiss at each other as we prepare to take Jannie to his party. Then, somehow, though we are still at loggerheads, a strategy emerges. We will drop our things at the restaurant this afternoon and if we cannot make alternative babysitting arrangements by tomorrow we will forfeit the trip to Sicily and get our belongings back when the rest of the group returns next week.

It is as good a plan B as any but we are still frosty with each other as we carry our packed bags down to the car and load it up. As is often the case, our heaviness infects everything; we get lost on the way to the paintball park and, when we finally find it, can barely summon the energy to be social with the other parents who are there. Behind a tall, netted screen, we can see snipers hunting each other with their weapons. Hear the pop-pop-pop of their guns. They perch atop wooden towers, flanked by russet crowns of autumn leaves. It is weird and ominous. Gorgeous Robbie bounds up to us to show us his back, splattered with green paint where he has been shot. He is overjoyed at his wounding.

We leave and drive to Giovanni's. It is sunny outside but inside our car we are still silently frigid. Peter cannot find a park on the street and, reversing impatiently, bangs into a pole. This inexplicably pleases me, and I hide my smirk as I jump out of the car before he has finished manoeuvring, not wanting to be subjected to any more of his bad mood, while lovingly nursing my own. Outside, in the garden adjacent to the restaurant, I see Older Giovanni, the landlord who runs the Epilepsy Foundation upstairs, shovelling weeds. I go over and say hello. He is a most learned man – his pedantry and knowledge is rich and relentless. The first time we ever met, at a party at the restaurant, when Peter and I were introduced as Australians, he took our hands and said solemnly: 'Thank you for the liberty'. And then he spoke so movingly about the bravery of our soldiers in WWII, and the part they played in the liberation of Europe, it was as though it had happened yesterday. Today, however, he berates me for not speaking to him in Italian. I go to Covid elbow-bump him and he tells me about the origins of the ancient Roman salute before it was appropriated by fascists: open palm held upwards at the shoulder. It meant, he said, that you come in peace. That your hand is empty. That you are carrying no sword.

When Our Giovanni emerges from the front door of his restaurant on the tail of my history lesson, I tell him the bad news we received at home; that our babysitter may have Covid, but we are still hoping to make the trip to Sicily. He shakes his head in a mix of disappointment and sympathy but is clearly amused as I describe my ensuing fight with Peter.

'*Molto arrabbiato*,' I say. 'Very angry.' (The Italian word for 'anger', by the way, is also the name of the fiery pasta dish from Rome, a blend of chillies and garlic and heat. It is, tellingly perhaps, one of the first expressions I was confident enough to use, having learned it from a Barilla sauce jar. It has since come in very handy.)

As if on cue, we spy Peter across the road, scowling at the front of the van. His angry driving has knocked the licence plate off the bumper bar and left it dangling towards the kerb, and we watch him pluck at it furiously. I motion towards my husband, raising my eyebrows in a wifely 'See?' expression.

Giovanni, always pragmatic, smiles wryly and shrugs.

'He needs wine,' he says simply.

He goes inside and brings out a bottle of Lambrusco and four clinking glasses, and while he does that, Older Giovanni fetches his toolbox and hunkers down in front of our van, screwing the broken numberplate back on. I realise how hungry I am, and wander down to the bar kiosk in the park, returning with a grilled cheese and ham flatbread wrapped in paper. I give Peter half and Older Giovanni has some. It is delicious, and we drink our fizzy wine, and everything starts to feel better.

I say sorry to Peter for being grumpy. He says he is sorry too.

Older Giovanni swears at us for going back to Australia. 'Fucking kangaroos, bloody,' he says, using words he has apparently learned in Scotland.

Peter's phone buzzes again and it is Veronica saying her cousin's friend will come to babysit until she gets the result from her test, and in the courtyard, in front of our lovely friend's restaurant, the sun gleams.

Our Giovanni FaceTimes Also Giovanni in Sicily and tells him we would like arancini rice balls for dinner when we arrive tomorrow night.

Those delicious crumbed and fried orbs are, after all, a Sicilian specialty.

And you know what they say: when in Rome, do as the Romans do.

Salute.

(My hand is empty. My heart is, again, full.)

We arrive in Sicily at night. At 8 o'clock it is dark, yet still ten degrees warmer than up north. The humid air, Peter and I remark to each other, is reminiscent of Asia, and as we assemble outside the main terminal to wait for the driver who will take us to our bed and breakfast accommodation at Taormina, the beachside town where we stayed last year, we divest ourselves of the jackets we needed when we boarded the plane.

I survey our fellow bike-pack. There are eight of us; two others are driving the borrowed bus from Bologna with our luggage and bikes. The group is all men, aside from me, and because this is Italy, two of them are older – much older. This is a phenomenon, by the way, I have rarely experienced in my pre-Italian life: that wherever you go, there will be elders mingling with younger people ('just like normal people', we are prone to commenting, which sounds odd, but it is so unfamiliar to us that it is a point of marvelling). Here, you see old and young together everywhere; in restaurants; in family groups on holidays; in shops; at basketball training; on the street. Such is the seamless melding of extended family with work and social life, we have met the parents of nearly every one of our Italian friends. In Australia, I realise, I have friends I have known for years, and yet have rarely spent time with – or even met – their parents. There is an undeniable age-apartheid in our culture, which does not seem to exist here. As my wise friend Adam Zwar said to me a month or so ago: 'It doesn't seem to be a crime to grow old in Italy.'

In that regard, I realise, at home Peter and I live much more along European (and old-fashioned Aussie) lines. Both our sets of parents know most of our friends and frequently socialise with us – not in a 'look-at-mum-in-her-crop-top-going-to-the-disco-with-me' kind of way, but as a significant thread in the tapestry of our lives. (My girlfriends Miranda, Mish, Sach, Alice and Georgie have stayed in touch with mum and dad while we are away.)

Anyway, among our holiday contingent are Carlo and Antonio. They are both blue-eyed and straight-backed and suntanned, and move with the characteristic grace of so many cyclists – all nimble knees and tight lumbar sections. Everyone is in high spirits, and this pair in particular seem to enjoy our unabashed surprise as Giovanni announces their ages, though Antonio is quick to shake his head when he is described as being 80. 'No,' he corrects Giovanni, holding up a corrective finger. 'I am not 80. I am 79 and ten months!' His friend Carlo, it transpires, is 75. Both of them will be riding every day, although Antonio has the option of employing the electric motor fitted to his bike, should the mountain climbs prove too much. We also have Bruno, a broad-faced, gorgeous, cheery chap, whose son Claudio has been entrusted with driving the bike-bus, and another couple of sinewy and quiet 'classic' cyclists.

En route to our accommodation, a giant cheer suddenly erupts from our van, and there – impossibly next to us at the autostrada toll-booth – is the bikes-and-bags bus, which in an execution of timing that would be deemed impressive anywhere (but particularly on a 12-hour, non-stop drive from one end of Italy to the other) has just arrived from Bologna. The two vehicles pull up moments apart at our accommodation, where Sicilian-Giovanni is waiting. It is good to see him again. As we gather round the bus, grabbing bags and bikes, he tells us to head upstairs, to the same room we stayed in last summer. Our tiled room is familiar and welcoming, simple but spotlessly clean, the bed made up with crisp white sheets under a thin orange quilt, and a terrace that in daylight overlooks the sea but tonight is hung with the low Sicilian moon. Peter and I are so exultant to be back, we have an embrace in the moonlight. We are weary but so, so, happy.

When we head back downstairs, only minutes later, the OG Giovanni is already on the tools. A pot of pasta boils on the stovetop next to him and I peer curiously into the bowl he is balancing over the sink. He is quartering small red tomatoes, which cascade onto a mound of sliced garlic, black olives, salt and olive oil. While he slices, he tells me a story about when he was cooking for the Tour du France with a French chef, who added garlic and oil, as well as pepper, to the boiling pasta.

'I ask him, what is this?' Giovanni recounts, still wounded by the memory. 'He says to me, "I have cook-ed in Marseille. That is Italy!"'

Marseille, by the way, is a gnarly seaside port town in the south of FRANCE. I know it because last summer, Lewis and I celebrated our joint birthdays there with the family, eating (impossible-to-find-in-Italy) Vietnamese food. It is a collision of cultures – Arab and African and Asian – so I understand the French chef thinking he had discovered the Mecca of food fusion. But there is another point to the story that goes unspoken. Who in the world would be arrogant enough to stand alongside an Italian and tell him how to cook pasta? (I think we know.) The other Italians drift in and out of the kitchen, translating the story to each other, variously roaring with laughter, and shaking their heads.

After a moment I ask Giovanni what he said to the French chef.

He shrugs. 'I say to him: "for me this is not Italy",' he replies, simply.

I am struck – not for the first time – by the Italian pragmatism and seeming lack of ego. Proud, yes. Prideful, no. Giovanni sends me outside to the pot of basil growing at the back door to fetch some pungent leaves, and ten minutes later we are sitting down to a feast.

We convene in the lounge/dining room, surrounded by the now-unpacked bikes, at two long plastic tables covered with cotton cloths – one printed with wisteria, the other with lemons. Giovanni brings his pot to the table – and, like hungry children in a musical about an orphanage, we hold our plates out to receive steaming helpings.

The dish, despite its fancy name – *penne con salsa crudaiola* – is the perfect quick meal: cooked pasta tubes with the raw salad ingredients stirred through. Like so much Italian cuisine, its simplicity belies its deliciousness. We dress it liberally with parmesan and I am so hungry, I foolishly abandon all thoughts of pacing myself. Although the servings are huge, the pasta, I know, is simply the *primi* – the first course. Even though we have arrived late, pasta alone would not be considered a full meal. Somewhere in the commotion, Also-Giovanni has sped off on his scooter, and arrived back with several pizzas. They are Sicilian-style, of course – the flat bases puffed and heat scorched from a wood oven, and adorned with different toppings to what we are used to: vegetables and hot salami, and most memorably, a *bianco* (white pizza) variety, baked with melted creamy cheese and crumbled pistachio nuts.

On the table is a spectacular centrepiece – a gold, fluted-edge takeaway cardboard platter adorned with the much anticipated and celebrated *arancini*. There are at least a dozen of them: large pine-cones of golden crumbed rice, stuffed with ragu and discs of barely-melted mozzarella. These, like the pizzas, are not home-made – some things are best left to the experts.

I have eaten *arancini* in Australia, often smaller versions served as finger food at events, and have never been much of a fan. It turns out I was wrong. Possibly because of the festive mood and our travellers' hunger but most likely because 'Sicily' – these are just delicious: a perfect combination of creamy, savoury filling and crisp shell. They are both delicate and substantial, and we gobble them up, accompanied by cask wine that has been decanted into a large glass jug and bottles of water, fizzy and flat. Then, when it seems we cannot eat another morsel, Our-Giovanni enters from the kitchen, like Mustafa from the Lion king, proudly carrying aloft an ornately wrapped package.

He places it on the table with a flourish. The northerners crowd around excitedly, undoing ribbon and peeling back waxed-paper, and when the contents are finally revealed, burst into spontaneous applause. There, nestled among the fluted edges of another golden platter, are the fabled *cannoli*. They are spectacular; fried pastry rolled around fat cords of sweet ricotta, drizzled with melted chocolate, and adorned with candied cherries. Another parcel reveals a dozen gleaming women's breasts – round, almond flavoured-sponge cakes cloaked in ricotta and a coat of thick, opaque white icing. Each one is tipped with a glacé cherry nipple.

It is a lot, and yet, not too much. We have coffee and liqueurs: for me a bottle of the rich and delicious liquid chocolate that Giovanni knows I love; for the others, bitter *Amaro* with the bicycle on the label. It is as glorious a meal as anyone could wish for. Full-bellied, we wish everyone a *buona notte*, and roll upstairs to our Sicilian retreat. The others stay downstairs, chatting and drinking. (We are going to bed before the 70-year-olds.)

Every morning, usually after breakfast, the cyclists head out to ride up Mt Etna. One day they leave extra early – wanting to get to the top of the volcano before the *Giro d'italia* cyclists, who will be making the ascent as part of their 21-stage race. Every afternoon when I have returned from the beach, Sicilian-Giovanni's mum arrives with his dad, sometimes in their little car, sometimes on the back of a *moto*. They are laden with bags Vincenzo decants in the kitchen, where Serafina begins her meal prep. No one is allowed to help, which is a treat, but it is rare to have Sicilian home cooking, and I am keen to see her magic firsthand. 'I am not a queen,' I say to her, to which she replies: 'But you are my guest,' and brusquely shoos me out of the kitchen. I have to content myself with the finished meals, which she serves to the 10 of us, and which are incredible.

Every night, we begin with a large shared plate of bruschetta: tiny tomatoes sliced on bread. The *pane*, I notice, is left over from breakfast, toasted thinly and brushed with oil. (How clever the Italians are with not wasting food. The whole concept of *aperitivo* is designed to use up the uneaten food from the day.) Then, of course, there is pasta: penne with eggplant and zucchini, or spaghetti stirred through with mussels and calamari. One night we have *zuppa* instead – a delicious thick porridge, made with rice and, Serafina tells me, 15 vegetables. (We all try to count them and can't get past 13, which amuses her greatly.)

The main courses that emerge from her one-woman kitchen are spectacular: crumbed chicken tenders, pan-fried with lemon and served with steamed potatoes and lettuce; *involtini* – skewered rolls of flattened beef filled with local cheese, herbs and raisins. One night she makes the classic Sicilian dish *beccafico*: small fish stuffed with fresh, sweet anchovies and baked under a crumb crust, separated with tender bay leaves. When she places the dishes on the table, there is always applause.

The morning before we are to leave I am having breakfast on the terrace, chatting with Vincenzo, when Serafina emerges from the kitchen. She has a small mesh bag with her, and shyly presents it to me. Inside is a gift, a necklace she has crocheted. It is a long strand of red woollen flowers, studded with pink pearls. It is beyond beautiful. I hug her tiny, strong and lovely self – I am a giant compared to her.

That night I wear my new necklace to dinner.

43

SIX MAKE A PARTY

There is always a point, in any endeavour, at which it seems you have made things worse, not better. It is like when you have a big spring clean and end up with everything in disarray – piles of clothes and drawers emptied and beds stripped – and you just have to keep ploughing through the chaos, even though you exhaustedly think, 'What have I done?'

I am like this now, only I am trying to clean and cook and ready myself and the children for a party we are hosting tonight.

There is a lot of pressure on this gathering. It has been a year in the planning. It had its genesis last year in the innocence of pre-plague times, when we first moved into our gorgeous palazzo apartment. Then, I found myself at a basket tournament with parents from Artie's team. Peter was in another town at another tournament with Jannie and the mothers had led me to a separate table at the restaurant in which we were gathered, away from their husbands, and were asking about our move. My Italian was so poor then that lovely Francesca (face like a peach) had to translate the details of our new abode but even without her expertise and my limited vocabulary, I could convey the apartment was something special. '*Molto, molto grande,*' I said. '*Anche molto elegante.*' (Very, very big. Also very fancy.)

I showed them some photos and shared the tale of how it was so big that I had to have a lie-down after sweeping the floor, and they laughed and oohed and aahed and passed the phone. I said: 'We will have an aperitivo party so you can all see it' and it was such a brilliant, fun thought we all clapped. And then Speranza (our delightful Albanian friend whose husband Daniele takes the team photos) asked 'Just the women?' and I boldly said: 'No! Everyone!' I was thinking that would be twenty people or so but the ladies did a maths huddle in rapid Italian and worked out that with children and coaches and reserves it would be more like SIXTY PEOPLE. What? Anyway, I had established space wouldn't be a problem so, after a slight gulp, I reiterated our party would be for *tutti* – all of us.

After much, much cross-referencing of calendars and debate about school nights (the Italian children have school on Saturday), match fixtures and general availabilities, and interruptions for Christmas and public holidays, our aperitivo party was set for March but Covid happened instead. Peter predicted two weeks out that our plans were unlikely to come to fruition; I was still hopeful. Then, a week out, we formally cancelled, which was just as well because by the time the evening in question rolled around, all of Italy was in lockdown. No one was having parties.

Seven months later, we find ourselves between eased restrictions and freedom, and longing to see everybody. After the summer holidays the boys have been allowed to resume basketball training but parents are still not allowed in the courts. We all drop our boyos off, each in our respective vehicles, waving to each other and sometimes joining a small cluster of parents to swap pleasantries, but we are denied that companionable time courtside (that, like a fool, I had once resented). And now, aware of how fragile our liberty is, I suggest to Peter that what we really need is a party.

Everyone is so into it. I speak to Ferdi to see if it is actually okay to have a gathering (Covid restrictions now being so ad hoc) and our former lawyer landlord says it is permitted. 'It is up to the people,' he says, which I don't fully understand but then he adds that he would very much like to come, which is the ultimate green light. So Petie and I work out a date and Francesca translates the invitation, I send a WhatsApp message to our playing group and we start planning our cocktail party.

Working out the menu is tricky. Aperitivo is the start of evening eating time – everybody is hungry by 6.30 pm in this non-snacking nation. Also, I want there to be a balance between the food our Italian friends like to eat but without me having to make pasta (I wouldn't dare) so we devise a menu that straddles both worlds. We will have Australian party staples: dips and chips (guacamole, if I can find the holy grail of ripe-but-not-rotten avocados), sausage rolls, sticky chicky wings and a pavlova for dessert. I will also get some gluten-free pizza bases for Artie's mate Spidi, whose mum has already contacted me to check her son will have plenty of food. Peter has spoken to Giovanni who, though he disappointingly cannot come (he is visiting his father for that week) is amused by the thought of us entertaining so many people. His restaurant will prepare platters of prosciutto and mortadella for us and have them ready for pickup on Saturday afternoon.

My preparations have actually started two weeks out, unusually, in the op shop around the corner. I love op-shopping, and the Italian stores, though uncommon, are full of gorgeous old things discarded in favour of the modern. It is fun to pick out plates, platters and embroidered serviettes and tablecloths. I find a pair of silver candelabra and carry them home in the basket of my bike.

Peter and I head to Esselunga, our favourite supermarket, and fill trolleys with soft drinks, beer and prosecco. In Australia, chicken wingettes are common; here they are not, so we buy kilos of cornfed wings and I joint them myself. I make litres of marinade and place the wings in the freezer in the old kitchen at the end of the house near our bedroom. We buy wedges of the best parmesan we can find – forty-eight months aged – olive oil, balsamic, fresh anchovies, olives and breadsticks.

Our party plans grow. Aside from the food, I have a vision: to line our sweeping front stairs with flowers and candles for our guests' arrival. At the local two-euro store, I find gorgeous red-glassed candles with pictures of saints on them and buy forty of them. My plan for flowers, though, is a bust: the shop is full of fake flowers but they are ridiculously expensive, too much for one night only, so I purchase a few straggling fronds of birds of paradise.

Perhaps because it has been so long between celebrations in this party-loving nation, Italian magic intervenes. That afternoon when I am on our front landing, sadly arranging the paltry paper stems, Ferdi appears (in his daily attempt to fix our aircon that is still not working from the previous summer). I explain my thwarted plan for decorating the stairwell. He nods slowly and says, 'If you like, I have many such flowers'. It seems ridiculous but I follow him upstairs where he has been emptying out his vacant attic apartments and, there, lined up in the hallway are a dozen bouquets: roses and wisteria and daisies and sunflowers. I am so happy, I hug him. Ferdi smiles, a little bemused I think, but helps me carry the floral arrangements downstairs. I dress the stairs with the flowers; interspersed with the crimson candles. It is perfect.

We have invited some of our language and international school friends; not too many because we don't want our Italian friends to be overwhelmed. One day when we are having aperitivo in the piazza with Irish Olivia, the school coordinator, and talking her through our plans, I ask her if she would like to sing at the party. She is too shy, she says, though she performs with bands around the city. She does know, however, of a brilliant pianist, Riccardo, who may like the gig. Peter calls him and he is available. He also has a singer, Daniela, who can come with him if we like. Of course, we like very much.

And now – the actual day of the party – we are crazy. There is always more to do than you think, and we are furiously cleaning and tidying. Sunday is sent to Tigota, the local cleaning-products store, and returns loaded with tea candles, scourers and disinfectants. Peter oversees our crew of child workers; everyone has to make sure their rooms are spotless, the same with bathrooms and floors. 'The Italians are coming!' we say repeatedly, in probably the same panicked tone Paul Revere might have used centuries ago to warn about the invasion of the British. The irony is, of course, that we wouldn't have to worry about cleanliness if we were simply expecting our English cultural cousins. The Italians, by contrast, have turned housework into an art form and we don't want them to be embarrassed for us, with our Australian untidiness, or the fact that we clearly use our bidets as extra storage in our bathrooms. They would be mortified. Also, the initial idea of the party was to show our friends the apartment, so every room needs to be open-for-inspection immaculate.

As well, I am cooking; slicing rolls of pastry I have filled with minced pork and beef and herbs, while juggling baking trays of marinated wings. Lewis and I made the pavlova the day before, a huge Stephanie Alexander rectangle that emerged from the oven perfectly puffed and peaked. My intention was to decorate it in Italian colours, with stripes of sliced kiwifruit and banana and strawberries but at the market I got distracted by the fact they had passionfruit – so much so I forgot to buy the kiwis. There is no room in our cramped kitchen. I have trays propped on every chair and flat surface. No matter what I do, there is something else to be done: cream to be whipped, glasses to be washed and polished. Petie is shifting his stationary bike out of the ballroom to make room for Riccardo, the piano player, and to set up a bar that will be tended by Lewis and his schoolfriend Helen. We need to find somewhere in the centre that sells bags of ice. I still have to shower and wash my hair. My back aches at the thought of it.

Our doorbell buzzes. I walk onto our front landing to see that one of the floral arrangements I have placed out there has grown legs and is walking up the stairs towards me. The flowers come closer, an enormous bunch of peonies, hydrangeas and blooms in summer colours. But how? And from whom? The bouquet's legs, it transpires, belong to a deliveryman. He hands over the flowers, then says in Italian he has to get something more. There at the base of the stairs are two rectangular white boxes. Peter comes out, and together we carry the booty inside. It is from our Italian basketball friends, thanking us for our hospitality and saying they are looking forward to the party tonight. In the accompanying boxes are bottles of alcohol: white wine, red, grappa, and assorted chocolates and biscuits.

That our modest friends, who have already shown us such kindness and generosity, would organise this is incredible. It brings tears to my eyes. Also, it gives us renewed vigour to keep going with our party prep. I had better whip the cream. Peter heads off to pick up our aperitivo platters. *Pronto, pronto.* The Italians are coming.

Our party is a sparkling, euphoric, magnificent success.

Everyone is so happy to be out and dressed up and celebrating. The apartment is glowing with candlelight; the music is perfect. And even though our guests are – literally – a worlds-collide bunch, it is incredible how much in common everyone has, aside from us. I remember, in the blur of laughter and playing hostess and dancing, a few key moments.

Sunday is with her girlfriend Bea. The two of them are whispering, convulsed with teenage giggles, and then my daughter comes up to me and says: 'You know the candles you put all over the stairs? They're actually funeral candles.'

Later, Peter and I have a moment of pure joy: Lewis and Helen have mastered the art of making aperol spritz and pouring wine. The bar is buzzing. The food has been eaten – Giovanni's generous platters with fried bread and meats, every sausage roll and chicken wing. Every room, it seems, is full of friends, dancing or chatting. There are boyos running in and out or chasing each other with basketballs. Robbie, the lovely son of our friends Monica and Riccardo, is watching the pianist Riccardo, who slides over to make room for him on his stool and together they plink out a tune. It is a beautiful moment: the maestro and the little man. The doorbell buzzes; someone has closed the front door so I head over to open it.

There, in the doorway, are three of Artie's teammates. The middle one, tall and confident Baiocchi, looks at me for a moment, takes in my baby-blue lace dress, my shining and happy face.

'*Ciao, bella*,' he says, his voice rising approvingly.

His greeting is cheeky, and so unexpected it makes me laugh. My son's friend has just said 'Hello, beautiful' to me. It's not that he is wrong. After all, we are in Italy, at a beautiful party, in our beautiful home, surrounded by beautiful friends. How could I not also be beautiful?

It's just that he is thirteen years old.

Later, several of our friends help me serve the pavlova. The Italians are mad for it. They nearly mob us as we slide wedges onto the pretty plates we have handed around. When they actually eat the dessert, they make noises of extreme undisguised pleasure. Speranza says it is the best thing she has ever put in her mouth, which makes everyone laugh. They discuss it with each other, holding it up to the light, analysing the meringue, the crust, the passionfruit, the cream. It is quite an amazing response; I am oddly proud of our national dish.

And of course, it makes sense. To us, pavlova is familiar and traditional; to the Italians it is exotic.

To all of us, it is utterly delicious.

44

TIME TO LEAVE

We are in lockdown again in Bologna.

This time it has come upon us slowly. First the country was divided into zones: Yellow, Orange or the dreaded Red, depending on the severity of numbers succumbing to Covid infections.

In Bologna we have moved to Orange, which means there are no bars or restaurants open but shops are still operating. Children from middle school (Artie and Jannie) are still allowed to attend school. There is a curfew on the streets after 10 pm and you are not allowed to travel more than five kilometres from your home unless you have an exemption. The streets are still busy during the day but deserted after 8 pm. Peter and I have started going for a walk after dinner, wandering down darkened laneways that would normally be packed with diners and drinkers. Most local restaurants are closed. Pasta, the staple fare served by most of them, is not a dish that travels well for home delivery, although there are a few that remain open to service regular customers who live in surrounding apartments. Outside the big McDonald's at the top of the main thoroughfare of Via Indipendenza, there is always a cluster of waiting delivery riders with their bikes; we frequently see the manager wander outside and order them to socially distance. They scatter for a minute, before returning to their previous huddle in the cold.

Down south in Naples, which first-time round avoided most of the Covid outbreak, the numbers are high. There are protests in the street – residual resentment and fear spilling forth from a population who have barely dragged themselves back to their knees after the first lockdown. The scenes on the news are confronting: hundreds, possibly thousands, of people assembling in the main piazzas of Milan and Rome and Naples, brandishing signs and banners. The police are not playing; there is footage of them picking up rocks and hurling them back at protesters who have pelted them. It is a peculiar irony that, even as hospitals are at breaking point trying to treat Covid patients, the streets are filled with crowds protesting the measures aimed at halting the plague.

In Bologna the mood is calmer, though it has something of a 'before the storm' quality. Last Saturday we wandered over to our Australian shoe-designing friend Lana's new temporary apartment (half-price, as landlords have dropped rents on empty Airbnbs) for low-key birthday drinks. She told us that she and her lovely Calabrian husband Dom got caught up in a noisy protest here and it was frightening. In the large piazza towards the station there have been several weekend gatherings, and though these have been less impassioned than those in other centres, there were still flares and police in riot gear; previously unimaginable in this quiet city.

In accordance with some immutable law of nature, everything goes wobbly at once. Giovanni has a bike accident. He spends three days in hospital before he is released home with a broken pelvis and collarbone, just in time for his restaurant to be shut for lockdown. In Australia, my father-in-law Bryan has a health scare; he has kept it quiet from my mother-in-law, and is now waiting for surgery in December. My girlfriend Georgie's mum, Joanna, a vibrant and exuberant former nurse who would often reduce us to laughter with her sense of drama, succumbs to a failing heart and dies in Sydney. I have been checking in with Georgie as she works bedside at the palliative ward; she sends photos of her beautiful pup Honey resting on her mum's bed. The death was inevitable, releasing my beloved friend and her brothers (and her mum) from months of home-caring, but also breaking their hearts. Joanna Harrop's funeral is reportedly a glorious celebration of her life. How I would have liked to have been there. There is a seeming stream of bad news. Two boys from Jannie's basket team test positive for Covid. Although they are asymptomatic, the training sessions (which had amazingly continued outside with social distancing) are suspended. Then another blow from the international school: two parents in grade four have also tested positive for Covid. As a precaution Jannie and his entire class are sent home for two weeks of isolation.

The message is clear: it is time to go. So we continue working towards our return home. Our flights are still booked and confirmed for December, as they have been since the start of the year. We have told the children that we are heading home, and they are so happy. They start to talk of what they will do when we are home; of their grandparents and friends, and Christmas. In the meantime, Peter and I are packing and divesting ourselves of surplus belongings in order to be ready to move out when the date draws near. We had originally intended to hire a shipping company to move our belongings back to Australia but the removalist's quote was so high, and given we have nothing other than a few precious souvenirs (including the ludicrously impractical, but precious ceramic heads we bought in Sicily last year), we have decided to leave everything behind, and just take what we can carry on the plane. The little boys have outgrown their clothes anyway, and since we are returning to summer, there is no need for winter apparel other than what we will need for the last month or so. In this regard, lockdown is a dark convenience. There will be no ski trips, no final dinners, no country outings; no all-in class birthday parties; no need then for more than the tracksuit pants and puffers they wear to school every day. Sunday and Lewis are homeschooling in accordance with the new lockdown guidelines so they don't need much either, and though I have left out a nice dress and boots (just in case!), most of my clothes are now so shabby from the first lockdown, I am looking forward to purging myself of them.

There is an element of sadness among our friends: there will be no rousing farewells, no final lunches or last suppers. My yoga group is confined again to Zoom sessions and everyone is uncertain about whether or not we are permitted to meet up in the flesh. In the event that we don't go to the next level of restrictions, we have a loose arrangement to meet at our apartment next week for a cup of tea and cake or even go to the piazza and sit on the steps of the big church with takeaway coffees. It is interesting, being part of a fraternity of expats. They are so used to people coming and going. Beautiful Johanna and her family are back in Sweden, where cases are soaring; lovely Vineetha has moved back to India. English Sophie is in Cambridge and in lockdown there. Our Aussie Bologna brethren, Rachel and Dave, are long-gone, back in Australia and ten minutes from our house, keeping us appraised of developments in our home state. Victoria has recently emerged from the world's longest lockdown, and is now embracing the freedom of a long-awaited Australian summer.

Tuesday morning, I wake at five-thirty, only to find Peter is – unusually – already awake in bed next to me, his face illuminated by the light of his phone.

'Do you want the good news or the bad news?' he asks.

This is a big question for so early. I weigh up my options. Decide on the bitter pill first.

'Bad news,' I say.

'Our flights are cancelled,' he says.

My stomach drops.

'The airline couldn't wait any longer for the Victorian government to open to returning travellers so they've pulled the pin. We don't have flights home until March.'

The lurch of my stomach is now eclipsed by a despair-rush of adrenaline, and a thousand crushing, futile thoughts. No flights. No apartment. How to break the news to the children; to our parents. No Christmas. Stuck in limbo.

I try to breathe. Then, human nature being what it is, I reach for the glimmer of light he promised.

'So, what's the good news?' I ask.

Peter pauses.

'I shouldn't have said that,' he says awkwardly.

'There isn't any.'

Even in this darkest hour, this hour before dawn, when the Italians say 'the sun has gold in its mouth', that makes me laugh.

45

THANKS FOR THE GIVING

Years ago, pre-children, I was on a holiday with my go-getting girlfriend Lou. She, a fellow Queenslander and sun-seeker, knew of a little cabin on the beach in Byron Bay (pre-Hemsworths and The Hollywood Invasion) when it was still a relatively quiet hippyish enclave and brimful of the most-easterly-place-in-Australia magic. I remember a few things from that escape. We had to get to the cabin by dragging our suitcases for a kilometre from the town along the dunes, and another friend, Julian, also came to stay. Louie and I shared the only bedroom while Julian slept on the couch in the louvred sleepout. We nicknamed him 'Pigpen' because wherever he sat, he left a little puddle of sand (mysteriously even at the local pub, The Rails, after a shower and being nowhere near the beach).

After four glorious days of waking up and wandering into the ocean, going into town to buy cream buns from the local bakery, Louie cooking chilli mudcrabs on the beach, and all of us downing numerous cocktails (my proudest invention featuring passionfruit, vodka and local honey from the market), we were desperate to exercise something other than our ability to indulge. In keeping with our resolve, Lou booked a surf kayak outing from a mob who operated from the park up the beach. So the three of us rose early one morning and convened with the local surfer boys, who kitted us out with life vests and sunblock, and gave us a basic briefing. The idea was that we would head over-water to a point within eyeshot called The Pass, from where we would start paddling furiously and catch waves into the shore. We had watched others do it all week from our vantage point on the shore; it looked like great fun.

We were divided into pairs. Lou and I were together; she was behind me in the long canoe, both of us armed with paddles. Pigpen, nose daubed with white zinc, was coupled with one of the brawny surfers. We headed out onto the water, which was glassy and smooth, but, water distances being hard to gauge, it turned out our destination was further away than we imagined. By the time we reached the spot where we were supposed to pick up speed to catch our first wave, Lou and I were both flagging. We were hot and thirsty; our arms aching from the unaccustomed exertion. Try as we might, we simply couldn't get up enough speed to catch a wave. Eventually the leader of our expedition asked if we wanted a bloke on one of the other kayaks to help us muscle our way onto a swell. Louie and I answered simultaneously.

'YES!' she said.

At the very exact same moment as I replied: 'NO!'

The stark difference in our responses made everyone laugh, even the surfers, and once our gallows mirth had subsided, we realised it had rendered us even more weak-of-arm. Around us, other kayakers were whooping with exultation as they caught waves and plumed their way into the shore; a far cry from us on our drifting vessel.

'We are strong enough. We don't need help!' I said to Louie, even as I sweated and flailed my paddle, propelling us nowhere.

Behind me, my friend shook her head. I didn't need to see her to detect the exasperation in her voice.

'We do!' she said. 'I'm not like you.' She paused, her frustration rendering her momentarily speechless.

'You're so . . . DUTCH!'

It was such an unlikely and unexpected pronouncement, it made us both laugh even more.

I remember the moment vividly because it was the first time I had really thought of myself as Dutch. Growing up, I was proudly the only member of my family born in Australia, but when questioned about my family genealogy, I always identified more with the Jamaican–American ancestry of my mother, than that of my dad. I guess the reasons for this are twofold: the eye is drawn to difference and while my Dutch father (one of 'the invisible migrants') could pass for any white-skinned Australian, my mother with her milk-coffee complexion and black afro, clearly didn't. This elicited curiosity. Also, my mum's gregarious personality was pretty alpha in our family, a complement to my dad's dry reserve.

It was not displeasing that Lou had pegged me as Dutch. No doubt, they are strong people, the Dutch. I mean, they wear shoes carved out of *wood*. And Louie's summation was pretty accurate, insofar as, while I am not drawn to physical challenges, I do not think of myself as weak.

My self-view is counter to the popular mood, I know, where many are swift to identify and embrace experiences that have rendered them victims. My contrasting ethos, incidentally, does not invalidate anyone else's life experiences, but it seems to me to provide a marker of how well people will navigate tough times. While I have undoubtedly been shaped by, for instance, leaving a restrictive religion in my late teens to forge a new life in the outside world without the support of any childhood friends or relatives, or nursing a son through the shadow of the valley of death of leukaemia, or even taking on a life in the public arena, with its attendant slings and arrows, I have nearly always felt confident in my capacity to face these challenges. I am a person who looks forward, who has faith that things will work out as they are supposed to (whatever that means), and there is a certain comfort in that.

This, by the way, is not a passive ideology. Of course, you reap the benefits of striving, of planning, of self-discipline, of staring in the gimlet eye of a frightening reality you would rather not acknowledge, of grasping opportunity when it is presented. There is also, cruelly, 'bad luck' that even the most blessed cannot evade in the living of a life. But my core belief is this: humans are resilient and resourceful and capable of enormous strength. I believe that of myself and my husband and children. I also believe that mental muscles are like any others: those you exercise the most will be the strongest. So it is that I look within myself to respond to situations with laughter instead of anger; to find a course of action, instead of the passive acceptance that comes with fearfulness. I discourage feeding the mental troll of anxiety; for it is never sated. I hate people subjecting others to the tyranny of their bad moods. ('Mood backwards is DOOM,' an acting teacher of mine used to say, and I often – no doubt annoyingly – repeat the maxim in our own family.)

This mindset is a gift that has stood me in good stead, but it is not titanium. I am fallible.

These last couple of weeks here in Italy have tested me, and I have found myself faltering. In the uncertainty of waiting to find out when (and *if*) we will be allowed to return to Australia, while being surrounded by Covid cases among Bolognese friends, and signing a contract for a new job when we return, which (though exciting) means for the first time in two decades I will not be working with my beloved and brilliant friends Hughesy and Sacha, and packing and paring belongings, and not being able to formally farewell our life of two years here because of lockdown, and washing and cooking for six in the winter cold and realising how many things we have still not done and yet have still to do, I am overwhelmed.

I am just so tired. I am weak. I am spent.

This week in particular has hit me hard. On Tuesday and Wednesday, after the little boys have gone to school, I can do nothing more than crawl back into bed. I have a headache and a stomach gripped by cramps. One of my eyes is red and swollen. It is all too much.

I just want to sleep. To shut out the world.

And then something happens that changes everything. It is not a big thing, and yet it is huge.

Thursday is Thanksgiving. I know, because when I dispiritedly check my school group WhatsApp messages, the American fraternity (three or four families) are swapping notes on their respective festivities. It is a reminder of last Thanksgiving, when our neighbour

Denise invited us to share the traditional meal with her own gang of six at their apartment across the palazzo courtyard from us. In fact, last year she had planned such a huge gathering that she asked if I could cook one of her two turkeys in our oven since hers was full to bursting. I was so happy to do that. I also volunteered to make gravy from the necks and giblets, an all-day simmering with onions and carrots and celery that resulted in a giant jug of rewardingly rich and unctuous sauce.

The Thanksgiving celebration itself was a revelation. There were twenty or thirty people in attendance, children running in and out, the sweetest harvest decorations (biscuits sandwiched together and iced to look like turkeys! autumn leaves!), a traditional-rivals gridiron match on the TV and a buffet groaning with food. As well as being plentiful, the spread was intriguingly foreign: sweet potatoes with brown sugar (the mythical candied yams?), cornbread bake, pecan and pumpkin pies.

This year, of course, lockdown means no such festa. Instead, my lovely neighbour has been sending me updates of her turkey quest. Restrictions on travel meant she was unable to source a gobbler through her US army contacts and had to order one through a local Italian butcher. When she picked up the bird yesterday, it was huge: eighteen pounds – the weight of three newborn babies. The Italian butchers, unused to the concept of cooking a full turkey, had thoughtfully already stuffed it. They had also liberally covered *the outside* of the turkey in stuffing, which Denise's husband Joseph (the bird wrangler) spent the morning removing, coating it instead in his own concoction of butter and sage. Denise sends me a photo of the turkey on the kitchen operating table; it looks more like a plucked cassowary. Indeed, her husband has accused her of buying a pterodactyl.

That afternoon, I wake reluctantly from an hour of groggy sleep-escape. The children are home from school. It is after five and winter dark. I am cold. I sluggishly try to assemble myself and my thoughts to tackle our evening meal. It feels like I am about to ascend Everest. I have nothing. No inspiration. No motivation. But I have six people to feed. I lie there, missing the feeling of myself. Minutes pass.

My phone pings.

'The lift elves have visited,' says the message.

It is a code that Denise and I developed during the first hard lockdown, when we would exchange books, jigsaws or birthday bottles of wine in our shared liftwell.

I walk past the lounge room. Peter is working on the computer. The boys are doing Mathletics. Everyone is hungry and asks about dinner.

I open the door between our apartment and our neighbours'.

On the wooden bench in our shared vestibule is a mirage.

On a large platter is sliced turkey breast, with a giant, golden-skinned drumstick resting atop. There is a stainless-steel bowl of mashed potatoes, still steaming. Another of green bean casserole. As well, there is a foil-wrapped tray of buns, made by another shining school friend, Patricia. She has drawn a smiley face on the alfoil and instructions to bake them for fifteen minutes. It is unbelievable. She and my neighbour have clearly colluded to deliver this feast to us.

Denise is standing, socially distanced, at her door. She is beaming.

'Happy Thanksgiving, neighbour,' she says. 'We thought you might need a meal in the middle of your packing.'

I can hardly speak. I am humbled and exalted and overcome. My eyes prickle with tears.

I call Peter, and after he, too, has marvelled at the lift-elves' bounty, we carry the feast inside. I make some gravy, and we find a jar of mustard fruits (spicy cherries and apricots in syrup) that we eat with the turkey, which is perfectly moist and delicious. The food is so unutterably good. The green bean casserole, creamy and dotted with mushrooms; the mashed potato, comforting and smooth. The bread rolls, from Patricia's mother's recipe, emerge from the oven puffed and buttery and golden. They are manna from heaven. Hearts lifted and bellies full, the six of us toast and take turns to go around the table and say what we are thankful for. When it comes to me, my response is simple.

I am full of Thanks for the Giving.

The Dutch, as well as being strong and resourceful, are known to be quite stubborn. This is sometimes to their detriment.

My girlfriend Louie was right, you see.

In the middle of that glittering Byron blue, under cotton-ball summer clouds and mocking gulls, she and I engaged in the ultimate indignity of swapping kayaks, awkwardly clambering across vessels so that we each found a place in front of a strapping, strong-armed man. The surfers were amused, good-naturedly telling us to brace ourselves before ploughing through the water as though powered by steam.

I remember a moment: my friend and I together but separate, squealing with delight as we were propelled across the top of the waves – the view from the crest of the swell before the surge. The sleek vessels flying, the power of the ocean hurtling us through the white-crested plumes towards the shore.

It was exhilarating. It was euphoric.

It would not have been possible without help.

46

THE LAST SUPPER

The joy of our Thanksgiving meal, a circuit breaker for the malaise I have found myself in, continues into the following day. It is Friday, and Riccardo has been speaking to Peter about plans for a farewell dinner.

This, though seemingly incredible, is permissible because of the strange disparity in lockdown rules which this time round are so random they are difficult to fathom. You can wait for five minutes at the bar of a cafe for your morning espresso but cannot drink it inside, though a cluster of people outside the front of the bars is common. You must wear a mask at all times, but not if you are smoking (or drinking your coffee). You may buy a gelato but you are not supposed to lick it on the street.

In a similar vein, because his hotel on the main street is still open for the few lingering and trapped international guests, Riccardo is also permitted to continue to run the attached restaurant. And because we are foreigners, he has organised a dinner for us there. We will dine early – at 7 pm – the idea being that we will be finished in time to head home before the strict curfew at 10 pm.

It is such a treat – the thought that we will get to see our friends for a festive farewell, and in a restaurant (not just any eatery, but Bologna's only Michelin-starred restaurant) seems too good to be true. All week I have been expecting the meal to be called off but as Peter, who has come to know his Italian friend intimately through myriad basketball training and travel arrangements, reminds me: 'When Riccardo says something is going to happen, it happens'.

And things are happening, for sure. That morning, I wake up early and, per my slavish 2020 habit, check my phone.

There is an email from our dedicated Australian travel agent, Frank from Benalla Travel. We always refer to him as Frank-from-Benalla-Travel as though that is his full name. Initially his being based in a country town in rural Victoria seemed delightfully eccentric – now, of course, we realise that he had the jump on the whole world at working remotely. Although his job must have seemed initially ho-hum when he booked our family's return flights to Australia way back in January, since their formal cancellation two weeks ago he has been trying everything to find us a route back to Australia. The options due to Covid restrictions are limited, and most of them are hugely expensive, but Frank (from Benalla Travel) has been working tirelessly to ensure we can get back home. In the course of one conversation, he says to me in his calm, assured manner: 'Kate, I have made it my personal mission that you will be back in Australia for Christmas. And I don't know if you realise this but I don't have a lot else on.'

His wry observation is funny because it is true. Travel agents around the world have ground to a halt. They are like the shuttered luggage shops we see dotted around Bologna; closed due to lack of need. True to his word, every day there are messages from Frank containing updates on the situation in Australia, his latest conversations with various airlines and government departments, as well as suggestions for alternate routes home.

The latter options are limited – all the more so because several Australian states remain closed to each other, and any way around the impediments requires a mental agility that is fatiguing. We may have to split the family into two groups of three to secure seats. Though this is obviously not ideal, we are prepared to do it; we are now willing to do anything to maximise our chances of getting flights. If the family divide is necessary, it is decided I will fly with the older teenagers and Peter will follow with Artie and Jannie.

Frank has been steady throughout, urging us to keep the faith. Our home port of Melbourne is expected to announce it will open to returning travellers in December and he is confident our tickets, from Bologna to Dubai, and then on to Australia, will be honoured. Waiting for this is like pinning all our hopes on a cosmic roll of the dice.

But Frank – dear, tireless, faithful, stubborn Frank – is proven correct.

The email I wake up to at five in the morning is that our Emirates tickets to Australia have been reinstated. We are leaving Bologna on 9 December at 2.30 in the afternoon. All of us, together.

What a relief. I read and reread the email to check that it is real. I feel such a surge of happiness, I cannot wait to wake Peter to tell him. He, too, is sleepily exultant. We make our way to the kitchen, where I make coffee, while he checks our overnight correspondence. It is true. We are leaving Bologna.

I know that people say blessings come in disguise, but this one is a double-bunger. It has been so difficult to secure flights and our return in time for Christmas seemed so unlikely, the news that we are finally confirmed to fly home has put paid to any sadness we have been feeling at the thought of leaving Italy. It is such a hard-won prize, we feel nothing but jubilation.

When we tell the children, they are euphoric. Lewis, as always, makes us laugh with his fist-pumping response, bellowing, 'Yes! The tyranny is over!'

Jannie and Artie dance around the kitchen, Jannie twerking and shouting, 'Hubba hubba hubba!' until his sister emerges to see what all the racket is about. Our calm and lovely Sunday is more measured in her response but nonetheless the smile that spreads across her face is pure joy. We all hug delightedly. Excitedly. Exhaustedly. The end of our Italian adventure is in sight. The next chapter awaits.

And in the meantime, we have our farewell dinner tonight.

It is already dark when we set off for the ten-minute walk to the hotel. It has been such fun getting ready to go 'out'. Our hosts' son,

Robbie, has come back with Peter and Jannie after their outdoor basketball training and, inspired by his Italian attention to grooming, my boys are also shower-fresh. This alone marks the evening as a special occasion. Jannie has spent ten minutes in front of the mirror, plastering down the cowlicks in his hair. Artie is wearing his 'good' shirt, a hand-me-down that fitted Lewis when we first arrived last year. I am wearing the one decent outfit I have left unpacked, a green knitted sweater dress I bought in Paris last year with my girlfriend Mac, but at the last minute decide not to wear the matching shiny boots in favour of a chunky, rubber-soled black pair that are slip-proof on the terrazzo paving. Even dressed up we stand out amongst the stylish Italians – we are an unusually large (and tall) group – and I don't want to draw even more attention by promenading down the main boulevard in high heels.

Our posse-walk down to Indipendenza is so pretty. Despite lockdown, the Bologna *commune* has strung up traditional Christmas lights, and every street is looped with golden bulbs. When we arrive at the imposing I Portici Hotel, it, too, is illuminated; a silver-blue waterfall of dripping lights that cascade down the front. In these muted times, these visual markers of the season lift my heart. It is something the Italians, with their deep and profound love of beauty, understand.

Our friends are waiting in the foyer. It has been a while since I have seen Monica, who is her normal chic-streetwear self. We all mill around, first elbow-tapping, then stealing furtive hugs before assembling for a group photo under the Christmas tree in reception. Apparently we are permitted to remove our masks for three seconds for our photo. I'm not sure if this is official health policy (I'm actually pretty certain it isn't), but nonetheless we all enjoy the high-spirited challenge as a prelude to the evening ahead.

While the hotel itself is a multi-storey, modern establishment, like so many businesses in European ancient cities, it has been retrofitted into a building steeped with history. We are ushered into the private dining room behind the main restaurant (which was once a French music hall) and when we make our way through the main room it feels positively vast, with a lonely clutch of couples at socially distanced tables.

The back room, by contrast, is like a glamorous smugglers' convention; under low canopies of pale stone arches, two tables are set for the mandated groups of four. On each table are flickering candles which illuminate the cavern. Underfoot are panels of thick glass, common in medieval buildings in Italy, and designed so that you can see through to the excavated area beneath. Often these will reveal diggings or archeologically significant stones or other treasures. Our floor reveals the restaurant's wine cellar; thousands of bottles of wine stacked in a climate-controlled series of antechambers. Like so many in this town, the building dates from the fifteenth century, when it was used by one of the popes, who later 'gifted' it to the city of Bologna.

It feels like a secret tunnel, Jannie observes, and Riccardo nods enthusiastically, explaining that the back of the hotel has hidden passages which lead out to the park behind it, which was once occupied by a grand papal palace. Tonight, however, it is a sleek (but empty) international hotel, with black-suited waiters seemingly as excited to have us there as we are to be here, ushering us to our tables and spiriting away our winter coats, before pouring welcoming water and wine.

The food is just beautiful. A couple of months ago, Riccardo had overseen the recruitment of a new chef, Gianluca Renzi, a culinary superstar who got his first Michelin star ten years ago (at the age of twenty-three) at another famous restaurant in Rome. Because of the rolling lockdowns, since September he has had few opportunities to show his cooking prowess. Tonight is his chance to shine. And he does.

There are plates of delicious tricks: small, whole tomatoes that turn out to be made of cheese; tiny crispy discs topped with mousse made from local mortadella; donuts that look sweet but are savoury. There is a delicate and lovely dish inspired by Gianluca's nonna's traditional cold tomato soup with old bread. We eat pasta tossed with anchovies and fruits of the sea, a dish Riccardo has deemed too intense for the children, who are instead served bowls of homemade tortellini buttons in broth.

Then, a surprise. In the spirit of artistic competition and collaboration, another chef friend of Gianluca's, Marcello Corrado, has turned up to cook one of his specialties: slices of melting duck liver topped with sweet scampi, on a purée of ginger-flavoured carrot. It is so stunningly perfect, we are all shocked into greedy silence. We eat roe deer cooked in spiced orange, a short column so dark and rich that it looks like a self-saucing chocolate pudding. For dessert there are several types of the Christmas specialty, panettone, light as air and studded with fruit.

It is a truly magnificent repast, one that we would be fortunate to eat at any time, let alone in this time of restricted freedoms, and we savour every mouthful. Even the children devour everything, entertaining the waiters by calling out when they recognise the flavour of an ingredient. This is, of course, no casual conversation to Italians, and the waiters take their time, listening carefully and then explaining where the flavours originate and the heritage of each dish. It is always remarkable how the Italians learn as they eat. Their enjoyment and understanding of their own cuisine is unique, and for my children to be a part of this adds another burnished glow to the evening. How these four Aussie kids have matured in their palates, I think. It is a far cry from nuggets and chips.

At the end of the meal, when we are drinking coffee and liquors, and Robbie has wearily drifted over to sit on his mother's lap and stroke her short blonde hair, Monica presents us with a farewell gift. It is a photo album of our time together: at basket tournaments (of course), but also the first time the three of them joined us for a 'pancake party' at our old apartment; photos of us at the beach. There are my parents eating pizza at their home and Peter's parents on the precious day Monica and Riccardo joined us at a farm we stayed at outside Bologna last June. Here we are, captured swimming in the pool under the chestnut trees and eating gnocchi in the restaurant, and napping in deck chairs while the children play soccer on the grass. It is a time capsule of our time in Italy, a composite of how we have come to know our thoughtful, hard-working Italian friends; a time before the whole world turned on its axis. Everyone clusters around to look at the memories. Peter clears his throat and, a little huskily, thanks our *amici* for their friendship. For their kindness. For everything, really. How we hope their fortunes turn and prosper.

The chefs, Gianluca and Marcello, emerge, still looking pristine in their whites, bowing modestly as we thank them and the waiters for an unforgettable meal.

And then it is time to leave. There is slight anxiety about this. We are now outside the official curfew, as Artie (always conscious of the rules) pointed out an hour or so ago. Riccardo, who has been in a huddle with his front of house staff, suggests that since there are now four plainclothes police (what?) outside the front of the restaurant, we should exit through the kitchen and take the staff entrance onto the street. We don our coats and make our way through the maze of corridors through the back of the hotel, joking that we are like Jason Bourne trying to give his pursuers the slip. While that makes us smile, we are all aware that we don't want to be caught breaking the law and land our hosts in trouble. Riccardo has offered for us to stay the night in one of the many empty hotel rooms but that would mean more work for our friends. Plus, we are only a ten-minute walk away. How difficult could it be to slip through the night to our waiting apartment?

So, after a hushed final farewell, we step out onto the empty streets, turning right – away from the secret police – where we silently shepherd the children across Via Indipendenza to the back streets that will lead to our neighbourhood. We stick close to the walls. We walk the opposite way up one-way streets. When we speak, we do so in whispers.

We have been walking this way for about seven minutes and are approaching the traffic lights at a large cross-street when we see, reflected in the windows across the road, the flashing of red and blue lights. Artie whispers urgently, '*Carabinieri!*' – the police that are a branch of the army. This is bad. Very bad. We all freeze. The children instantly duck down behind a large industrial bin. Jannie, always dramatic, does a rolling lunge that makes everyone hiss in disapproval. Peter and I press against a brick wall, hiding in the shadows. We swiftly weigh up our options, then double back, quickly, quietly, into the darkened street behind us. We have decided on another detour. It will add several minutes to our trip in a direction we're not entirely sure of but we clearly can't risk attempting our normal, straightforward route home.

It is sobering, this fearful journey. It is a strange, new-world-order postscript to our beautiful, stolen evening.

We silently pad our way along our new route for another quarter-hour or so, Lewis leading the way. On the silent, lead-grey streets, we see few other people, save for a couple of food delivery guys who pedal past us, breathing fog, and one or two civilian cars.

There are a couple of heart-in-mouth moments: one, where we have to make our way around a huge open roundabout; and another, in the final metres of our journey travelling up the narrow one-way street that will pop us out at the piazza near our local church. We are so close to home by now but tired. I am so glad I wore my flat boots, though we have walked so much further than we intended to that even they are starting to rub. We are still in single file, darting in the dark from doorway to doorway, buoyed by our proximity to safety, when sudden headlights illuminate us from the rear. A police car drives up from behind and pulls up on the street alongside us. Peter, who is now at the front of our pack, quietly murmurs, 'Don't look at them. Keep your heads down. Just keep walking. Keep an even pace.'

So we do. And while the *polizia* slow to a heart-stopping crawl beside us, we look resolutely ahead, maintaining a measured but purposeful stride. We can feel the police looking at us from their vehicle, but, in true Italian style, we simply refuse to acknowledge their gaze. Eventually, their car speeds up to pass us, and we are once again alone on the empty street. It is an impossible relief. My heart is pounding so loudly it must surely be echoing around the deserted piazza. But apparently not, because then we have turned the final corner and Peter is opening the giant doors to our palazzo and the children are galloping up the stairs to our apartment, and suddenly we are all in the kitchen, puffed and panting and shining with adrenaline and exultation and the laughter that comes from sheer relief.

The next morning, I am making recovery corn fritters, a Lewis–Langbroek family staple in good times and in bad. I am mixing the traditional 'special sauce' to go with them, using the last of the gherkin relish I brought back from my June trip to Australia with Lewis, and mentally noting there is no need to ration it anymore because soon we will be back there, with jars aplenty. As we all drift to the table, we are discussing the brilliant dinner last night, and our consequent curfew-busting walk. Artie, our beautiful, cautious, good-citizen son, the most diligent brother and teammate who would normally rather break his leg than break a rule, loads up his plate and says, 'That was so much fun last night.'

I am happily surprised to hear this. I was half expecting him to berate us for taking such a risk; for breaking curfew; for risking getting caught.

'You know what it was like?' he says, shovelling corn fritters. And I know what he is going to say before he utters the words.

'It was like that movie *The Sound of Music*,' he says. 'At the end, when they were all trying to escape from the Nazis.'

And it was, my beloved son.

In some ways, it really was.

47

THE BIG ARRIVEDERCI

Sometimes we are so busy negotiating the alternating whirl and grind of everyday life, we forget to appreciate the very people who make that life so special. And sometimes, it is only when they leave (for a new job or location – or, god forbid, permanently) that we realise we have failed to acknowledge what they meant to us.

This phenomenon – this taking for granted those who are precious – is curiously common in my industry. Showbiz is unusual work and one of its many rewards is a strong social element. Whatever job you are undertaking is likely to be inherently fun, and bookended with impromptu gatherings; a drink at the airport, perhaps, or a meal after a gig. These spontaneous assignations are great, but also unwittingly highlight a lack: the vast difference between planning an event because you like each other versus simply hanging out because it is convenient post-performance. Of course, not all our showbiz friends are like this – the radio and music subset are particularly wildly, gloriously social, and we have enjoyed many unforgettable World Best Practice parties and music festivals together. But comedians often tend to be more insular and self-oriented, and I have been at more than one funeral where my funny friends have looked at each other sadly and said, 'Is this what it took for us to get together?'

But a cavalier attitude towards friendship is not a problem for Italians.

The Italians are famously the masters of love. They are good at painting it, playing it, feeling it, expressing it, losing it, mourning it, celebrating it. It comes from their generosity, I think, for a stingy person cannot fully love. Loving is giving, and Italian hearts, as we have learned in our time here, are bountiful.

When we announce we are leaving Bologna, we get to experience the full flight of our friends' expressions of regard for us, in an outpouring that is deeply touching. The eloquence and unabashed sentiment is overwhelming. The boys' basket-team parents, with whom we have shared endless hours on hard benches or travelling to tournaments around Italy, praise our sons – not only for their sporting skills but also for their physical beauty, and who they are as people. There are compliments on our family and our very spirit as Australians. It is heady stuff, but it also means we have to rethink our exit strategy. Because we have been in this current incarnation of lockdown, and because I don't really trust my own emotions, I had figured we could just ghost our way out of town. This influx of messages puts paid to that. Our leaving is a big deal. Of course it was always going to be significant for us, but it seems the Italians cannot, and will not, let us depart without fanfare.

(I recall the rotation of early-morning drivers who would drop me at my radio studio, right back at the beginning, and how they taught me the importance of farewells in this country. *Salve*, they would say, as I exited into the still-sleeping street. *Buona giornata. Ci vediamo. Ciao. Grazie mille. A domani. Arrivederci.* If a seven-minute trip elicited such a litany of salutations, it is not surprising our two years here will not pass without some fanfare.)

On Friday night – five days before we are to fly – we are home, packing and sorting, packing and sorting, when there is a ring at the door. It is William, his Spanish wife Begoña and their strapping son Luis, one of Art's Bologna Virtus teammates. The trio are at the top of our stairs, unannounced and beaming. They are still breathing fog from the cold air outside and brandishing a rare bottle of champagne (not prosecco – actual *French Champagne*) and a large, festively wrapped panettone. Peter and I, a bit grimy and dazed, are taken aback but also thrilled to see them, and usher them inside. As it turns out, we only thought we were exhausted. What we actually needed was the combined tonic of our friends' warmth and cold French bubbles.

I have been determined for the last week to empty the fridge and freezer so I am actually in the final stages of preparing dinner when they arrive. It is not quite 6.30 pm, which is deemed ludicrously early for dinner here, so we end up turning off the oven, clearing some of the chaos from the kitchen table and having our aperitivo there. The giant panettone, it turns out, is *salata*, a savoury version of the domed Christmas cake-bread, sliced and filled with ham and the weird mayonnaise-rich carrot and potato Russian salad the Italians are so partial to. With the champagne, it proves strangely moreish. The boys, in between wrestling and gaming, drift in for the sandwiches and before we know it, music is playing, the panettone is demolished, and the grownups are a couple of bottles in. It really is TGIF.

We convince our friends to stay for dinner but by the time the children have set the table and we move to the lounge room, it is nearly 10 pm and the chicken wings I left in the oven are as dry and brittle as sparrow's bones. I counter their shortcomings by making a quick gravy, an exercise in lipstick-on-a-pig futility. The damage is truly done, and there is no disguising it. Nonetheless, our guests are, in true Italian style, nothing but complimentary: '*Molto croccante!*' (Very crispy!) beaming Begoña says more than once, trying to chisel her way through an incisor-snapping wing. The meal is unremarkable (actually *terrible*), but the company at the table is so joyous, our visitors end up staying well past curfew and leave nervously just before midnight; an echo of us the previous week when we snuck home from our Michelin feast.

Peter and I seem to have adopted an unspoken ethos – people before packing – and it seems the more we embrace this, the more Italian magic attends us. Not with regard to the teetering piles of clothes and books and *things* that taunt us from every flat surface. But with having resigned ourselves to leaving behind whatever we cannot fit in our cases (aside from the bicycles – fark me, those bicycles!) comes a certain freedom.

Three days before we leave it is announced that, despite climbing Covid numbers around the country, our region, Emilia-Romagna, will come out of the *Arancione* (Orange) lockdown zone and back to the less-restrictive Yellow. This, incredibly, means restaurants and bars will be allowed to reopen to serve lunch. The news is a huge boost to everyone's morale. It also catapults us into a frenzied receipt of last-minute invitations – but there are only three lunches before we leave.

On Sunday we all head off to Bottega Portici. It will be our final walk to the piazza at the foot of the landmark Two Towers, the last time we see the magnificent bookstore Feltrinelli, our ultimate meander past the Roman spring-fed spigot, giant trough and the ornate bronze clock that blooms proudly under the pharmacy portico. It is a glorious lap of honour. The broad and handsome boulevard of Ugo Bassi is closed to cars, as it always is on weekends. Overhead is roped with garlands of Christmas lights. The church bells ring as we walk – extra tolls for sacred Sunday.

Although shops have continued lockdown trading, the last weeks have been quiet. Today, however, the wide pedestrian precinct is filled with people. Christmas shoppers are out in force, a cheerful and determined army of puffers and boots, bikes, strollers, wheelchairs and shopping bags. Everyone, it seems, is re-energised by the thought they can break up the chilly day's activities with lunch and an indoor coffee. Bars are full; patrons spill onto the street, accommodated at an array of tables. Chestnut sellers toast their wares at kerbside braziers. Buskers are strumming. The crisp air is humming. Inside restaurants, golden-lit groups can be seen laughing and talking animatedly over glasses of wine and plates of food. A soaring, sixteen-metre silver fir in Piazza Nettuno is lit up with a thousand lights, shining hope and joy alongside the statue of the

King of the Sea. It is as though the business of Italian life (which is simply 'life') has never been interrupted.

Bottega Portici is bustlingly full. We press past the masked crowd, sort-of-socially-distanced and queuing outside, and head upstairs, where our friends are waiting at Covid-mandated tables of four pulled close together. It is heartening to see the place abuzz. Everyone in Bologna, it would seem, has been longing for their regular fix of homemade tortellini or platters of prosciutto and mozzarella. We are especially happy to see the brisk business for our beloved Riccardo and Monica, who are hosting us. Lockdown around the world has been a stop-motion nightmare for restaurant and bar owners – my husband included.

The lunch is with Jannie and Robbie's lovely basket coach Valentina, along with some other teammates and parents. During this second lockdown, the coach and her husband have somehow kept team training going by moving it outdoors, despite encroaching winter and constantly evolving restrictions. For us, this involved reams of forms filled out for every session; what it has meant for them, navigating the Escher-like landscape of Italian bureaucracy, we can only imagine. But they have – through sheer grit – maintained a routine for their junior team, and we deeply appreciate it. It is a source of double happiness that Jannie adores Valentina, who is at once firm and gentle, and has taken an obvious shine to our littlest son's lisping cheekiness and fierce competitiveness. He gives a shy farewell speech in Italian, and presents her with a delicate potted orchid. She cries. She gives him a team hoodie with his name printed on the back. He cries. They hug many times. Hair is tousled. Cheeks are rubbed. Eyes are moist all round as we toast each other with Lambrusco. The junior contingent of basket-buddies clink bottles of their favourite local brew, Mole Cola, a name that always makes me smile. *La vita*, we say. To life.

Afterwards Peter heads around the corner to the pub (how comforting that wherever you are in the world, there is an Irish pub) to meet other friends. After walking him there, I head home, ostensibly to do more packing but really to sneak a lie-down. Home is far from restful though, with our bed littered with clothes and my mind full of jobs, so I hop on my bike with the hand mixer and stick blender I am gifting to a friend, and head back to the pub for its final hour before closing. Our upbeat mate Andrea gives a cheer when I enter and orders me an Irish coffee that is so delicious, it instantly fixes all maladies. When the pub closes at six, we wander to some other friends a couple of blocks away for another instalment of what feels like the everlasting farewell.

The last-minute resurrection of our social life (and the subsequent mornings-after) mean that our moving plans loom in our near future like ogres, big and foreboding. In honour of the country that has given us so much, practicality must, however, defer to emotion. On Monday Peter takes the final two bikes to get boxed up for their trip home (he has left his till last so he can cram in a few more laps of his beloved Bologna hills) while I see my yoga friends for a farewell hug and lunch. Antonella, my lovely doe-eyed friend, gives me a pair of earrings and then, shyly, a copy of the book she wrote about the Australian Saint Mary MacKillop, the book she told me about at our first unforgettable lunch together. (Saint Mary, who performed one of her miracles at the children's hospital where Lewis was treated for leukaemia, has more than one hundred years later forged this bridge of faith and understanding between us: Italian and Australian.) The moment itself feels like a minor miracle. Antonella and I both drip tears into our Chinese food.

That evening, friends drop off homemade pasta and Christmas baubles. There is a constant procession of the older kids' school *amici*; Lewis tells us his friends want to see us. Bemused, Peter and I venture from our room and there they are, assembled at the oval table in the entrance hall, at once awkward teenagers and eloquent young friends. They are beautifully mannered Julian, luminous Lucy, sweet Spanish Elvira and clever, reed-thin Andrea, who Peter early on nicknamed 'The Forty Pound Man'. The latter leads the charge with a farewell tribute and awkward hugs. (It is impossible not to hug and be hugged by our Italian friends, even in these socially distanced times. A week later, when we are in hotel quarantine in Australia, we will hear that Andrea's mum has tested positive for Covid.)

Veronika and Filippo, our landlord's delightful daughter-in-law and son, stop by with Edo, a baby when we first arrived, now a mop-topped boyo who regards us with permanent suspicion. As he plays peekaboo behind the door, his parents present us with a delicate pen and ink panorama of Bologna, featuring the *porte*, the ten surviving gates in the ancient city wall we have entered and exited so many times. We give them a Christmas panettone in a Dolce & Gabbana colourful painted tin. There are more hugs, and promises to return.

So. Tomorrow is our last full day. We haven't finished packing. Instead we are doing the maddest, most impractical thing. And we can't wait.

A couple of weeks ago, Giovanni asked where we would like to go for our last meal, which seemed a fantasy question, given lockdown. Nonetheless, Peter and I were unanimous in our answer: the seafood restaurant in Cesenatico.

It was there last February, only weeks after we arrived, we had the first of the many magnificent meals we have shared.

After stopping at the Marco Pantani museum (closed for siesta) so that Peter could pay his respects to one of Italy's greatest cyclists, we found ourselves in a most northern hemisphere phenomenon, a seasonal beach town totally shut for winter. It had the eerie, slightly mournful air of an abandoned theme park. But there, discreetly positioned on the ground floor of a freestanding apartment building, was our destination, a restaurant called Casa Tua ('Your House'). From the outside you wouldn't know it was there – the only clue on the grey street outside was an incongruous smattering of gleaming

Ferraris and Maseratis. Their owners, as we would soon find out, were already inside enjoying the fabled Casa Tua hospitality. Giovanni giggled and nodded when we exclaimed at the fancy cars. As we emerged from his own slightly battered vehicle, he turned to me and said, 'You know the restaurant owner does not like communists. If you are communist he will not serve you.'

It was an unusual pronouncement: a perfect starting-pistol shot for an unusual day.

Everything was amazing, even before the food. The room, a large and light-filled U, was a study in the high-low design the Italians do so well; the way they can marry a Murano-glass chandelier with a bunch of plastic grapes and it will be breathtaking.

Here was the same alchemy. An oversized gilt throne at the doorway, heaped with purple velvet cushions. A giant fibreglass giraffe towering in the courtyard. Gleaming monogrammed crockery and glittering glassware, and flowers and ornaments crowding every table. The most effusive welcome from our bustling host Silvio and his grownup but – like him – diminutive daughter And then, when we had settled, glasses of prosecco in hand, the other diners: OMG. The people.

Sitting near us, a couple sheltered from view by a discreetly placed screen. Him, bearded, in his sixties, with a distinctly academic vibe – leather patches on his corduroy jacket and a briefcase at his feet. Opposite him, a girl; late twenties, long hair brushed but unadorned, dressed simply in neat but slightly worn jumper and jeans. She was not racy, not even default Italian sexy-sassy, but was nonetheless vibrating with a frequency that ruled out the possibility she was his wife. He was tutoring her, it seemed, passing her wine to try; a morsel of food on his fork. Italian seduction.

Beside us, a group of half-a-dozen men, imbued with the casual authority of the mysteriously rich. (Mafia 'made men', I think, though we have already learned it is discouraged to speculate about this in Italy.) The whole room, in fact, is full of men of all ages savouring lunch and each other's company. They are so impeccably groomed, a casual visitor might assume all of Italy is a giant Grindr meet, but this is a cultural trick. They are also men who will overtly look you up and down as you walk past them to the ladies' bathroom.

Giovanni, who is clearly enjoying our enjoyment, has, after a rapid-fire exchange with Silvio, ordered without even consulting the menu. (I love it, by the way, when people do this. It shows such confidence. And it is so nice to not have to make any decisions). Peter and I had assured our friend we loved seafood and, true to his word, seafood began to arrive. Fresh, gleaming, straight-from-the-trawler, practically-still-flapping seafood. We knew exactly how fresh it was BECAUSE IT WAS ALL RAW.

This was, to say the least, a surprise. We have eaten raw fish before – we are not barbarians. But we have had sushi and carpaccio, never an entire array of uncooked creatures of the sea. This was the most stunning seafood platter imaginable, entirely *crudo*. Oysters, naturally, but also three types of prawns – white, violet and red – (the proverbial raw prawn!) which were astoundingly delicate and sweet. Then octopus and scampi. Raw. Clams. Raw. Sea urchins. Raw.

In between courses, Silvio's daughter magicked some stunning cooked plates onto our table – polenta with clams, fried calamari and tiny crisp anchovies – but the most memorable things we ate that day were raw.

The climax was a whole fish (snapper, I think) brought to the table with some ceremony atop a large platter. It was gloriously fresh, its skin shining silver and eyes sharp and clear. Which was just as well, because – raw. Giovanni peeled back the skin of the fish, and inside it had been finely crosshatched. The flesh was the palest pink and mince-soft. It didn't taste even slightly fishy. We ate it with bread and olive oil and salt, and sparkling white wine, and it was one of the most delicious things in the world.

Afterwards, we joined in as the un-made men next to us had a firecracker cake at their table and sang 'Happy Birthday' in Italian. Silvio's daughter brought us creamy, cold dishes of gelato, topped with sweet and sour cherries in a dark crimson syrup. They were so deliciously sweet and mouth-puckering, I stole Peter's and was sniffing around for more when Silvio brought the huge blue-and-white ceramic serving bowl straight to the table so I could help myself. Amarena, he told me the cherries were called. They came from near Bologna.

Twenty months later, then, it is a miracle – or some kind of madness – when Giovanni tells us he has procured a booking at Casa Tua for our final farewell meal. It is a miracle because there is no lockdown and also it is a festa day, the Feast of the Immaculate Conception, a public holiday in Italy. It is madness because Giovanni still has a broken clavicle and pelvis from his bike accident, yet insists he will pick us up for the two-hour round trip, since Peter is returning our leased VW van that morning.

The lunch is magical. Astounding. Brilliant. Incredible. Glorious.

The restaurant is as much a glittering oasis as it was on our first visit, only today it is packed to the gills. Halfway through the meal, Silvio – who it turns out is also a DJ – stops by the decks he has set up between the two dining rooms and an old skool techno tune starts blasting. Everyone is mid-meal but the music is so loud, it is hard to ignore. Soon half the restaurant is standing at their seats, arms pumping exultantly. Giovanni waves his crutch in the air, which makes us all laugh.

EDM gives way to Christmas Mariah, to some Rat Pack classics, and then to Italian folk songs; the whole room singing in unison, glasses held aloft. These are songs we have heard so often now, even we can join in. Tables are moved so people can dance with each other unconstrained. The food, of course, is sublime. It makes its way to us unbidden: white-fish and tuna *crudo*; grilled octopus on mashed beans puddled with oil; fried prawns; creamy risotto strewn with truffles; citrus-daubed scallops on the shell. Giovanni's mate Paul and his girlfriend Kika order a bottle of 'the best Champagne in the world'. We don't argue. We are at the most unexpected, euphoric restaurant-dance party ever. People start smoking and vaping at their tables. Opposite us, a dapper man in his seventies moves into the middle of the room to keep dancing with two women who are enjoying his moves. The trio twirl and dip, flanked by a group of enthusiastic teenagers, who are cheering them on. Giovanni beckons Silvio over and yells something to him over the soaring music.

Silvio nods, then disappears. Moments later he pops up beside me. Places a bowl of vanilla gelato in front of me. It is crowned with Amarena cherries.

That night, after the Greatest Lunch on Earth, Giovanni drops us off at the front of our palazzo. I am in the back seat and have fallen asleep on the way home, lullabyed by the hum of the autostrada. I don't wake until we enter the old part of Bologna. When Giovanni pulls up at our giant wooden gates five minutes later, there is already a car impatiently idling behind him. We kiss, and thank him for everything. Our friend says gruffly: 'We will see each other soon'. There is no time for anything more, which suits us all.

Peter and I enter the courtyard, where I grab my turquoise bike and take it for a final ride, around the corner to the Elektrobau. Grace is there in her usual position, standing behind the bar with Eddie. Her face lights up when she sees me and the bike. I tell her I hope it will change her life, as it did mine. In a walking city, to have wheels is to have freedom.

She walks me out onto the street to say goodbye. She is so sad; sad she can't get back to Australia.

And I am sad; sad to be leaving.

How strange the world is.

The next morning, Ferdi comes by. I have been anticipating, but dreading this moment; this farewell that will mean our departure is imminent. Our landlord takes a moment to marvel at the huge pile of bags and suitcases we have spent the night packing before joining us in the kitchen, where I am making coffee at the stovetop. Behind me is the wall he patiently had repainted twice last year after explosions with the very coffee-maker I am now using. Ferdi is noticeably subdued. He shifts from foot to foot, apologises for not removing his knitted cap. We understand how he suffers in the cold.

We know this and so much more about him, and as he proffers his formal goodbye, I find myself with tears in my eyes. I have become so fond of him. I will miss his gentle gentlemanliness, his wry, thoughtful conversation and humour, his random history lessons. I will even miss him dropping by every three days to try to fix our air-conditioning, or fiddle with some plumbing, or bring over some new marble tiling.

He has, he says quietly, brought us a farewell gift. It is a black and white postcard of the palazzo, a shot from the street into the interior courtyard. At the top of the frame, you can just see the shutters of our apartment; our beautiful Italian home. In his elegant hand, our landlord-friend has written a message on the back which makes my eyes well.

Ferdi, watching me read, is also moved. He clears his throat.

'I think, as you know,' he says in his careful, deliberate manner, 'that Americans are amazing people, but you Australians are most like Italians.'

It is, for us, the ultimate compliment. Peter and I understand completely what he means. There is a *simpatico* between us; a shared humour, pleasure in socialising, respect for nature, a stickybeaking curiosity. The result is a mutual, often bemused, love.

'There is always room for you here,' Ferdi says, and we hug tightly, before he moves to also embrace Peter. He reaches into his pocket and presents me with a white box. Inside, folded in crumpled-smooth tissue paper, is a silver picture frame. It is clearly old and slightly tarnished, which only adds to its splendour. It is also, as Ferdi explains, a little too small to actually fit the postcard it was meant to hold. This revelation makes me laugh through my tears.

The gift, you see, is beautiful and heart-warming and romantic and impractical and thoughtful and generous and funny and precious and unforgettable.

It is perfect.

It is just like Italy.

POSTSCRIPT
THE RECIPE FOR HAPPINESS

2023

Ah, this book! This pretty, sometimes-gritty, sometimes-witty show of my heart. How many beautiful encounters I have had with people who have taken the time to read it – on holidays, on audio (the tears!), at book clubs – and how I love it when someone approaches me (often shyly) to convey their appreciation of the travels we have now shared.

Bella Italia and its adventures and inevitable lessons continue to vibrate within me like a shining secret, even as I reembark on my Australian life. Work. Children at school. Chores. Friends. Service to family. It is comforting and familiar to be back home, but it is also a grind. I am like a donkey that has broken free of its enclosure for one brilliant, mad (two-year) gallop, only to be rounded up and returned to my corral. Some mornings I wake with the responsibilities of the day jumbling out of the shadowbox of my mind; obligations and appointments crowding out trinkets of memory and joy. But if I close my eyes, I find myself walking down a cobbled lane, past the steps of an ancient church, Italian blue overhead, brown and russet around me, bells tolling, and I am so vividly transported back to the country that taught me so much about beauty and giving myself the gift of time.

And then I rise. I literally drag myself out of bed, body first, spirit trailing. I make my way to the kitchen and spoon ground coffee into the little metal moka percolator that always sits on the stovetop. It takes SO LONG to brew, which is of course part of the resetting of my impatient, heavy-headed self, and while that magic happens, I potter around, folding washing or making school lunches. And always, like breathing, I am thinking about what I am going to cook.

One of the reasons I love cooking so much is that it makes us all capable of performing miracles. Truly, you can be the most novice, tentative derp in the kitchen, but if you drop an egg into boiling water for five minutes, then decapitate it and sprinkle it with pepper and salt, you will find you have performed a sort of alchemy that makes the heart sing. As you greedily dip your toast soldier deep, deep – into the very soul of that egg – and pull out the buttery baton coated in unctuous, warm, sunshine-hued egg-innards, you will marvel at what you have done. By the way, I personally find this practice abhorrent; I hate runny yolk (liquid chicken!), which I know is regarded as sacrilege by most people I have ever shared a breakfast table with. Liking hard yolks is almost akin to liking your steak well done. It makes that group of borderline bullies who describe themselves as 'foodies' all trembly in the jowls. But really, I think, the chicken has gone to a lot of work on your behalf. You may as well enjoy your eggs as you like them.

The other superpower of food is that it speaks directly to you. Like music, it can be high or low, popular or classical, but its taste and smell can transport you to a place and time, release the dam wall of memories. Several seasons ago, I was watching a cooking show where dozens of nervous hopefuls were lined up at their kitchen stations, hoping to win an apron that would see them go through to the next round of the competition. They had been given a brief: to cook a recipe that defined their family. One of the girls made a dish that featured mayonnaise. (I can't remember exactly what it was. Pasta salad? Mac and cheese?) She served it in a casserole dish and explained that her family ate it at every festive gathering, and to her it was not just a meal. It was love. When it came time for the judges to taste her family tribute, one of them shuddered and said disgustedly, 'You used mayonnaise out of a JAR for this?' She nodded meekly and the judges all shook their heads like my maths teacher did in grade 10 when I got 19 per cent in an algebra test, disappointed and grim, and she was booted from the competition. The injustice of that has always stayed with me. Because that's how her family made this dish. They weren't drizzling and whizzing and whisking and dipping a pinky finger in to test the piquancy of their 'emulsion'. The judges had asked for a family favourite, and when their fledgling contestant did as they asked, they punished her for it. Which struck me as not only being unfair, but also very food-snobby. (I actually like jar mayonnaise, by the way. Ditto tinned food. Of course I do – I'm not running a restaurant. I'm feeding a family.)

See, a favourite dish is not only nourishing, it is comfort and history and a linking monkey-grip between generations – which must be, now I think about it, why every son loves his mother's lasagne. I discovered this in my past life, when I was at acting school with a group of other students from around the country. One day we were in our common room, and the talk – unusually – turned slightly homesick. Suddenly, all the boys were reminiscing about their mothers' cooking and every one of them seemed to speak dreamily of their *madre's* lasagne: what their mums did that made their layered pasta dish so memorable. Chicken lasagne or vegetarian. It was a moment so sentimental and gentle and personal, it was almost religious. And then (TRIGGER WARNING FOR ANY ITALIANS ABOUT TO READ THIS) one strapping boy from a log-felling town in Tassie got all misty-eyed talking about his mum's lasagne – which she apparently made with tinned tuna. The whole room was stunned into silence, as we (much like my friend's imagined family) tried to digest this offering. And I know it sounds so weird (and really, is that even *lasagne*?) but if you think about it, in that remote setting, his mum would have often been cooking with cans from her store cupboard. And she did it so faithfully and so well, that years later, her cherished son, far from home, had a hankering for what many would consider an abomination.

I think about this often when I am cooking for my own family – how I will love it if one day my three boyos tell their mates they have to come to our house to try my lasagne. This projected future happening, by the way, makes me tear up – a reaction borne partly from sentiment, but also from the imaginary numbers at my table (when your baseline is six, more mouths at the table is a blessing, but also a test of stamina). The basis for my lasagne, naturally, is the meat sauce – what the Italians call *ragu* – and now I make my bolognaise from a recipe I learned in the town it got its name from – beautiful Bologna. And here is an inherent irony: the Italians are the greatest food snobs of all – yet I love them for it. God forbid they ever see you attempt to put parmesan on a seafood dish.

Peter and I once incurred an hour-long lecture from a 78-year-old waiter by the beach in a quiet port town in Puglia. It was a classic Italian seaside scenario – a little joint that looked bleak by day, but seemed to pop up in the evening sparkling; just plastic tables and chairs on a concrete slab, made beautiful (always) with cloth serviettes and polished glasses. Our waiter, aged like bronze and with a face creased by *molto, molto* summers, was wearing a crisp white long-sleeved shirt and floppy slip-on leather loafers. It was his uniform for the evening shift, which he clearly had been doing for decades. It was perfection. There were barely any foreign tourists that summer because of worldwide lockdowns, so we were already a novelty in the town – and the restaurant – and the air was perfect and we were mid-summer tanned ourselves. So relaxed and happy. Sea-marinated holiday hungry.

Anyway, we ordered oysters, as we had spent our summer doing, and when they arrived, glistening in their shell-baths, we thought it would be nice to make a little vinaigrette to adorn them, so we asked if we could have one of the little glass bottles of *balsamico* we could see on an adjacent table. The old cock serving us, who clearly suspected we were up to no good, was curious; did we want the vinegar for the bread? No, we said. For the oysters; the *ostrica*. He made no effort to conceal his horror. 'No!' he said, shaking his head. 'No, no no!' Then he leant over Peter, jabbing at the oysters with his deep-tanned knuckly fingers, and shook his head some more. '*Limone, si. Aceto, NO!*' he said. Lemon, yes. Vinegar, no!

His reaction was so unexpected, and his indignation so undisguised, it actually shocked us into laughter. Also, we were a little confuse-ed, because isn't lemon just an acid like vinegar? Naturally, there was no way we would say that out loud because our waiter was clearly upset, so instead we found ourselves trying to placate him. Which was hard, partly because we were both trying to stifle giggles, looking fixedly down at the table, only sneaking peeps at each other to see who was best equipped to deal with what had become 'a situation'. And our waiter clocked this, of course – our strange behaviour making us seem not only like simpletons – but obstinate ones, at that. Petie finally gathered himself and took charge. In Italian, he agreed it was a foolish idea, and that we wouldn't pursue it, it's just that in Australia (where we came from) it was not uncommon to have a vinaigrette with oysters. But of course the molluscs were perfect just as they were, and maybe we could just order some more wine? The old guy, however, couldn't let it go. He circled our table, fully agitated now, rattling off a list in Italian of all the toppings that are permitted on oysters ('salt, pepper, lemon, oil ... but never, never, NIENTE vinegar!'). And then he wouldn't even leave us to get the wine but called out to the kitchen and a guy in a cooking apron came out sweating with a bottle of *vino*, and the waiter shared with his colleague the story of us and the vinegar and while the kitchen-*signore* didn't seem as perturbed as our old friend they still both tsked and shook their heads and we sat there slightly shamed but mostly it was funny and insane. Because our waiter's upset was FOR THE OYSTERS. And because he now knew he couldn't trust us to do the right thing for the food – or ourselves – he hovered over us, shifting from one leg to the other, till the oysters were finished.

At the end of the night, when we left, we found our man on the street-side of the trattoria. He was with a couple of t-shirt-clad guys from the kitchen, hunkered over a glass of grappa with a cigarette.

We thanked him for the meal, and he gave us a broken half-smile and returned our wishes for a *buona serata*, but he was clearly shaken to his core. In fact, he could barely meet our eyes. It is fair to say he will never forget us.

I share this with you because you need to know what a risk it is for me to pass on the recipe below. Food to Italians is not small talk. It is big talk. And recipes are precious: they are family and history and heirloom and region and season and passion. There is no experimenting; at least, not in a traditional family kitchen, not with a foundational dish like ragu. Yet there are as many variations as there are *mammas*: red wine or white, milk or no milk (always milk in Bologna, and sometimes even cream). No garlic, but if you must – a sliver half the size of your little fingernail. The meat is kind of greyed, not deeply browned, so as not to lose the moisture. Not too much tomato – maybe even no *passata* at all – just some tomato paste. And, of course, *Bolognese ragu* is never never never served with spaghetti. That is American!

This sauce – *ragu alla Bolognese* – has made its way around the world as bolognaise (and is now the most popular family meal in Australia). In Italy, it is served over tagliatelle, for only the wider pasta holds the prized bounty the way it should. It is markedly different than the mincey, tomatoey sauce I grew up with. (My beloved mum would often add a tin of Heinz Big Red Tomato Soup at the end for some sweetness – which I know sounds shocking but is also delicious and slurpily good. Not authentic, apparently. Who knew?) The following recipe is a prized souvenir from our time in magnificent Bologna, the ultimate gift. It is a simple dish, made complex by simmering. I have written it pretty much as it was dictated to me by our friend Stefano's nonna. She was mystified I didn't have my own recipe ('What do they eat?' she asked her son as we sat in her tiny kitchen). Now, of course, we eat this.

OUR FRIEND STEFANO'S NONNA'S RAGU ALLA BOLOGNESE

Ingredients:
Three or four slices of pancetta (or bacon), not smoked!
An espresso cup of olive oil and a big spoon of butter
One onion, two carrots, two ribs of celery; diced fine like the pearls on a necklace (this is called *soffritto*)
One big, big man's hand of beef mince; one smaller lady's hand of pork mince
One cup of wine; red or white doesn't matter, but not sweet
One cup of passata (or two tablespoons of tomato paste – water added later)
One cup of milk with all the fat
Salt and pepper
Tagliatelle (or any wider egg pasta)
Parmesan

Preparation:
Finely dice the pancetta to match the pearls of your *soffritto*.

Over a low flame, sauté the pancetta till the fat melts, then add the olive oil and butter. Add onion till it is softened (and clear like a window!). Add the carrots and celery and cook until the vegetables are soft and maybe a little bit browned.

Turn the heat up and add the ground beef and pork. When the meat is just starting to brown, and the fat is coming away, pour in the wine and cook till the alcohol is gone and the liquid with it.

Add the crushed tomato passata (or if tomato paste – stir through and then add a cup of water).

Slowly, slowly (*piano, piano!*) stir in the milk and cook low for an hour or so, stirring occasionally.

Taste and then add salt and pepper.

Put a lid on your pot and continue for simmer for four or five hours, always visiting it to stir.

Cook your pasta in plenty of salty water, but do not throw away all the cooking water when you drain it.

Add a splash of the pasta water to another saucepan, then add a big spoon of *ragu* for every serving of pasta and stir it through. The pasta water makes it creamy. Add your cooked pasta to this pot and mix the sauce till it coats every strand of pasta. Not too much sauce, but the pasta should be shining.

Shave plenty of parmesan over the top, the best you can afford.

Close your eyes. Breathe in. Then eat.

Like my friend Lorenzo always says: a glass of wine and bowl of pasta fixes everything. But there is not always time to visit the butcher or stand by the stove simmering. And in times when comfort is needed quickly, you must have the following recipe. It is from my girlfriend Rachel; her mum would always make it on Sunday nights, because it was quick and cheap, and could be expanded to feed a family of seven with ease.

LEWIS-LANGBROEK CORN FRITTERS
Ingredients:
A tin of corn (or two)
A cup of flour
An egg (or two)
Enough milk to mix the above into a thick (not runny!) batter
A pinch of salt
(You can also add cheese, or grated zucchini or onion, but none of this is necessary)
Oil – a centimetre or so in a frypan, hot (not olive oil, or your fritters will not crisp)

Preparation:
Drop spoons of the corny batter into the hot oil and fry till golden and sealed on both sides.

Drain on kitchen paper. Salt liberally.

Mix a bowl of unsweetened yoghurt with some gherkin spread (from a jar!) to a pale green 'special sauce' consistency.

Dip fritters in the sauce. Eat with greedy fingers.

High and low. Quick and slow. These, my friends, are the days of our lives.

Xxxx Katie

ACKNOWLEDGEMENTS

I never thought I would write a book. But then, I never thought I would live in Italy. And when you have a dream, I have discovered, some people will support it, and others will not. Self-interest always reveals the truth of motivation, and us moving to Italy made those around us – in big ways and small – rearrange their own lives to make room for our absence.

There are so many people to thank; many of them Italian Australians who we have always loved, and did not realise it was because of the generosity and humour in their DNA. Nonziata and Priscilla and her family, Lady Johnny and his family at Pino's. Gianna Rosica. Santo Cilauro, whose view of the world I always found so appealing. My incredible parents, Anne and Jan, who left their countries behind and chose Australia, the land that has given me everything. They find pleasure in small things, and make friends wherever they go. Peter's family, my beloved parents-in-law, Maree and Bryan, and Paul and Anna, who love an adventure. Mark and Bee and Sue and Rob, for keeping the home fires burning. PB, for bagels and godfathering and unwavering love and friendship. Pierluigi Trombetta and Maria and Roberto at the Italian consulate in Melbourne, who helped us navigate the complexities of visas with humour and vigour. Paul Garwood, Maria Carpenzano, Dr Greg French and Margaret Twomey at the Australian Embassy in Roma, for repping Australia so faithfully. My friends who sent packages (or tried to!) – especially when we were in lockdown – my sister-in-law, Stacey, my brother John-Paul, beloved, beautiful Alice and

Juz and Miranda and Trudy and Flooze and Michelle 'Moomies' Bennett and Georgie Damm and Carla – my Feelthy – and my other shining Georgie, Harrop. BT, whose people come from a heady mix of Taranto and Gippsland. Timmeh and Mon. Michael Williams, for The Knowledge. Sophie Braham, herself a brilliant writer, who lit a torch for me in the dark.

Thank you to the teachers and admin at St Kilda Park Primary School and Albert Park College, for believing that education doesn't just happen in a classroom, and for farewelling our children and welcoming them back with the same love. Thanks to Anne Grigg, who first introduced us to Italy via her retirement gift – a school trip organised for a bunch of ten-year-old state-schoolers. Our national treasure, family man Gerry Ryan, with whom we spent an unforgettable couple of days in Bologna watching our countrymen pedal the Giro. Robbie Sitch and Janie Kennedy, who had boldly chased the sun with their own brood, and for generously sharing life and tips about travelling with a multitude. Annie Peacock, for infinite kindnesses (in fair weather and foul); for the talisman I wore in good times and bad. Nicklebob and Kanye, for somehow being a part of every adventure – we will pick you up by the roadside in Chianti anytime. Ange and Peter Scanlon, for knowing what we needed, even from afar, and for lending us Romituzzo. My Mac – who ran with me up the stairs of the Royal Children's Hospital behind Lewis that miraculous day, for always being behind and in front of me. To Drs John Heath and Simon Gibbs. To our friends who came to stay, and to those who never made it to us in Bologna (Jock and Brigid, Batz and Katie, Shane D and Maha, Emma Lewis and Chloe Langbroek) – one day we will all be free again. To my radio bosses Gemma and Grant, for persuading me to do my radio show from afar, before 'working remotely' was a thing. To Duncan, who first audaciously suggested it. To Hughesy and Sach, for nearly everything. To DB and Mel and Monty, for then and now.

I am so grateful to my snap, crackle 'n' pop manager Dean Buchanan, whose enthusiasm should be bottled. And to Dan

Ruffino for believing there are not too many books in the world. I owe the hugest thanks to my editor Fiona Henderson (and Randy), for reading my chapters over aperitivo drinks as I would send them through, for her flint and grace, her delicious laugh and storehouse of anecdotes, her forensic nose for detail. Thank you also to her team: Katherine Ring, Deonie Fiford for copy editing (truly, god is in the details), and for making sure my book can be judged by Christa Moffitt's beautiful cover and design. Thanks to Tina Smigielski for her gorgeous photographs of me, and to Nat Vincetich for her makeup artistry and vision.

None of this would have happened without my own family; the one we made. My heartsong Lewis. My enchanted woodland creature Sunday. My crying-game soulmate Artie. My snuggle-pot, dancing elf Jannie. And Peter Allan Lewis. Pierre. Pietro. Petros. The rock. How I love you, my darling. And how well you love me. Thank you for trusting me with your lives, as I entrust you with my own.

Of course, of course, I have to thank Italy, and the angels who made that glorious boot, and filled it with people of courage and character, faith and generosity and humour, and a soul-affirming love of beauty and carbs. (It is entirely understandable they forgot to teach them how to form a queue.)

I remember reading, years ago, that in the olden-days, when missives between lovers were delivered by hand, love-letters bore encoded messages in case they were intercepted. One of those codewords was ITALY: I Trust And Love You.

And I do, ITALY. I do.

ABOUT THE AUTHOR

Kate Langbroek is one of Australia's most beloved media personalities. Her ferocious wit, playfulness and irreverence have made her an audience favourite in a career that has spanned prime time television, top-rating breakfast and drivetime radio, acting, scriptwriting and journalism.

Kate first came to our attention on Triple R in the mid-1990s and then as a regular on *The Panel*, one of Network Ten's longest-running shows. She went on to guest on other popular shows like *Thank God You're Here* and *Dancing with the Stars*.

In 2001 Kate helped catapult start-up radio station Nova 100 to instant ratings success. Along with co-host Dave 'Hughesy' Hughes, Kate continued her stellar radio career on SCA's Hit! Network and is now on the ARN Network. She broadcasts nationally every weekday on KIIS FM's 3pm *Pick-Up* and is a regular guest on Channel 10's *The Project*.

While juggling a frenetic career, marriage and parenthood, Kate and her husband Peter decided to make life even more interesting by packing up their four kids and moving to Bologna in Italy. The result is Kate's first book, *Ciao Bella! Six Take Italy*.

You can find Kate on Twitter @katelangbroek and Instagram @katelangbroek.